MORAL PASSAGES

MORAL PASSAGES

TOWARD A COLLECTIVIST MORAL THEORY

KATHRYN PYNE ADDELSON

ROUTLEDGE

NEW YORK   LONDON

Published in 1994 by

Routledge
29 West 35th Street
New York, NY 10001

Published in Great Britain by

Routledge
11 New Fetter Lane
London EC4P 4EE

Printed in the United States of America on acid-free paper.

Library of Congress Cataloging-in-Publication Data

Addelson, Kathryn Pyne, 1932–
    Moral passages : / Kathryn Pyne Addelson.
        p.   cm.
    Includes bibliographica references and index.
    ISBN 0-415-91020-X — ISBN 0-415-91021-8
    1. Ethics.   2. Collectivism.   3. Feminist ethics.   I. Title.
BJ 1031.A33   1994
170—dc20
                                                            94-20583
                                                            CIP

To my grandson, Sean Pyne Moran

There is a conviction that we are under a moral obligation in choosing our experiences, since the results of those experiences must ultimately determine our understanding of life. We know instinctively that if we grow contemptuous of our fellows, and consciously limit our intercourse to certain kinds of people whom we have previously decided to respect, we not only tremendously circumscribe our range of life, but limit the scope of our ethics.

—*Jane Addams*

Contents

Preface

THIS BOOK DEVELOPS several feminist principles—principles of criticism as well as positive principles of theory and practice. My aim is to present a more general feminist philosophy that leaves behind the partisan, oppositional approach that was suited to the women's movement in the United States in the 1970s. My own thinking was formed in the movements of that time, and my own intellectual struggle has been to change my thinking to ways suited to the 1990s.

One theme of criticism that I develop concerns the *individualism* that lies at the root of classical, market economics and classical, liberal politics and ethics. It projects the image of a public world rather than the world of intimate relations with particular others. Feminists have argued convincingly that the individualist ontology has been suited to a masculine experience of life and world—in fact, a higher-class, Westernized experience.

Another criticism concerns what I call the ideal of the *judging observer*. In epistemology and ethics, this is the theory of the detached knower who poses at an Archimedean point, the judging observer who is separate from time, place, social position, body, and intimate relations. Judging observers require a certain kind of world, a world of objective, independent facts, principles, and laws. It is a world in which prediction and retrodiction are supposed to work, and a world in which one can justly fix blame on individuals and punish or cure them. And so it is a world that requires a particular understanding of time, nature, and human action and moral development.

I offer a different theoretical basis, one that brings together philosophy and sociology. I can sketch it in slogans. "It is in collective action that time and world are created." "The unit of meaning is the collective act that generates self and social order." "The knower is not a judging observer but a participant."

I also use positive principles of the women's movement of the 1970s. The principle of taking women's experience seriously is particularly important. Some theorists see in women's experience not the separation of individuals but a creative interaction among selves in relation, particularly relations of care. Women are creative agents generating a world through nurturance and love. The dangers in this "caring" approach have been pointed out time and again—the ideal of the nurturing woman belongs to the same individualist framework that divides public and domestic, masculine and feminine. And perhaps worse, it may be an ideal developed for white "middle-class" women, echoing not only the gender order but the race and class orders as well.

Still, the principle of self in relationship may be sound and fruitful if it is understood in the context of a more general theory of human nature and society. The trick is to see how the face-to-face relations relate to the generation of a social, economic, and political order through collective action. This is empirical as well as theoretical work, and to do it I need to join philosophy with sociology.

There is also the important question, How do we know such a dynamic social, economic, and political order, created as it is out of collective action? We know it as participants, not as judging observers. But this means the mode of our participation is all important to consider. And here I can give some more slogans. "Knowledge is made in collective action." "Truth is not discovered, it is enacted." "The social order is revealed as it is enacted in collective action." In saying these things, I preserve other feminist principles, ones that found meaning in the women's movement of the 1970s, ones that were developed by some of the "standpoint" theorists. Properly understood, a "feminist standpoint" is created and understood in action, and a standpoint epistemology has to do with *learning how* the social order is regenerated through collective action and *knowing how* to make changes through collective action. This, I believe, is Dorothy Smith's understanding of a standpoint in her sociology for women (Smith, 1987).

A feminist standpoint has usually been interpreted in a way that is oppositional, or liberatory, or requiring commitment to a group claimed to have agency to make progressive change. The idea was developed for knowers who participate in making knowledge in certain ways—as political activists in a movement, for example. The feminist principles I use came alive at a time when there was a mass women's movement and that sort of standpoint analysis was plausible. The feminist principles functioned as calls to action, and feminist researchers were sisters to all women in action. Then, a fight for women's studies and feminist theory was a fight for women's liberation, and responsibility was settled in the context of the movement. But today, in the 1990s, I must ask whether academic feminists—or professionals of any sort—are participants in making knowledge in those activist ways? Or does the position of professional in the social, political, and economic order require a more complex discussion of responsible knowledge making?

The feminist principles lived on after the movement faded away, and we are left with a question of what feminist research might mean in the 1990s, or even the twenty-first century, in these radically changed historical circumstances. The question is a serious one, because for the most part, feminist researchers and other feminist professionals hold positions in established institutions of the very social order that the activists of the women's movement criticized. These are institutions which carry authority in the collective action of enacting truth; they are institutions crucial to regenerating the social, political, and economic order.

The cognitive authority of professionals has traditionally been legitimated by claiming that they give us "the best knowledge of the day," or even that they give us the way to truth and the good life. I do not see the participation of professionals as a question of legitimating their authority as knowers of truth. I see it as an issue of how professionals, feminists or not, are to do morally and intellectually responsible work in these changed times. The issue concerns all researchers, of course, not only feminists. And so, of necessity, I must consider issues of truth. And so too, I must consider issues of responsible work in this book—in a certain sense, issues of professional ethics.

I do have many people to thank for their support during the years it took me to write this book. Where possible, I have expressed my gratitude in the chapters where saying, "thank you," was most clearly called for. There were several people who read the whole manuscript through or otherwise helped me to shape the book as a whole. For this support, I thank Howard Becker, Philip Green, Shiv Visvanathan, and Judy Wittner, and the anonymous reader for a university press, who gave me invaluable advice and support. While I was writing this book, Anselm Strauss was writing *Continuous Permutations of Action* (1993). We read each other's manuscripts, and I have made my best effort to refer to him in the appropriate places. I'm pleased to know that my work was also helpful to him. I also want to thank Susan Visvanathan, Caroline Whitbeck, and Frederique Marglin for their comments and encouragement. Most of all, I thank Rosemary Haughton and members of the Work and Vision Workshops at Wellspring House for being partners in the enterprise. And of course Dan Hall who prepared the index and Ruth West who did the artwork for Chapter 5.

I also have institutional thanks to give. Smith College has been more than generous, in terms of leaves and sabbaticals, funding and support services. The members of the philosophy department have been unfailingly supportive of my work, even though it sometimes seemed not to be philosophy at all.

I could not have gone on without their sympathy and tolerance. I have received funding from a number of sources, including the National Endowment for the Humanities, the Mellon Foundation, and the Luce Foundation.

I am also grateful to my daughters, Kay Pyne Moran and Shawn Pyne, not only for helping me with the intellectual work of the book but for opening magic windows on the world. My husband Richard has shown patience, courage, and charity in living day and night with the obsessions of a writer. I owe a great deal to the thought and experience that has grown between us, day after day, year after year, as we have lived our lives together.

Many sections of this book were written or rewritten at the home of Jeanne and Herbert Addelson in Nova Scotia, and I am grateful for their love and hospitality and their continued encouragement. It was with my own parents, Joseph Etchells and Catherine Newton Etchells, and my grandmothers, Mary Thompson Etchells and Mary Casey Newton, that I received the treasure of knowing suffering in a hard world and the spirit to carry on.

1

A Philosopher's Question, "How Should We Live?"

ONE MAIN PHILOSOPHICAL QUESTION I'm concerned with in this book is, "How should we live?" The question of how we should live has deep roots, reaching far down into prehistory. It is the core question to which animism, theism, secular humanism, and science, politics, economics, art, and music offer answers. In everyday life, we all work out answers in living our lives together. We pose and answer the question in the moral passages of our lives.

I say that I'm concerned with a philosophical question because I'm interested in ways the question is answered, rather than in giving an answer myself. Answers to how we should live are created in the process of living. My hope is to propose a moral theory (and an epistemology and ontology) to shed light on the processes, and even on myself as a theorist proposing the theory.

Some philosophers have written that all moral or political theories presuppose a theory of human nature.[1] If that is true, then my own theory of human nature is that our lives are passages of discovery and creation. As infants we open our eyes and ears, mouths and hands to the new world that is ours to make. As elders we close them on the new world we have made with others. In between, we discover and forget, uncover and hide. We live through childhood with its paradoxical bonds to home and independence, adolescence with its secrets of love and sex, and later, the commitment to partners and

---

1. So many philosophers have claimed this that it seems a platitude. For a good, clear, feminist discussion of human nature and moral and political theories, see Jaggar (1983). It goes without saying that science also requires a theory of human nature. In my discussion of R. C. Lewontin below, I suggest that science requires the same theory of human nature that I offer for a moral theory. Some philosophers have also said that every moral theory presupposes a sociology, and if that is true, then my own collectivist moral theory at least wears its sociology on its sleeve.

children and the satisfactions in making a home community and doing our work. We learn, sometimes slowly, sometimes all at once, the meaning of human time and the meaning of suffering, loss, and death. If we are fortunate, we eventually learn the wholeness of life. The passage of life is a process of veiling even as we unveil. It is a process of enacting truth as we enact the social order and the self. If these are the ways we answer the question of how we should live, then a philosopher has to respect these ways.

It may sound romantic to say that our lives are passages of creation and discovery. Perhaps I seem to contradict the hard-headed truths of science, for example, that we are products of the dual forces of outer environment and inner genetic structure (or perhaps inner forces of the conscious and the unconscious). In such a context, in speaking of creativity, I may seem to disinter the old Christian relic of free will, or fantasies of the free individual artist or *übermensch*. But I should correct that misimpression. I'm not concerned with the creativity (or determinism) of the individual. I'm concerned with the creativity of a collectivity through which the patterns of culture and the social, political, and economic systems are generated and regenerated.[2] I'm concerned with freedom in the sense of collective possibilities within which one creates oneself and one's personal life in joint action with others. That kind of creation is a particular, everyday matter, and it takes place through processes that can be empirically discovered and with people that can be named—though the discovery and the naming require appropriately respectful methods of research.

Far from being romantic and unscientific, supposing that human and animal nature is fundamentally creative can behead some of the serious problems in twentieth-century science. For example, the dualism of organism (or inner genetic structure) and environment makes evolutionary theory incoherent, and the idea of objectivity that parses a scientist as an observer rather than a participant makes science itself incoherent. But let me cite an authority.

R. C. Lewontin is a leading geneticist, holding the Alexander Agassiz chair in zoology at Harvard University. His thesis is that the relationship between organisms and environments is a dynamic interaction, continually changing, in which organisms and environment create each other. This thesis is a different approach to evolutionary theory from those in which individual organisms are either subjects or objects of evolution. In "transformational theories," like Lamarck's, species change because each individual changes,

---

2. I thank Frederique Marglin for suggesting I use the term "generative," which I use throughout the book. She has used it herself in speaking of the generative community, and the term carries a concern with procreation and a rather organic and creative view of social change. Together with Christina Platt, we gave a short presentation on the generative community for the Alternative Economic Visions subgroup of TOES (North America).

triggered by elements in the environment (a model that is also used in developmental theories like those of Piaget or Freud). In variational theories, like Darwin's, organisms in a population differ genetically and a species changes through selection by environmental forces. Both approaches involve a dualism of inner and outer forces, of organism and environment. Even to find out an organism's environment (Lewontin writes) it is necessary to consult the organism.[3]

The dualism of organism and environment must be put aside. But so must the idea of the objective, judging observer. Human beings are, after all, living organisms who create their environments—who even, in that sense, create both society and nature. In the United States today (and elsewhere) one of the important ways human beings create nature is through science itself. Scientists are participants in the process, and the knowledge they produce ought to reflect that.

Accepting that human beings and other organisms collectively create the world has very great implications for scientific work. For example, the much-touted human genome project operates on a philosophical foundation of inner cause (genetic structure) and outer cause (environment), with ample room for irresponsibility for the moral outcomes of biomedicine and ecology. It would be absurd for me to deny the influence of genetic structure on our lives. My issue is with the philosophical foundation of the dualist, materialist, individualist, causal framework. My issue is with the objectivist idea of knowledge that makes it difficult for researchers to do responsible work. In this book, I call that framework the individualist perspective, and I contrast it with what I call a collectivist perspective, one that takes living beings as creative and the knower as participant in creating what is known.

Certain moral and political theories are included in the individualist perspective, particularly those that focus on individuals and the inner causes (whether rational or emotional) that act on them, and the outer, environmental forces that shape them, whether through socialization or through dominance and oppression. My own commitment is to finding a way to see how individuals are collectively created, and how the patterns of socialization and the structures of dominance are generated in collective life, as people do things together. To do this properly, I would have to include the collective action of all living organisms, even those minute organisms of the soil, air, and water upon which larger flora and fauna depend, including humans themselves. I can't do this of course, due not only to my own limitations but to those of the learned professions of the twentieth century. And so I'm restricted to discussing human creativity in collective action, and even that only in the United States.

---

3. (Lewontin, 1992). See also Levins and Lewontin (1985).

Making a "We"

"How should we live?" One of the significant terms in the question is "we." The "we" is not something given but something that is enacted. One way to make a "we" is through the bonds that grow among people doing things together in everyday life. Another way is to establish some knowledge as "our" truth; for example, the public knowledge of morality, the church, or science. This is presupposed when speaking of "our" norms and values, "our" race or gender, "our" world, or even of "nature" itself, as distinct from "us." I believe that a "we" is often made by giving some knowers authority over others, as adults have authority over children. In this case, the others' knowledge does not disappear, it is hidden. Hiding it sometimes means suppressing it or declaring it false or superstitious, but most often it means ignoring it or overlooking it.

Often, in making a "we," some ways of doing things are named as "our ways"; for example, the nuclear family, or public education, or free enterprise capitalism, or liberal democracy. In the United States, these are sometimes called "our traditions" in an effort to give them legitimacy or authority. There are also dissenting traditions, like feminism or fundamentalism. But of course there is the question of whose knowledge defines the traditions and whose is hidden—always leaving open the possibility that what everyone knows may be hidden under the public definition.

Civil war and genocide have been waged over the question of who "we" are and who we ought to be. The peoples of the republics of the former Soviet Union are struggling with the issue here at century's end, and there has been the horror of ethnic cleansing in the former Yugoslavia. South Africans are straining for a political resolution, and so are many of the nations of the world—nations being one way of defining a "we" by implicit or explicit force. But questions of national governance are far from being the only issues involved in the "we." Within the United States, there has been conflict over who "we" are from the beginning, and only rarely has it been framed as a problem of national governance. Over the past century and a half, it has been more a problem of making a "we" out of native born and immigrant; white, red, brown, and black; men and women; young and old; rich and poor; scientist and spiritualist; and a thousand more. These are disputes over who represents what is normal "for us," and who speaks "our" consensus and prescribes "our" truth and goodness.

Artists, visionaries, politicians, priests, and scientists all take it to be within their territory to prescribe the true and the good. Is the free market the way to the good life? Or is it the welfare state? Is it New Age myths and medicines, or healthy childrearing (as prescribed by the Surgeon General)? Should we leave behind our virulent (or self-indulgent) individualism and return to the old-time religion and the old traditions, or should we improve our "moral ecology" and take responsibility within "our" institutions—family, school, community, corporation, church, synagogue, state, nation—while still acknowledging the importance of "civil society" as a corrective to a market and state run rampant?[4] All of these are suggestions acted on today in the United States.

But I must ask who these artists, visionaries, and scientists are addressing. What means do they use to have their knowledge enacted? How do they know which institutions and traditions are "ours"? Where do they get their authority to speak for "us"? Whose knowledge do the old institutions and values hide? What deep problems and solutions do these experts place behind a wall when they give their proposals on how we should live?

In the old days, when there was one truth, one beauty, one goodness, the experts' authority rested on solid ground. In the United States today, there is a tendency to argue that all knowledge is relative, and so we are stuck inside our own culture and can't get out. Some experts have insisted that given where we are stuck, we have no choice but to embrace Western liberalism. They say that, in its institutional as well as its ideological manifestations, it is simply the best (indeed for "us," the only) place to move on from—"the relatively decent, free, progressive political culture characteristic of the North Atlantic democracies" (Rorty, 1991: 6). That proposal, of course, includes accepting the expert's expertise.

Other intellectuals have argued otherwise. Marx, after all, was pretty explicit about showing that the abstract, liberal framework legitimated the dominance of the capitalist class, and that the revolutionary standpoint of the proletariat was available for "moving on." Anarcho-syndicalists believed that through direct action, workers could learn how the force of the state stood behind capitalist owners, politicians, priests, and the upper classes, and in the process, they would learn how to make the new, classless, stateless world. Multitudes of twentieth-century feminists in the United States have written that knowing from a man's perspective is quite different from knowing from a woman's perspective, and that taking the man's perspective as the normal one simply establishes male dominance. Other intellectuals (and activists) have said that the knowledge and the very self of the colonizer are essentially different from those of the colonized.

But these analyses also presuppose a "we"—like all "we's" it is a promissory "we" that must be continually generated and regenerated in collective

---

4. Bellah et al. (1991) suggest that we "reappropriate elements from our biblical and civic republican traditions." "Our" biblical and civic republican traditions? Some of "us" are Buddhist, Hindu, and Islamic—to say nothing of atheist. Jewish and Christian biblical traditions differ, as do the traditions of different sects within each.

action. Ideally, this oppositional "we" grows out of building consciousness and solidarity. It is certainly a "we" that is defined against a "they." But it is a "we" nonetheless, the "we" of the subordinated or dominated, the "we" that might make a different future. Like all "we's," these are made in action, including the action of making some knowledge public and hiding other knowledge, by privileging what some people do over others. The "we" is a commitment to a way of knowing the past and making the future. The analysts are arguing for a commitment to a way.

Are people, of necessity and at root, part of a "we"? Is that what it is to be a social animal? Is it an illusion to believe that people's lives are passages of discovery and creation of a human world together, not simply a commitment to a way? Answering these questions means taking a serious look at what people in fact do together to make a "we." I believe that uncovering what we do together might leave, as a gift, all the freedom of creation that is in fact our own.

What Am I Doing Here?

Having scrawled these dark remarks about artists, priests, politicians, and scientists, I should at least say something about how I hope to avoid being blackened by my own ink.[5]

First, I need to distinguish the way I am asking about how we should live from the way writers embalmed in the philosophic canon have generally asked about it. My question is different from those asked by Plato or John Stuart Mill or John Rawls. They gave their answers in terms of just or good or well-ordered societies, offering a public world that suited their well-honed tastes. My concern is rather with how those public worlds are made (or might be made) and what part these philosophical artists, these cognitive authorities, play in making them.

The question of how we should live has many faces. According to one respected story, the philosophical question is expressed as "How should *one* live." That question is said (by Bernard Williams) to have simpler forms of the sort, "What should I do?" or "How should I live?" or "How should a man

---

5. Much is hinted at but hidden in these remarks. I did indeed scrawl the original sentence (in pencil, in a lined book for schoolroom use that I bought at a store selling damaged or discontinued items). But as it appears here, the sentence has moved away from the original scrawl. In that incarnation it was full of information on its genesis and development through crossings-out and inserts; and full of information on me as to whether I am an optimist, a good manager, honest (those things that handwriting interpreters find out). Its first significant reincarnation was into the bland electronic record of my computer. After it emerged from the printer, it left me behind to follow life on its own, finally emerging from editor and "typesetter" to find flesh as sentences do, in words on pages that I have never seen, purified of its history and my self so that we both become stereotypes, it, of a thought, and I, of an academic thinker.

live" (see Williams, 1985). Setting the question in these ways also sets a framework for answering the question, an ontology, an epistemology, a politics, a reading of history. Bernard Williams would agree to some of that at least—he writes his ethics for the modern world, because "the demands of the modern world on ethical thought are unprecedented," and not to be satisfied by the ideas of rationality in the *usual* moral philosophy. The usual Anglo-American moral philosophers also set a framework, of course. But it seems to me that most philosophers do not properly question their own place in offering their ethics, nor do some of them question the periodization of history that underlies the idea of "the modern world." And there are analogous problems for those more unusual and refreshing moral philosophers who turn to friendship and compassion as basic moral concepts, or intimacy and trust, or the mothering relationship, or an ethics of care. Philosophers set themselves as authorities on "our" concepts and behavior.[6]

I do not mean to say that these philosophers don't locate themselves at all. Some locate themselves "ethnocentrically" within the Western democracies, or in a feminist mode as women in a gendered world. But the location that is most important is the place that we philosophers ourselves occupy, as workers, qua professional philosophers. Finding a proper way to set that place is crucial to framing the question of how we should live. It is the one way I might avoid being blackened by my own spilled ink.

I ask the question of how we should live from a particular social position, as a professional philosopher in the United States in the 1990s. I do not make that position *ab ovo*, whatever I believe about freedom and creativity. My position is collectively created with collective meaning in a historically and politically developed institution within a particular social order—and of course I participate in that collective creation. I am a knowledge maker, however humble, and a transmitter of knowledge, however flawed, because of my position. I am a cognitive authority, however small. Among sophisticated academics, it is now generally accepted that there is no Archimedian point from which to make knowledge.[7] But it isn't enough to accept, or to write, that we are all historically, institutionally, and politically located. The reality of it must be integrated into the method and the making of the knowledge itself. It must be enfolded into myself and my work.

---

6. On history, see Dye (1979), and Lerner (1979), especially chapter 12. On epistemic privilege, see Bar-On (1993). For a review of alternative moral theories, see Tong (1993).

7. Harding (1986); Jaggar (1983); MacIntyre (1981) are widely circulated examples, but there are multitudes of articles and books that cover the topic. Rawls (1971) makes an interesting use of the Archimedean point in his "original position." I am concerned not with intellectuals per se but with professionals in institutions and their place in producing knowledge, or more directly, my place in producing knowledge. Dorothy Smith faces something like this question, though she slides off the point by identifying her work with a political movement, the women's movement. See Smith (1987).

One obstacle to doing intellectually and morally responsible work is an "individualist perspective" that legitimates professional practice. It also serves as a basis for epistemology, ethics, politics, and the understanding of truth and the very nature of time itself. The individualist perspective has two poles. At one pole are the individuals who act, decide, think, judge, and vote. At the other are the customs, norms, rules, laws, moral principles, beliefs, and meanings that the individuals are said to share, and the facts and truths that individuals are said to discover and then share. This is one version of the separation of organism and environment, inner and outer, that I mentioned above.

The basic difficulty with the individualist perspective is this. "The freedom that is in fact our own" is a collective freedom. What it creates are collective possibilities—collective, not egalitarian. The individuals are products of collective action, and so are the customs, norms, beliefs, and meanings. The facts and truths are collectively enacted—which is not at all to say that they are illusions or mere beliefs. This book is a product of collective action, made out of collective work in my discipline (and others). It includes not only the collective work of training me, but also the work that goes into making journals and books and conferences, and the collective effort of creating whole library systems and colleges and universities, and all the technologies that lie behind them, and all the practices. My students and colleagues have taken part in the collective action of making this book, and so have newspaper columnists and television commentators and makers of movies. And of course all of the people involved in the elaborate practices of publication and distribution and review. And so, of course, have the readers of the published book itself. To say that I am the creator of this book is a *façon de parler*. To say it is ultimately individuals who exist and think and create is a *façon de parler*. I realize that my remarks may sound absurd or eccentric—the individualist perspective is deeply embedded in life in these United States. Some philosophers even take the individualist perspective to be "folk psychology" (see, for example, the papers in (Greenwood, 1991). In the course of the following chapters, I trace some of the ways professionals are implicated in this "folk psychology."

Whether or not my remarks sound absurd, the collective freedom must at least be considered if I am to do responsible work within an institution that sets my responsibilities in the narrow sense but hides them in the larger sense. It is a question of doing work that is respectful of the creativity of others as they enact truth and take part in making the meaning of the world. The trick is to do this from my place within an institution that is an official enactor of truth and a producer of official meanings, an institution that hides what people do together as part of its task of regenerating the social order. An institution that usurps the freedom of creation that is in fact our

8

own. Given the established modes of making and transmitting knowledge in the United States, it isn't possible to be fully respectful of others in a book like this, nor is it possible to be fully reflexive about my own part in enacting truth. I'll say more about this below and in chapter 7. Here I want to talk not about contradictions or impossibilities but about difficulties, because difficulties often open windows to new possibilities.

One of the most serious difficulties has to do with the issue of intellectually and morally responsible work. The work is collective, not individual, and so I need a moral notion of responsibility designed for collective work. Fortunately, some philosophers have developed the beginnings of an appropriate notion in professional ethics and environmental ethics (Ladd, 1975; Jonas, 1984). I'll more or less use that moral notion. I'm recommending it to professionals, not claiming it is one of "our" moral concepts and not recommending it to everyone, and not even doing much analysis of my own on the moral notion per se.

Making sense of that notion of responsibility does require an analysis of human group life as collective action. I will try to set out that analysis in this book. To do so, I have to face the difficulty that the individualist perspective is embedded in the everyday ways of answering the question of how we should live in the United States. But that difficulty opens a window: I'll use the collectivist perspective to show how the individualist perspective is embedded, and how it is that individuals, with their thoughts and actions, are created in collective action, at the same time that they create their worlds.

So my need to do intellectually and morally responsible work leads me to give both an analysis of human group life as collective action and a revelation of the individualist perspective as it is enacted within the United States. The double effort requires a new philosophical approach to "the moral institution of life." I'll start by saying something about the old approach.[8]

---

8. This part of my work might be called "ethnophilosophy." Anthony Appiah wrote of ethnophilosophy as an attempt to explore and systematize the conceptual world of Africa's traditional cultures (Appiah, 1992; 1992–93). In Appiah's sense, ethnophilosophy amounts, in effect, to adopting the approach of a folklorist or ethnographer doing the natural history of "traditional" folk thought about human life, the world, and nature. In its own self image, and in its practice, philosophy is usually distinguished from ethnophilosophy. Philosophy is taken to span centuries and cultures, going back to Plato and Aristotle (or beyond) and collecting writings along the ages, bringing together East and West, Gandhi and Quine (though not usually in the same college courses). Understood in this way, philosophy (without the prefix) is something that has a canon, criteria for entry, a methodology of sorts, and practitioners. In short, philosophy is a professional discipline in the United States and some other places. But this itself must be taken account of, and one way to do it might be to do ethnophilosophy, not of "traditional culture" but of a modern or progressive society as complex as that of the United States. And I've tried to take a few steps toward doing that.

Traditional and Progressive Society

One of the great presuppositions of twentieth-century professionals is the distinction between the modern and the traditional. Bernard Williams used it in remarks I quoted above. One way he used it was to mark a difference between ethics that is reflective and that which is unreflective.[9] Being reflective is (according to Williams) a mark of modern institutions, and he insisted upon it being a mark of ethics. But the distinction has more uses than this, as Williams would admit.

Another way of describing the modern is to call it progressive. In his introduction to Margaret Sanger's *The Pivot of Civilization*, H. G. Wells described the battle for ownership of the twentieth century as one between "Traditional or Authoritative Civilization" and "Creative and Progressive Civilization." The one (he wrote) discourages criticism and enquiry, while the other is the civilization of enquiry and experimental knowledge. The one (he wrote), declares "Let man learn his duty and obey." while the other asserts, "Let man know, and trust him" (Sanger, 1922). Wells favored socialism, not capitalism, but the contrast he drew suits both of those economic-political approaches to how we should live.[10] The contrast is partisan, of course, progressive society painting its own portrait and projecting its own shadow. But Wells based it on the science of the day, not only as a progressive mode of knowledge but particularly in the evolutionary story of the descent of man, which Wells read as social, moral, and political as well as biological (Wells, 1920). The contrast offers a way to step into the question of morality and the philosophers' answers to how we should live.[11]

Traditional society offered the "other" to progressive society, the rigid father against whom the vigorous son measured himself. In an analogous way, the philosophical idea of heteronymous morality forms the "other" to autonomy. Autonomy involves the responsibility of giving oneself a moral law and choosing one's own life plan; i.e., it is the basis of letting a person

---

9. Another was to distinguish the thin moral concepts of modern society (rightness, obligation, rights, justice, goodness, all bare and remote from from the specificities of daily life) from thick moral concepts embedded in what people do. I'll spend most of the following chapters with concepts embedded in what people do, and that includes ways in which "thin moral concepts" are used to maintain the social and economic orders in modern society.

10. The contrast has been drawn using a variety of terms. Over the past 10 years, many academics have used the term, "the enlightenment orientation" or "the modern" instead of "progressive society." "Progress" reaches deeper into the way of life outside professional circles. I quote Wells' remarks from the introduction to Sanger's book (rather than someone else's) because of the important place Sanger's early work has in setting out my perspective in this book.

11. Wells wrote of traditional and progressive civilization, and I will use the word "society." There are significant differences in the two terms, historically and theoretically, but I will ignore them.

know and trusting him. [12] The heteronymous person learns his duty and obeys. Intentionally or not, John Stuart Mill gave one description of the morality of traditional society when he wrote,

> We do not call anything wrong, unless we mean to imply that a person ought to be punished in some way or other for doing it; if not by law, by the opinion of his fellow-creatures; if not by opinion, by the reproaches of his own conscience. . . . It is a part of the notion of Duty in every one of its forms that a person may rightfully be compelled to fulfil it. Duty is a thing which may be exacted from a person, as one exacts a debt. (Mill, 1951: 45)

In comparing duty with contract and debt, Mill took a particular Protestant, bourgeois look at morality. But his description brings out some features that are shared with a variety of philosophical analyses. The idea of morality is individualistic, and it requires an understanding of time, truth, and meaning that is suited to judges and judgment. It also uses a psychology that has recently been called "folk psychology" by a group of philosophers working in problems of cognitive science.[13]

First the judge. Although duty concerning future acts is included in traditional (or heteronymous) morality, the responsibility involved is essentially retrospective, or backward looking. It concerns liability for one's actions. It is a juridical responsibility suited for judges passing out sanctions (including the "reproaches of [the actor's] own conscience"). As "progressive" society came to dominance in the U.S., moral liability and punishment were gradually played down. A more therapeutic approach came into favor: the causes of the deviant's behavior should be uncovered in order to correct them so that the error won't happen again. The causes might be inner (an addiction, neurosis, post-traumatic stress syndrome, lack of knowledge) or outer (drug culture, gangs, ghettos, dysfunctional families). In the United States today, the direction is toward rehabilitation of the errant person and the "medicalization" of deviance.[14] The direction is toward a clinical perspective (see

---

12. Anglo-American theorists distinguish the theory of the right (or duty and obligation) from the theory of the good, which includes questions of virtue and the good life. Both give answers to the question of how one should live, and to the question of the "we." I will not use the distinction, although I will discuss its use in academic ethics, particularly as it enters into formulating political solutions to social problems.

13. Greenwood (1991) contains articles by major philosophical disputants in the philosophical world of folk psychology/cognitive science, and it includes a helpful introduction by editor John Greenwood and articles on the current range of philosophical positions.

14. The move is not as simple as I make it out here. For example, the proponents of "progressive society" continue to rely on moral liability when it involves rewards or positive sanctions. But I'll discuss this at length throughout the book. For a discussion of a distinction between liability and causal responsibility, see Ladd (1982, 1975). For a discussion of the medicalization of deviance, see Schneider and Conrad (1980) and Conrad and Schneider (1980).

chapter 5). However the rehabilitation approach was also used by groups of "good Christians" throughout the nineteenth century (Gusfield, 1976; Smith-Rosenberg, 1971b). All in all, it represents an attempt to take account of collective action within the individualist perspective by distinguishing individual and environment, and inner and outer causes. It is a framework shared by many biological scientists, as I said earlier.

Both liability and rehabilitation explain human behavior as something caused by the individual's inner thoughts, feelings, and attitudes (or even genetic structure or hormonal state). The inner cause is also presupposed in the progressive morality that uses the notion of autonomy—giving oneself a moral law, choosing one's life plan.

There are two sides to morality as Mill presents it above. One side concerns the individual and his or her inner thoughts, feelings, character, decisions, commitments, etc. The other concerns the moral principles, rules, or norms according to which the individual's behavior is judged. In his remarks, Mill seems to presuppose that there is some sort of consensus on the form and content of morality, one that supports all the praise, blame, and punishment. What is this consensus, and what is the source of the "we" that Mill refers to? I'll begin by looking at "traditional society," though consensus is an issue with progressive society and with oppositional approaches as well as those supporting the status quo.

The We and the Others

Some theorists have supposed that the "we" is defined in terms of a relationship to the group rules or customs. H.L.A. Hart once wrote that we may *describe* a moral system or a group's moral rules by taking an "external" viewpoint suited to a scientist or philosopher. But he noted that when our own moral customs are involved, we take an internal view of the rules in the sense that we *use them* (Hart, 1981). Presumably, in traditional society, those who constitute the "we" take an internal view of the group rules. Some theorists would say people are socialized in this way, and that the rules are internalized. Presumably these rules and customs constitute (or legitimate) the authority of traditional society and justify the sanctions.

Hart's distinction between the internal and external viewpoints captures the paradox of trying to do responsible work as a professional scientist or philosopher, work that respects the fundamental creativity of others. Knowledge of the sort professionals produce, i.e., knowledge certified for public use, has to be made "as if" the professionals were not actors within the folk activities, "as if" the professionals were judging observers. This is the idea of objective knowledge. It is as if their participation were limited to producing knowledge and truth. But of course the professionals are actors in the collec-

tive activities, not only gathering "the facts" but formulating them as knowledge to be used by others as well as themselves. Social scientists, natural scientists, and philosophers all participate. After all, biologists not only take
part in the collective life of the human and natural environment as they do
their work, they produce knowledge that changes the collective life, i.e.,
changes the social and natural environment, for good or ill. Current work in
genetics offers striking examples, with consequences for procreation and
genetic engineering, and for the moral categories of life itself.

The conflict between objectivity and political bias (for that's what it is)
shows in taking "our moral rules" to be rules that define who "we" are. Feminist philosopher Annette Baier has written that professional philosophers
have taken the point of view of the powerful in their work, because they
focus on rule breakers (as Mill did in the quote I gave above). She wants to
look at the rule makers "from the underside" to see who can be trusted. In
the process, she offers a substantive ethics of trust (Baier, 1985; 1986). However, both making and breaking rules are processes that are important in
making a "we," and so they are important to any understanding of ethics,
including Baier's.

Hart did take a closer look at use of moral praise and blame—a look that
shattered the "we" of traditional society. He wrote that in any group, there
may be some members who are "hardened offenders," i.e., members who
reject the rules, or at least continually violate them and do not consider
themselves at fault. As I read Hart, these hardened offenders are not
respectable people who are part of the consensus who, through some weakness, transgress and then repent. Nor are they the "non-powerful" who insist
on trust in making a "we." The hardened offenders refuse to be part of the
consensus. They will not be part of the "we" except as outsiders, rebels, the
marginalized, or the oppressed. They reject the moral scheme. Though they
may be compelled to pay the price, they reject the duty.

The hardened offenders are interesting. If they reject the morality of the
group, what morality do they operate under?[15] Are they simply disobedient,
ignorant, sick, or vicious, as the group would have it? Or might they have
their own rules, forming a different "we" with its own identity? Might they
have their own answer to the question, "How should we live?"

To suppose hardened offenders have their own rules runs the danger of
reducing the problem of the hardened offenders to a problem of relativism:
we simply have two different ways of life, two different sets of rules, perhaps

---

15. I discussed aspects of this question in Addelson (1973), bringing in Nietzsche, Kuhn, and
the women's movement in the United States. The question seems to me to be a crucial one. It
is, of course, a Nietzschean kind of question, though I couldn't accept a Nietzschean kind of
answer.

even different concepts of truth and duty, leaving no rational way to resolve a conflict. But this relativism ignores the *relationships* between the hardened offenders and the respectable members of the group. It ignores the relationship between the insiders and the outsiders (Becker, [1963] 1973). It ignores relationships of authority and power. As a philosophical thesis, relativism depoliticizes morality.[16]

There are alternatives to relativism being offered today that do take account of relations of authority and power. Feminist theorists have offered one alternative with the concept of "women's perspective"—something I'll call a "point of view" for terminological reasons.[17] Women can't clearly be called "hardened offenders" in most social worlds. Yet in many, they do seem to be deviant when the norms and ideals are based on men's experience and men's lives, as they have been in much of the literature of the West. Let me give an example.

The anthropologist Edwin Ardener has provided cases in which outsiders were given descriptions of group practices based on the point of view of men of the group (even when women gave them). Descriptions based on the women's point of view (he claimed) were very different—not only of the culture of the group but of nature itself (Ardener, 1975, 1985).[18] The men's point of view yielded the public knowledge, in the sense that it defined the group to outsiders. It legitimated the group as an object that had to be acknowledged and taken into account *in certain relationships* by both outsiders and insiders. It defined the "we" *for certain purposes*—purposes which counted as more or less "public" in Western eyes. Ethnographers entered that relationship and represented it as the scientific description of the group.

The women's knowledge was hidden from the public eye, though not hidden from the women. This difference cannot be understood as a case of rela-

---

16. "Ethnocentric" positions like Richard Rorty's politicize morality but in a way that preserves the social order. The claim is that "we" cannot escape our Western, democratic culture, so we should embrace it and rather than assuming consensus, jawbone our way toward consensus and solidarity through conversation (Rorty, 1979). Many feminist efforts also politicize morality, but many run afoul of the question of the "we."

17. I'll use the word "perspective" to name a theoretical approach, for example the individualist perspective, the collectivist perspective. I'm not using "point of view" in any technical sense here, because I suspect the idea can't be coherently analyzed. Bat Ami Bar-On (1993) gives an interesting review of "perspective" (or "standpoint") work in feminist philosophy. The idea of a standpoint may admit of a coherent analysis; see my remarks in the text.

18. In complex, modern societies, this problem of authority is one that many feminists have described in terms of patriarchy or male dominance, and that Marxists have described in terms of dominant ideology. The moral system and the very world are described from a dominant perspective. In this light, women, the working class, and many other groups have at times been dealt with as deviants—deviants who may be treated kindly, or even educated out of their ways, but deviants nonetheless. Moral revolutionaries are also treated as deviants (after all, they are a notable variety of hardened offender).

tivism or ethnocentrism—men's conceptual schemes vs. women's—without altogether fracturing the political and moral life of the group.

As in the case of the hardened offenders, the women's "point of view" cannot be analyzed as an alternative public knowledge because it is precisely what does not project the group to [male] outsiders (though of course anthropologists in their reports to other audiences may compare groups according to the women's points of view). The women's ways may have made a "we" of the women (and sometimes the children and men) for doing certain things, but they did not make a "we" of the group for outsiders. And if the men's ways did make a "we" of the group, then that seems to be a matter of authority or politics, a "we" for doing certain things with others. The "objective" report of the social scientists and the very philosophical model of norms, rules, or principles (or of "our moral concepts") is biased toward dominant groups.[19] The professionals participate in defining the groups, and that is a political participation.

Something similar can be said for other kinds of subordination—race, age, ethnicity, religion, nationality, physical difference, and many others. The point for a collectivist moral theory is to investigate the processes through which the social order is generated and regenerated, and through which the normal and the deviant are enacted.

As I interpret it, the idea of a feminist standpoint is different from what I called a point of view.[20] A standpoint is enacted in the process of a political movement, and it requires changing the social worlds in which subordinates live, challenging the dominance order, and creating new answers to how we should live. A standpoint involves issues of agency, of a collectivity as actor. Although I don't use the term, the anarcho-syndicalist process I describe in chapters 1 and 3 was a process of creating a standpoint. It is a more or less self-conscious liberatory process, in contrast to the everyday processes

---

19. The bias is much more blatant than my remarks indicate. For example, research in sociology has concentrated heavily on the doings of dominant groups (see Acker et al., 1991; and Smith, 1987). When "the others" have been studied, it has often been as deviants, i.e., through the lens of the dominant groups. The bias runs through the research professions and many of the service professions. See, for example, the gender, class, ethnic, and race bias not only in using white, higher class men as subjects of study in biomedicine, psychology, etc., but devoting porkbarrels full of research to their diseases and problems. The difficulty has been noticed in some fields, particularly biomedicine, but it has hardly been remedied.

20. The idea of a feminist standpoint is often a development of a Marxist idea, though much transformed. My understanding of a standpoint is compatible with that of a leading standpoint theorist, Dorothy Smith. To cite another authority, Alison Jaggar's explanation in the widely read *Feminist Politics and Human Nature* (1983) is consistent with my understanding here. Jaggar uses the contrast of perspective and standpoint (personal communication), where I speak of "point of view" and standpoint. Sandra Harding (1986, 1991) interprets "standpoint" differently, and her criticisms of standpoint theorists, particularly of Dorothy Smith, miss the mark.

that generate the social order. Professionals may participate in the process of creating a feminist standpoint, as they did in the 1960s and 1970s, but their participation presupposes that there is a feminist movement to participate in. Participation thus requires changing the relations between professionals and folk, something which Dorothy Smith stresses in her sociology for women.

I've used the words "dominant" and "subordinate" here. The terms have been used very well in feminist literature, and other literatures of resistance and dissent. I find a difficulty with some ways the terms are used, a difficulty that opens a window to new possibilities. It has to do with issues of responsibility, blame, and reparation.

I mentioned two kinds of responsibility in discussing John Stuart Mill's remarks—the traditional liability idea and the causal and rehabilitative version that came to be favored in progressive society. They are both "backward looking" senses. They are designed for the question, "Who (or what) is responsible for this?" In the case of social problems, there are answers like, "Drug dealers are responsible for crime in the inner cities, and so they must be punished"; "Welfare mothers are responsible for rising costs of social services, so they must be rehabilitated to become proper working citizens."

When the backward-looking sense of responsibility is used in issues of dominance and subordination, the answers may be something like, "Men are to blame for the subordination of women"; "Whites are to blame for the subordination of blacks"; "The ruling class is to blame for the subordination of the working class"; "The white patriarchy is to blame for oppression." And so punishment (or reparation) is to be exacted, as a debt. Or (more conservatively) the situation is to be cured through enforcing equal opportunity or through rehabilitating individuals by educating them out of their prejudices. In certain circumstances, this rhetoric may have a liberatory force, and it may provide tactics that work in a given time and place. But except in times of mass movement, when participating professionals are transformed into intellectuals swimming like fish in the activist sea, I don't believe the rhetoric offers a basis for responsible work.

And here I have come again to the notion of responsibility, now turned back upon itself in a reflexive way. My earlier question was about my own responsibility as a professional, acting as a cognitive authority, in the collective work of making knowledge in the United States. The question I have come to after wandering through a few simple ideas about morality (based, I must say, on the individualist perspective) is about responsibility in more general terms—responsibility in generating the social order, in making the "we," in answering the question of how we should live. That turn is appropriate, since the question of my doing responsible work is also a question of my responsibility in regenerating the hierarchies of the social order.

A Word on Responsible Work

In progressive society, responsible work by professionals was legitimated in two ways. One way was based on an abstract ideology of truth and objectivity: there is one world, one truth, and although anyone might know it, the professionals are the ones who are trained in the methods of discovering (or applying) it. The professionals are trained to deliver (or use) certified knowledge. This part of the explanation makes truth a criterion for the professionals' knowledge, not in the sense that the theories and data are guaranteed true, but that they are "the best" candidates for truth so far (according to methods of test, falsification, etc.). According to this part of the explanation, truth is the measure of knowledge and the professionals are the bearers of the methods of measurement.

The second way responsible work was explained was in the ethics of the professions themselves, including the common good that the collective, professional work was supposed to serve. Unfortunately, the professionals had a large hand in defining what good they were to serve, and how they were to serve it. John Ladd once wrote that professionals often took it to be part of their job as professionals "to be moral arbiters of what, in respect to professional services provided, is morally good for their clients and perhaps even of what is morally good for society" (Ladd, 1983: 12). What professionals judged morally good for society usually required leaving them a monopoly on the services that were necessary to achieve that good.

Professionals also had charge of defining what truth is and how knowledge is to be certified. Philosophers have been roundly criticized for analyzing truth and knowledge in a way that preserved their monopoly: for example, in Richard Rorty's well-circulated criticisms of foundationalist analyses (Rorty, 1979). Many other professionals, particularly in the sciences, simply operated "as if" what they produced according to disciplinary practice was the best candidate for public knowledge. For the most part, they simply *assumed* that the ideology of scientific work described the professional work itself— though of course they would insist that in practice, there are always human failings in an imperfect world.

In chapter 7, I propose a different understanding of scientific truth and of the relationship of professional knowledge makers to the knowledge they produce. I'll use the notions of sensitizing concepts and the discovery of grounded theory (Blumer, 1969; Glaser and Strauss, 1967). Using these notions, I'll understand knowledge not as a body of would-be truths, or as a method, but in terms of *sensitized people*. Questions of the intellectual responsibility of professionals concern both the way professionals are sensitized and what they are sensitized to.

The main criterion I use for judging the adequacy of my own work in this book is not the criterion of truth but that of intellectual and moral responsibility. Being morally responsible requires foresight in acting from *one's place*, foresight on the outcomes of the collective activity in which one takes part (see Ladd, 1975). Being intellectually responsible requires, for professionals like myself, devising theories and practices that can make it explicit what the collective activity is and what some important outcomes of the activity might be.

I believe, like many others, that professionals are always politically engaged because of their *positions* in the social order. The question is how to understand that engagement in a way that allows professionals to do responsible work. The answer requires less a sociological or political description of the social order than a starting point that will eventually let me show how professionals contribute to generating that social order. That starting point must be in the larger world in which professionals act, not in the narrowly defined worlds of their disciplines.

My goal in the book is to show that our lives are passages of discovery and creation, and that, in living them, we answer the question of how we should live. My problem is where to start. Because I believe that as an academic, I participate in generating the social order at this historical time in the United States, and that I myself and my academic work are in some way generated within that order, there is certainly no "Archimedian point" from which I can investigate my questions. I am not a judging observer. But because of my place in the social order, there is no dissident political point from which to do it either—not the alleged standpoint of the proletariat, or women's standpoint, or any of the others.[21]

On the other hand, I must say that I am not trapped within any conceptual scheme or ideology either. I am not determined in my actions by the social structure. There is no monolithic way of life, only monolithic, official stories. In everyday life, conflict, difference, and misunderstanding abound. My strategy will be to highlight what people do, particularly in cases that show conflict, difference, and misunderstanding. I'll do it by giving case studies. All of them concern ways of answering the question, "How should we live?" And they concern ways of making a "we."

I also chose a moral subject matter, something that is necessary to select my cases in a coherent way. Anglo-American philosophers (and the philosophers of their canon) have generally been preoccupied with issues of governance, broadly conceived so as to include not only governance of the group but governance of household and self. Thus Annette Baier's complaint about rule makers. Feminist scholars and activists have found reason to believe that

---

21. I want to emphasize that I am talking about my academic work here. I do intellectual work with community groups outside the academy, but it has a different form and point. Even so, it is not aimed at creating some standpoint.

these traditional approaches use male perspectives as a paradigm, I'll use procreation as my own subject matter. I'll take a moment to review some of the feminist work, to show its important contributions and to distinguish what I mean when I say I chose procreation as my issue.

Some Feminist Approaches

From the beginning of the "second wave" of the women's movement in the United States a quarter century ago, there was a growing criticism from feminist scholars in many disciplines. At the core of the criticism was the accusation that scholarly work had been focused on men's lives, men's world, men's work. And so it had either ignored women, thus making them invisible, or it had defined them in terms of men's relation to them. Scholars had usurped the freedom of creation, and even the selves and humanity of women. So ran the charges. I discussed feminist Edwin Ardener's criticism of the public definition of the "we" in traditional society as anthropologists reported it. Feminists have also given a criticism of the public definition of the "we" in progressive society, and they have done it from within.

The criticisms were sometimes framed in terms of the nineteenth-century distinction between men's sphere and women's sphere, sometimes in terms of the distinction between the public and the domestic, sometimes in terms of the later, twentieth-century distinction between the public and the private (or personal). According to these divisions, the public is the locale of state and market (though also of much that is included in "civil society"). In any event, the criticism was that philosophical ethics represented men's perspective, or a perspective from men's sphere, or even (in Carol Gilligan's criticism) the thinking of men of higher classes in industrialized societies. Even the defenders of the "modern" or progressive ethics admitted its natural place was in the secondary institutions of society—in other words, in what had been called "men's sphere."[22]

The ontology of "progressive ethics" is, as I said above, individualistic. Its paradigm is the autonomous, individual self, the one that gives itself a moral law, makes a life plan, and then follows it. Morality is a matter of choice and action. The individual's relations with others are external to himself, not morally constitutive. The relations are claimed to be freely chosen, often contractual. The individuals are basically competitive and oppositional, even when they are taking part in a collective activity (the idea of contract presupposes this). The ethics for progressive society takes individuals in the public sphere as the paradigm—the political man of the Western democracies, the

---

22. See Elshtain (1981); Gilligan (1977, 1982); and my discussion in Addelson (1991). For the admission concerning the secondary institutions of industrialized societies, see Kohlberg (1969, 1981).

rational economic man of the marketplace. But that is abstract theory. The attempt to put the paradigm into practice yields nothing other than the ideal of an impartial, detached professional, the one who makes knowledge without caring how it will be used, the one who gives care without caring.

Over the past twenty years, work in philosophical ethics in the United States has been moving away from the rational, individualist paradigm. Instead of ignoring the emotions, some philosophers have seen compassion, friendship, and intimacy as integral to morality. Anger has been analyzed as a moral stance that places subordinate on equal moral footing with dominant, allowing the underlings to be moral judgers of their "betters." Emotions have been taken as keys to the moral and political order.[23]

Some of the feminist (or feminine) moral philosophies have taken a new route, using mothering and the mother-child relation as a moral paradigm. One of the earliest, most original of these feminist approaches was Caroline Whitbeck's.[24] Whitbeck took the mother-child pairing as a paradigm to begin writing a different ontology for moral theory. She wrote about the self in relationship—she called it a "self-others" model to contrast with the oppositional "self-other" of the individualistic ontology. Using the mother-child relation as paradigm, the "self-others" relationship is not based on the contractual act of an individual. Rather, it is involuntary and permanent. The self of Whitbeck's ontology is not self-contained, fitted out with rights and liberties. Rather, people's selves must be mutually realized. In this, Whitbeck's ontology is supported by Jean Baker Miller's work in psychology, and the work of others at the Stone Center at Wellesley College (Jordan et al., 1991).

In this moral ontology, one cannot become a human person without relationships—quite a different understanding from the abstract definition of a person (see, for example, the usual philosophical arguments over abortion). Accordingly, Whitbeck uses an ethics of responsibility with her ontology, rather than an ethics of obligation (Whitbeck, 1983; Ladd, 1975). It is through responsibility to others that the self grows. All in all, her work gives a greater depth to Gilligan's "care and relationship" ethics, and to the various feminist (or feminine) ethics involving caring or mothering.[25]

There are things that I feel are very important in the work of these feminist philosophers, particularly in Whitbeck's work. The mother-child paradigm

---

23. On emotions, see the review in Tong (1993) and also Blum (1980); Jaggar (1989b); and others discussed in Tong's book. On anger, see Spelman (1989) and Jordan et al. (1991).

24. Beginning in the early 1970s, Whitbeck presented her work at meetings of the Society for Women in Philosophy and elsewhere. Whitbeck (1989) argues against the public-private distinction and Whitbeck (forthcoming) extends her analysis to moral problems in engineering, so that my criticisms below do not apply to her.

25. See, for example, Noddings (1984); essays in Treblicot (1984); Ruddick (1989); and Held (1987).

makes it clear that emotion and bonding must be included not only in morality but (I will argue) as part of the process of knowing. The emphasis on relationship realizing self and world is also important. But there are serious problems.

Both the "masculinist" individualist ethics and the feminist, relational ethics of care implicitly rely on the public-domestic distinction (men's sphere/women's sphere). In both, the domestic sphere is the locus of sexuality and childrearing, and it is associated mainly with women. In this sphere, the "we" arises from bonding and intimacy, and the bonds (as Whitbeck wrote) are not freely chosen and are permanent. The public sphere is where the grand sweep of history takes place, the sphere of economic, political, and ideological systems, and it is associated mainly with men. The "we" is territorial. But for my own work, I should show how the division between public and domestic, or public and private, is generated in collective action. As a matter of fact, I should show how men and women are generated, and gender relations as well. I cannot presuppose these things.

My own difficulty with the framework of the feminist ethics of care, relationship, and mothering can be framed in a variety of ways. If you will bear with me, I'll use the term "public" ambiguously. In my own, general use, what is made public becomes a matter of "common concern"—using Charles Taylor's phrase though not his analysis (Taylor, 1989). My own primary contrast will be between what is made public and what is hidden, and I will focus on these processes throughout the following chapters. In the individualist perspective, the contrast is between what is public and what is private, for example, between public policy and individual choice of lifestyle. In the feminist use, the contrast is often between public and domestic, a distinction that initially rested on a division into men's sphere and women's sphere.

In terms of the public/domestic division, there is a question of representing the perspective (vs. the standpoint) of women's sphere as a basis for public knowledge, when the very perspective that publicly represents women's sphere is that of men's sphere. It is from the vantage point of men's sphere that women are the sources of care and nurturance and intimacy. But in my opinion, the greatest problem has to do not with the *ideology* of men's and women's spheres but with the more material ways in which the social order is regenerated. The division between public and domestic hides the ways in which political and economic activities generate the network of intimate relationships, by representing them as external factors. Conversely, it makes it difficult to see how the intimate relations of mother and child (and family) regenerate the gender, race, age, and class orders.[26] Responsible work requires

---

26. See the introduction to Collier and Yanagisako (1987). They discuss the public/domestic dichotomy in terms of theoretical and empirical work in anthropology and sociology.

showing these things, not hiding them, and showing the part that professionals play in the regeneration, not hiding it.

I believe that Whitbeck's ethics, and those of other feminists, require an analysis of life as collective action, just as the ethics of the individualist perspective do.[27] But I also believe that Whitbeck's alternative ontology and her emphasis on intimate relations is important. Because I hope to avoid the pitfalls of the dichotomy of the spheres, I'll take procreation as my substantive topic not mothering, not parenting, but procreation as something that is the collective concern of a group of intimates or a community or society or nation. When I say that I take it as my substantive topic, I mean that I will discuss cases involving procreation, by which I mean not only the bearing and raising of children, but the health and welfare and future of the group itself.

Toward a Collectivist Moral Theory

In developing a collectivist theoretical approach, I'll work from the sociological school called symbolic interactionism, modified by what is called ethnomethodology.[28] The interactionist tradition names John Dewey and George Herbert Mead among its founding fathers, and in a sense it is the rightful heir of American pragmatism. The ontology rests on the slogan that the unit is the act, so that individuals, institutions, norms, rules, and "we's" are products of a process of social interaction, which process must be understood. Interactionists offer useful case studies, gathered by more or less anthropological methods of field study and interview. The tradition offers a variety of sociological concepts as well as the beginnings of an alternative understanding of truth and knowledge. However, these things have been developed for use by professionals doing research in a traditional academic setting, professionals who operate within institutions that grant them cognitive authority. In the end, I have to face that fact and try to understand how to move out of a traditional academic perspective in order to do responsible research. The move requires a substantial change in symbolic interactionism, which I'll discuss in chapters 6 and 7.

Taking the unit to be the act moves the focus in ethics away from individ-

---

27. I believe Whitbeck would agree.

28. The canonical reference for ethnomethodology is Garfinkel (1967). See also Turner (1974). I like much of what John Kitsuse and Joseph Gusfield do, and they are sometimes classed as ethnomethodologists (see Gusfield, 1981; Spector and Kitsuse, 1977). In overall aims, I am most sympathetic with the work of feminist Dorothy Smith (1987, 1990a, b). My relationship with symbolic interactionism is more *en famille*. I took a field methods course with Howard Becker in 1974, and I have been a member of interactionist circles ever since. I have learned a great deal from Joseph Schneider, Judy Wittner, and Arlene Daniels, as well as Anselm Strauss, Adele Clarke, and Joan Fujimura.

ual actors, decisions, judges, and praise and blame—that obsession that was displayed so well in the quote from John Stuart Mill that I gave earlier. That individualist focus carries with it a definition of past and future that suits the judging observer. It is an objectification of time that belies the lived experience and *assumes* what is most in need of explanation. In the service of praise and punishment, it forces a symmetry of time between judge and doer, in the sense that they are both assumed to be living in a public time, an objective time, an impartial time, a time in which the act lies like a fly imprisoned in resin. But so far as morality goes, I believe there is an assymmetry that needs looking at. The actors look forward to an open future in a freedom of creation, while the judges look back at a closed past, as if that past were made of dead events, as if history had a meaning all its own rather than a human meaning that is made in collective action, and made anew at every moment. Hidden in that story of objective time is the way the authority of the judges comes to birth as well as the fact that the judging observers are doers as well, in the same course of action that they judge.

To capture the assymmetry and the essential creativity of both doers and judges, I will talk about *moral passages*. These are processes that include judges and actors and their interactions.

The method I use is to analyze a very large number of cases, particularly in chapters 2 through 5. This isn't a method that philosophers generally use, but I do so both to provide illustrations for the more recognizable sort of theory I present in chapters 6 and 7, and to sensitize the reader to this dynamic way of viewing self and society.

In chapter 6, I set out the philosophical/sociological ontology of a collectivist perspective. Or to use more everyday language, I look at human group life as a collective process of moral passages in which people interpret each other's meanings and interpret the past in the process of creating their present institutions. These are passages in which people create their answers to how we should live. I do not mean this in any idealistic, democratic sense, because the public meaning and definition of what is going on belongs to authority as well as group action, as I indicated in the discussion of the hardened offenders above. This is as true in the most participatory democracy as it is in the most oppressive dictatorship. That people enter into collective action together does not at all mean that they agree on official definitions of what they are doing, or that they share the meanings of their "rules" and language. It does not mean they have the same point of view. These differences are what must be sought out in order to understand the processes by which a "we" is made. These differences are the root of conflict, oppression, and freedom.

In chapter 7, I try to face the fact that I am a scholarly authority producing knowledge in this book. I do so by suggesting an epistemology that is suited for those who make knowledge as professional researchers, beginning with some very fruitful ideas from sociologists. One basic thought is that professional research sensitizes the researchers to certain features of the social and natural world. In a sense, it is a theory of concept formation rather than one of scientific truth or confirmation. That is, the point of research is not to discover objective truths and timeless laws and facts (as in the individualist perspective, or the "enlightenment orientation") but to find ways to discover concepts that sensitize researchers to the processes of making an answer to how we should live. I should say that these processes include our interactions with "nature," and so sensitizing concepts are suited for the natural sciences, not only the social sciences and humanities. Rather than giving criteria that define a set of objects, sensitizing concepts work by using particular cases to illuminate more general themes. This is an epistemology suited for a dynamic world in which organism and environment create each other.

And of course that is the epistemology I use in this book. I am not claiming to give the truth about the social order, nature, or morality. I am trying to sensitize myself and the reader so that we are better able to be intellectually responsible in our work. That is why I devote so much space to discussing cases before "settling down" to do theoretical work in a more conventional sense.

There are several sorts of moral passages I'll present. I have taken procreation as base point for a philosophy of human nature and society, on analogy with the way Dewey and Aristotle took politics, particularly democratic politics, as their base point, and Marx and Engels took work and the economy as theirs. My basis lies in procreation, not narrowly in the sense of having one's own children, but broadly to include the ways in which both human and animal lives and communities are created and continued into the future.

One sort of moral passage I'll consider has to do with making moral problems public—the process that has been truncated as "issues of public policy" by the loyalists of modern ethics. In interactionist sociology these have been called social problems or public problems.[29] The more or less local passages of making moral problems public are both the mirrors and the engines of change and stability in the moral passages of the nation, and they are also loci of public conflict. Insiders and outsiders come to be labeled in these passages. "Our" values and what is normal are designated. Authorities are created and legitimated. These passages come to have institutional and systemic importance. I'll cover a number of examples in chap-

---

29. Spector and Kitsuse (1977) give one classic discussion of social problems as well as an interesting history of theoretical understanding of the phenomenon within sociology. Their own account has been well criticized. I find their account useful but theoretically and politically limited. Gusfield, (1984, 1981) takes a broader approach. Nathanson (1991) is probably closest to my own approach, but it is a work in sociology while mine is a work in philosophy, and that makes a great difference.

ters 2 and 3, including cases of making public some moral problems of abortion, sex education, and gay rights.

Personal moral passages are the second main sort that I'll discuss. Personal passages concern the making of the self in collective action, and so the making of the social order. This is the self in relationship that Caroline Whitbeck and Jean Baker Miller wrote about. But the nature of the relationships is an integral part of the social order (as is Whitbeck's self). These passages show the generation of selves and the moral and social order to be dynamic, full of conflict and turning points and dangers. Selves cannot be explained by talking of individuals being socialized into an existing cultural or moral system. These living selves generate the system. They give the meaning to the relations that constitute the social order.

Some of the personal passages I'll take up are institutionalized passages, even status passages; for example, the passages of pregnant teenagers and high schoolers in chapter 5. In that chapter, I discuss the transformation of the concept of birth control, from Margaret Sanger's original idea to one that suited an individualistic ethics of autonomy and life plans. This ethics came to be attributed to the "middle class" in the United States, though it was a professional invention (as was the "middle class" itself). Through the cases, I suggest some ways the respectability of the middle class was upheld and how, in the process, poor black communities and the white working class have sometimes been labeled as deviant. My point here isn't simply to show the dynamics of the social order but to illustrate how thoroughly even virtuous philosophers and professionals of good will may be implicated in regenerating the class, race, and gender orders of the United States.

In order to show a personal passage from the point of view of the person making it, I use a fictional character, Edna Pontellier, hero of Kate Chopin's *The Awakening*. In retelling that story, I can indicate how the knowledge necessary to life and self may be hidden (and discovered) among the hardened offenders. The story also lets me show some of the ways available to the higher classes to preserve themselves and uphold the social order. Most of all, it shows a person finding herself, and overcoming her self, in the process of creating new relationships and a world.

Researching my earliest and most substantial case involved me in doing some revisionist history. In chapters 2 and 4, I trace the early work of Margaret Sanger in founding the birth control movement. In the official history of the birth control movement, Sanger's work has been represented as progressing toward an individualist autonomy and planning ethics. However, when the movement began in the radical years before World War I, Sanger worked with the anarcho-syndicalists of the International Workers of the World. I'll sketch the syndicalist ethics of birth control and contrast it with the autonomy and planning ethics of the individualist perspective. The syndicalists (and Sanger) were interested in implementing an ethics, not in describing it in the philosophical abstract, and so my discussion in chapter 2 focuses on the dynamics of enacting a vision of how we should live, using Aristotle's ethics, the syndicalist Sanger, and the autonomy/planning ethics as examples. It is only by understanding the ethics as something to be enacted (not as an abstract theory) that it is possible to see how the ethics contributes to the generation and regeneration of a social order, thus how it makes an answer to how we should live. My point in chapter 2, as throughout the first five chapters, is to sensitize the reader and lay the background for the more strictly theoretical work.

The anarcho-syndicalists advocated revolutionary social change through direct action. Direct action was a paradigm of knowing and doing, and direct action was a *collective action*. Knowledge was needed to make the change, and knowledge was made in direct action. Coming to have the knowledge required the emotion and bonding necessary to a "gestalt switch," because new relations had to be made, and a new kind of self. The knowledge wasn't "objective" in the sense of being open to any individual (as in the individualist perspective). In the syndicalist view, it had to be created by the working class in action. The future wasn't predictable; it had to be created in the collective action. The past had to be understood anew. The syndicalists didn't simply have a different opinion (or theory) on politics and economics. They implicitly had a different paradigm of what it is to think, and know, and act that was embodied in what they did together. That makes the Sanger case very useful for my purposes, and it forms the basis of my major analysis of an ethics that is counter to the ethics of autonomy and planning. It is an analysis in which human nature is understood as creative, and so it offers a good example to test my collectivist moral theory.

2

Three Answers

The Revolution came—but not as it has been pictured nor as history relates
that revolutions have come. It began in my very being as I walked home
that night after I had closed the eyes and covered with a sheet the body of
that little helpless mother whose life had been sacrificed to ignorance.

Margaret Sanger (1931: 50)

DURING 1911 AND 1912, Margaret Sanger lived in New York, working
with socialists and syndicalists. From time to time, she took temporary
employment as a home nurse. Sometimes she worked on the Lower East
Side, in the homes of immigrant Italians, Jews, Irish, and Germans—those
who could afford care for a time after the birth of babies. Sanger herself had
been raised among the working classes in Corning, New York. Her father was
an artisan and a man of intellect and politics. Her Catholic mother managed
a houseful of children.

On the Lower East Side, Sanger saw the desperate poor of "the submerged,
untouched classes which no labor union, no church . . . ever reaches."[1] Of
these hidden masses, she says,

---

1. The quote is from a letter she wrote as she fled to England after being indicted under the
Comstock laws for publishing *The Woman Rebel*. My information in this section comes from
Sanger's two autobiographies, and from letters and unpublished sources in the Sophia Smith
Collection and the Library of Congress. I am grateful to Dorothy Green for her very generous
help to me with the Sophia Smith sources.

Ignorance and neglect go on day by day; children born to breathe but a few hours and pass out of life; pregnant women toiling early and late to give food to four or five children, always hungry; boarders taken into homes where there is not sufficient room for the family; little girls eight and ten years of age sleeping in the same room with dirty, foul smelling, loathsome men; women whose weary, pregnant, shapeless bodies refuse to accommodate themselves to their husband's desires find husbands looking with lustful eyes upon other women, sometimes upon their own little daughters, six and seven years of age.[2] In this atmosphere, abortions and birth become the main theme of conversation. (Sanger, 1931: 48)

When Sanger made these observations, abortion had been outlawed for two generations. Outlawing abortion didn't mean that there were no abortions, of course. It meant that abortion was not available to most people through legitimate medical channels. Because "Comstock laws" labeled abortion and birth control information obscene, home health manuals no longer gave instruction to their readers. Even most medical school texts did not carry information on birth control methods.

The women of the Lower East Side used more or less violent home remedies to solve their problems, and they lined up outside of "questionable offices well known in the community for cheap abortions." In her autobiographies, Sanger said that her crusade for family limitation occurred after her patient Sadie Sachs died from a "cheap abortion." According to Sanger, Sadie had asked her doctor how to prevent pregnancy. The doctor had prescribed abstinence—"Tell Jake (Sachs) to sleep on the roof." Whether prudery or ignorance or fear of the Comstock laws sealed his tongue is not clear (Sanger, 1931: 48); (Sanger, 1938: 88–89).

Sanger's confrontation with the moral problem of abortion occurred before the First World War in a society beset by social problems due to industrialization, urbanization, and massive immigration. The Lower East Side was so densely populated that it is rivaled today only by Hong Kong. In Sanger's political circles, the Socialists were gaining strength and electing people to office. Labor "unrest" was rampant, and Sanger contributed her own efforts to the successful textile strike in Lawrence, Massachusetts organized by the syndicalist Industrial Workers of the World (the "Wobblies").

For Sanger, the moral problem of abortion was always a problem of women and their place in the world. She wrote in her diary,

Shall we who have heard the cries and seen the agony of dying women respect the law which has caused their deaths? Shall we watch in patience the murdering of 25,000 women each year in the United States from criminal abortions? (Margaret Sanger, October 19, 1914)

---

2. An interesting reference for sexual abuse in earlier days is Arnold (1989)

It took Sanger some time to understand how to name the problem to which she would devote her life. In 1914, she and a company of friends named it birth control. As the years passed and social conditions changed, the "Reds" suffered suppression and she worked with other groups using other means. In the process, she developed and modified her analysis of the moral problem of abortion.

Hers was a political analysis which, like the Anarchist and Socialist analyses, included its own strategy for social change. She worked to bring what was hidden to light and to make the problem public. Her analysis and strategy changed as social and political circumstances changed. She began in 1914 with her magazine, *The Woman Rebel,* using the Anarchist-modeled "direct action" of advocating abortion and birth control. In 1916 she opened an illegal birth control clinic. Then came American entry into World War I and the suppression of the "Reds," and with it, the collapse of the movement in which she had taken part. She changed her strategy with the times, and by the mid-1920s she had organized a medically supervised clinic—the Birth Control Research Bureau. She moved from working with "the women of the poor" to working with the women of the wealthy and the middle classes for the women of the poor, and for all women. In the end, the laws on contraceptives were changed and The Birth Control Federation of America was formed (shortly to become Planned Parenthood Federation of America), though by then the organization had parted company with the singular Sanger. She busied herself with other projects, one of which resulted in the development of oral contraceptives.

Through her years of political work, Sanger came to define the moral problem of birth control through what we might call a philosophical analysis, based on the goal of a world in which human beings could make good lives for themselves and their children. In her one philosophical book, *The Pivot of Civilization* (Sanger, 1922), she named two major arenas of complementary problems. One arena was economic in a traditional sense centered on men and their work. Socialists, Marxists, and even the more conservative union organizers concentrated on this arena for the solution to moral problems of economic injustice. But Sanger insisted that they had omitted the second arena, that of the "large family" problem, which includes the problem of sex, and the problem of woman and child. She wrote:

> In spite of all my sympathy with the dream of liberated labor, I was driven to ask whether this urging power of sex, this deep instinct, was not at least partially responsible, along with industrial injustice, for the widespread misery of the world. (Sanger, 1922: 7)

As she reasoned it out in *The Pivot of Civilization*, abortion was one face of a problem that was as deep as the problem of the laboring classes under capitalism. If men and women workers might gain freedom and humanity by struggling for a union or forming a revolutionary party, then women and men might gain freedom and humanity by struggling for birth control. She argued that both struggles were necessary for a better, more morally accept-able world in the future, and both were necessary for the moral development of men, women, and children in the present world.

In the course of her career, Sanger managed to legitimate the birth control problem to the point that "respectable" and influential people, and profes-sionals in medicine and other fields, worked with her. She made the moral problem of birth control public. In the end, Planned Parenthood became an organization dominated by "professionalized" thought and action. Birth control was reduced to contraception and planned spacing of childbearing. It was officially understood in terms of the abstract "individual choice" of an ethics in which sex was divested of moral force. It was no longer Sanger's birth control that was to allow women to discover their sexual passion while they took responsibility for procreation, not only in their personal lives but in family, community, nation, and world, so that women, children, and men might flourish.

Governance As an Answer

Margaret Sanger was a doer more than a thinker, an activist more than a philosopher. And yet *The Pivot of Civilization* showed a basic philosophical concern. Birth control was Sanger's answer to a philosophical as well as a social problem—the problem of how we should live. Birth control offered a means to responsibility and self-fulfillment and it did so in a way that answered the question of the good of each person's life as that life con-tributes to the good of the whole and future generations. In Sanger's eyes, it concerned the future not only of the person and her community but of all humanity. It linked the personal, the domestic, and the political; the woman, the man, the child, and the family, and the community, the nation, and the world. It did so in a distinctively new way that embodied the hopes of the twentieth century, and Sanger had a prophet's eye for some of the cen-tury's major social and moral problems. In distinction from most other philosophical ethics, birth control, as a complement to industrial justice, was an ethics for a radically changing society. As a moral idea, birth control included the process of making the "we." And because of this, it was her answer to the hidden conflict of class and gender dominance. It was also a way of answering fundamental questions about the morally good life and the common good.

The question of the good life was one of the first questions posed in West-ern philosophy. According to Plato, Socrates asked how one should live. Aristotle answered in terms of the virtues of the man of practical wisdom.[3] The wisdom of this virtuous man was right reason—orthos logos—that bound together the personal and the political, and that unified the good in his own life, the good of his household, and the public good. Aristotle's answer has often been treated as if it were an abstract, philosophical answer to timeless puzzles of how we should live. In fact, it was designed to be implemented in a world in which most issues of how we should live were already settled.[4]

These civilized Greek men, Socrates, Plato, and Aristotle, believed that rational reflection was important to answering the question of how we should live. Through wisdom and rational reflection, the wildness of human nature could be tamed and order could be brought to anarchy. The men were, after all, pinpoints of reason in a dark world of barbarism. They were beacons that lighted the way to Western civilization. They were reasonable men in an Athens that wallowed in the rough seas of direct democracy. They were patriarchs trying to hold together households and communities that were bloody with the irrationalities of birth and death, sex and lust, abuse, incest, and subjugation, war and greed. They faced the dark powers of nature and struggled to tame them. Their task was not, after all, so different from Sanger's. But the solutions were very different.

The keystone of Aristotle's ethics was the man of practical wisdom.[5] The man of practical wisdom was an ideal that made sense of the ethics. It was a way of presenting the ideal so that citizens could understand it. In terms I'll

---

3. For the most part, I'm talking about the Nichomachean Ethics here, with some background from the Politics. There is a vast secondary literature on Aristotle and I am not pretending to add anything to it. My point is rather to illustrate how I understand morality in terms of collective action.

4. In Bernard Williams' philosophical explanation, the Greek philosophers' answers were about a manner of life, not simply about what I should do now, or tomorrow, and not simply about my career plans. And they were about a whole life, one that (presumably) would be a life worth living for anybody, or at least anybody to whom they were addressing themselves. The search was for the good life for human beings, and the belief was that the good life would also be the life of a good person (Williams, 1985; 4–5, 20). This seems to ignore the patriarchal nature of the Greek Ethics.

Williams writes that it was important for philosophers (including the ancient Greeks), to justify morality, to give a rational, compelling argument for accepting, embracing the moral. Williams would say, "the ethical" here, for he uses "morality" in a narrow sense that covers systems like that of utilitarianism and Kantian ethics, and he uses "ethics" in a broad sense that includes Aristotelian sorts of ethics and many others. That use is bound to the philosophical canon, and it won't work for me. I use "an ethics" or "a morality" to refer to a substantive proposal to be implemented (or already implemented) as an answer to how we should live. I use "moral theory" to refer to the work of epistemology, ontology, methodology, etc., that allows professionals like myself to investigate an ethics or morality. In this sense, Marx and Engels were doing moral theory as well as proposing an ethics (though an ethics quite different from the bourgeois ethics they criticized).

5. My discussion of Aristotle was developed in part for the first Eunice Belgum memorial lecture at St. Olaf's college, 1978.

use in this book, the good life for man, family, and community was an out-come of collective action, the action of virtuous citizens and members of their households in a democratic city-state. Citizens bore a special responsi-bility for that outcome: the responsibility of the statesman and the father (in the guise of head of household).[6] They bore a special responsibility for seeing that other members of the community developed the virtues appropriate to the parts they played (or were to play) in the collective action. Aristotle approached morality from the point of view of the rulemakers and gover-nors. He was particularly concerned with framing an ethics that could be implemented in his social and political world.

Aristotle was concerned with how one comes to have the excellence of character that is the basis of moral knowledge. To learn to lead a good life, a man needed proper education in childhood and youth. As part of the process of gaining practical wisdom, the grown man needed a certain position in domestic life as well as civic life—the position of a head of household as well as that of a citizen of a democracy. Proper training and experience gave him a "natural authority" in *managing his kind of life from his kind of social position*. He knew through experience how to live his kind of life well. Others could see that he knew. The moral knowledge of the man of practical wisdom, and his place as the keystone of Aristotle's ethics, was based on his having natural authority in living that kind of life. His social position and his relationship with others were the sources of his responsibility as statesman and father, and they were also the sources of the knowledge he needed to fulfill the responsibility. They were the source of his moral empowerment. Aristotle's man of practical wisdom was a patriarch of his ancient civilization, not by accident of birth but essentially.

Although Aristotle did speak about virtuous women, he didn't analyze a woman of practical wisdom—in fact, I believe the idea of an Aristotelian woman of practical wisdom is incoherent because practical wisdom is tied to the perspectives and lives of free men of his ancient society.[7] As a result, the virtue of birth control was hidden, along with all the knowledge of the mys-teries women had charge of in his ancient world, all those matters in which women had natural authority in the situation. I like to think of the keystone of Sanger's ethics as the woman of practical wisdom. Sanger wrote *The Pivot of Civilization* (her "head book") as a theoretical work, and birth control seems to me a route to "the woman of practical wisdom," and to a more self-conscious "man of practical wisdom." It offered a way for poor and immi-grant women to bring reason into the seething Lower East Side, to light up

6. Hans Jonas (1984) takes statesman and parent to be paradigms for a theory of responsi-bilty.

7. To speak of the child of practical wisdom is even more incoherent.

the hidden secrets of lust, incest, and abuse, to bring fresh air to the dark and odorous intimacy of the household, and to put a rein on the bloody powers of birth and death. It offered this to educated and wealthy women as well, for their households and lives held the same secrets and they were subject to the same bloody powers. Sanger's ethics made these moral problems public. Aristotle's ethics hid them.

Aristotle's ethics hid women's knowledge. He (and his fellow patriarchs) hid the knowledge of children, slaves, and barbarians, even though that knowledge might have led them to define some moral situations differently from the way the man of practical wisdom defined them, sometimes even more reasonably, sometimes out of better acquaintance with the situation, even with greater natural authority. It was by hiding these things that the knowledge of the man of practical wisdom could be given authority over the knowledge of women, children, slaves, and barbarians.

Natural authority requires considerable experience in the kind of situation in question, a recognized know-how. A person with natural authority is well sensitized to the relevant features of the situation and to what the outcomes of choice might be. In contrast, cognitive authority is based on social position; in this case, the patriarchal position of the man who is head of household and, taking turns with other free men, head of state. Aristotle's discussion of the training needed for moral excellence and his explanation of moral knowing legitimated the cognitive authority of patriarchs relative to other members of their world. Among the patriarchs themselves, the ideal of the man of practical wisdom legitimated the natural authority of those who excelled; i.e., who had recognized experience and know-how in fulfilling the patriarchal work and life. In his scheme, this made them trustworthy "rule-makers"—or policymakers and judges. It also encouraged able patriarchs to develop excellence of character in themselves, their sons, and other male youths, and to develop virtue in their women. Given the way Aristotle connected ethics and politics, it also encouraged the patriarchs to support an appropriate kind of democratic state.

Aristotle legitimated the cognitive authority of the patriarch by his ethics and by his philosophical account of moral knowledge. He argued that there was one correct solution to a moral situation a person or community faced, thus one correct moral definition of a situation. It was the man of practical wisdom who assessed moral situations correctly—who saw the truth of the situation and the truth of its solution. Although anyone might have an opinion on the situation, the man of practical wisdom had knowledge. He knew the correct definition and solution not only for himself, and not only for men like himself. He knew the correct definition and solution for the moral situations of the women, children, slaves, and barbarians in his vicinity. His knowledge made a "we."

This view on the objectivity of knowledge made the moral and political knowledge of the man of practical wisdom *public* in a certain sense. It was the knowledge used to formulate and resolve moral problems; to educate the young; to reform the deviant; to define the lives and characters of all and sundry; to define the "we" and the "they." Public knowledge in this sense is not what "everybody knows" or what has become public after being hidden. Rather this public knowledge is called truth, and it is used to govern. The theory of moral knowledge legitimated the cognitive authority of the civilized patriarch. Thus patriarchy was justified as being necessary to the welfare of the whole community. Thus the good life of the civilized man was justified—in philosophical theory at least.

The "moral scheme" of the ideal Aristotelian democracy, or its "moral consensus" was not one which every member of the city-state needed to accept, understand, or even follow. To call it "the morality" of Aristotle's ideal society is to give ownership of the morality to the man of practical wisdom.

Aristotle himself defined the good for human beings, and how we should live. In very general terms, that common good was the ideal outcome for which the men of practical wisdom were responsible for articulating. Virtuous women were not in a position to define or criticize that outcome, for the straightforward reason that it was the responsibility of male heads of households and statesmen, in theory and in fact. There were other outcomes of the collective action in the good life of Aristotle's democracy. They included the massive subordination of women and those who were not free citizens. They also included hiding the responsibilities of procreation that women understood, as well as the responsibilities of people of the lower orders.

One obvious difference between Aristotle's ethics and whatever ethics I might devise to cover Margaret Sanger's work is that Sanger was concerned with bringing light to some of the things that Aristotle would tame by hiding.[8] She dealt with women's mysteries, something the patriarch did not bring his rational floodlight to. It wasn't simply that she made an alternative philosophy. As a reformer, she made the hidden public. Her ethics of birth control centered on eros, not logos.

Birth Control As an Answer

In ancient Greek myth, before the beginnings of Western philosophy, eros named a force of nature, the first to emerge from chaos, to unite all in a mar-

---

8. In discussing Aristotle and the good life, Bernard Williams (1985) does not discuss having and raising children as parts of the meaningful life, even though they are the most important parts of men's and women's lives and the greatest contribution to society and the future; even though speaking of having and raising children would recast some of the philosohical puzzles. The same is true of the dominant traditions in Anglo-American philosophy, though feminist philosophers and some philosophers in applied ethics explicitly deal with having and raising children.

riage out of which the gods were born.[9] The double face of eros binds the blind frenzy of passion and the order and sanctity of marriage. From the two come procreation, the orderly community, and the future of life. In this light, eros was not simply a force to be tamed. It was a deep mystery of life to be plumbed.

In the later myth of Psyche and Eros, the force became personified as the son of Aphrodite, a young god with the power to inflict love's passion on gods and humans alike. According to the story, Aphrodite is in a righteous snit because men have begun neglecting her temples and worshiping the beautiful, human maiden Psyche. She condemns Psyche to be wed to a monster, and she orders Eros to take Psyche to the desolate rock where the monster is to claim her. But Eros is scratched by one of his own arrows and falls in love with the beautiful mortal.

Eros then hides Psyche away in a splendid palace, possessing her for himself, isolated from the world of humans and the wrath of his mother. He comes only at night, and he forbids her to look upon him. Over time, Psyche grows to love what she believes to be an unseen "monster." She begins to feel that she must see the forbidden face of her lover, no matter what the risk. When her sisters are allowed to visit her, they support her feeling. One night, she lights a lamp and discovers the sleeping god—unfortunately waking him in the process.

After he discovers her looking upon his face, Eros abandons her. But Psyche is committed to her lover. To regain him, she must discipline herself to perform heroic tasks—including a descent to the underworld, that realm of death, the past, and the unconscious of the race. Throughout her heroic passage, she is "with child," bearing the future within her. She makes the journey together with her unborn daughter.

By the time the journey is over, Psyche has come to know herself. She also understands her husband and love itself. In the end, she humanizes Eros and gains divinity.

Like any human being, Psyche begins to know eros, the force of nature, by loving a particular person. The erotic morality is particularist not in being *reduced* to emotional bonds and relationships among particular creatures in the world (as an individualist ethics would have it). It is particularist in the

---

9. The matter is philosophically more complicated than I indicate in this section. See, for example, the discussion in Nussbaum (1986) and references in that book. See Peters (1967) for philosophical definitions. Apart from the philosophical literature, there is a large literature on eros and the erotic.

I see the standard philosophical interpretations of Plato as one extreme of a male viewpoint on eros, arguing that its development requires leaving behind sexual passion for the mystical, passionate embrace of the Forms, and ignoring the creativity of men, women, and children in procreation. I'm analyzing birth control as a development from sexual passion to the erotic bond with children, with partners over the long term, with the community, and with brothers and sisters in a movement.

sense that one comes to know the force of nature, the universal moral center, the "archetype," through the love of particular creatures. Eventually, through his love of a particular woman, the young god Eros comes to know the sacred force whose instrument he is. It is in this way that he is matured to a human morality, which is far deeper than the morality of the pagan gods. The process requires a heroic journey by Psyche to begin with, but it is a process that continues with the reunion of the two, the birth of their daughter (whom Apulius claims humans call "pleasure") and, presumably, the process of making a marriage and a home place through all life's changes. The erotic passion is transformed as it grows to include children and community, in the process of enacting the common good. In this sense, moral knowledge and its practical wisdom come through a lifelong process in which people grow to know the universal moral center in practice, through bonds with particular people, as they make a world and a future together. Psyche has been made divine, and the pagan gods have been made humane.[10]

Psyche's virtues are not those of governance, nor are they the "virtues" of altruism and self-sacrifice. They are virtues of courage and commitment, love, and procreation. It is through her relationship to Eros (and perhaps her sisters and her daughter) that Psyche is empowered. It is through their relationship with Psyche that Eros and the pagan gods are empowered. All of them gained in moral wisdom.

In Margaret Sanger's ethics, I believe birth control tamed Eros by freeing women's and men's sexuality, in the same movement in which it tamed procreation. I say procreation here, rather than reproduction, because it involves not animal birth as the biologists define it but a social activity that includes the care and love and raising of the new generation. This is the work of the community, not merely of the parents. It is procreation in the sense of carrying on the work of the past in generating the future. It has to do with the good of the whole in a number of ways—the future of the community and world, including the education, feeding, housing, and humanizing of the young as well as temperence in childbearing, what is now redefined as population control (a definition from the point of view of governance). Birth control covers the mysteries of sexual, maternal, and paternal love, and the love of other kin. This is procreative responsibility in a different sense from that of Aristotle's statesman or head of household.

Birth control was the virtue (or cluster of virtues) that would come from, be created from, knowing the face of eros. A woman's knowledge of self, sex-

---

10. Some time after I wrote my original discussion of Psyche and Eros for this chapter, I began reading Carl Jung's work and eventually attended the two-week summer workshop at the C.G. Jung Institute in Boston. My discussion here benefitted from my work there. I particularly thank Manisha Roy for her discussions and for giving me the reference to Neumann (1956). My use of the myth has a different point, however, and accordingly my interpretation is somewhat different.

uality, marriage, childbirth, nature, and life itself depended upon it—according to the myth and Sanger's ethics. But so did a man's. Sanger wrote,

> In increasing and differentiating her love demands, woman must elevate sex into another sphere, whereby it may subserve and enhance the possibility of individual and human expression. Man will gain in this no less than woman; for in the age-old enslavement of women he has enslaved himself; and in the liberation of womankind, all of humanity will experience the joys of a new and fuller freedom. (Sanger, 1922: 212)

There is a "supreme morality" of mutual and reciprocal joy in the most intimate relation between woman and man. The joy Sanger described accompanied a bond of unity that grew with the passage of life, as human beings ripened in practical wisdom.

Birth control in Sanger's sense brought together what are separated today into problems of "sex" (including homosexual and teenage sex as special problems), "reproduction," "childcare," "population problems," and a dozen others. In the public morality of the United States today, some of these things are left to private and subjective choice while others are brought under government policy—and birth control has been reduced to a contraceptive technology.

Sanger included the twentieth-century emphasis on self-development of the person in her idea of birth control. She wrote,

> Birth Control is an ethical necessity for humanity today because it places in our hands a new instrument of self expression and self realization. It gives us control over one of the primordial forces of nature, to which in the past the majority of mankind have been enslaved, and by which it has been cheapened and debased. It arouses us to the possibility of newer and greater freedom. It develops the power, the responsibility and intelligence to use this freedom in living a liberated and abundant life. . . . By knowing ourselves, by expressing ourselves, by realizing ourselves more competely than has ever before been possible, not only shall we attain the kingdom [of heaven within us] but we shall hand on the torch of life undimmed to our children and the children of our children. (Sanger, 1922: 21)

In her early work, Sanger's idea of responsibility and self-development was quite different from current liberal views, not only because she included sex as part of public morality (rather than personal choice), but also because she took class conflict to be important. Birth control, in her original vision, was the complement of industrial justice. Syndicalists called the conflict between labor and capital a fight for "industrial justice." The working classes were the agents of social change for both industrial justice and birth control. These agents of change were also the groups who had moral knowledge (or rather,

37

the potential for moral discovery and learning) in the syndicalist epistemology. Although Sanger does not say so, I believe that in the course of revolutionary action, the erotic bond would be transformed and extended to brothers and sisters in the movement. It provided the force that would make possible the creation of a common future and a common good.

The anarcho-syndicalist vision was anticapitalist as well as antistate, and the goal was a stateless society in which the coordination necessary for social life on a large scale was to be carried on through federated worker syndicates.[11] In the United States, the International Workers of the World—the IWW or Wobblies—were the proponents of the vision, and Sanger worked with them.

The syndicalist means of social change were through direct action, a mass challenge to established rules and particularly to the law. Their strikes were only one sort of direct action. Sanger's understanding of birth control before World War I included direct action. The most striking example was her advertising and opening a birth control clinic, knowing there would be a confrontation with authorities. Women came by the hundreds, and Sanger's belief was that they would fight for the clinic, thereby taking an important part of social life into their own hands.

I'll discuss the syndicalist epistemology at greater length in chapter 3. In brief, the idea was that in a direct action of a strike, workers would learn the repressive nature of the capitalist-democratic state, not in abstract theory but by seeing how the police, the government officials, and the priests and ministers supported the owners to crush the strike. By acting, workers would see capitalism in action and learn how to change it. In the course of organizing the strike and relief committees, supplying food, housing workers, caring for the sick, the infirm, and the children, the people would learn together how to make a new moral and social order. They would come to learn the grand stateless society in the process of making it in their communities. The general strike, built upon the experience of multitudes of local strikes, would finally shut down the capitalist-democratic state and make way for the new order. It would also shut down "civil society" and the old institutions with a process of making new ones. The action was collective and the freedom they were looking for lay in the collective possibilities for human good. Empowerment lay in the relationships created in the collective action, empowerment of the person as well as the working class. Empowerment lay in the erotic bond of revolutionary brotherhood and sisterhood.

As with Aristotle's epistemology, moral knowledge is here placed with

---

11. The one, large-scale test of something like this organization was during the Spanish Civil War, though syndicates became less important and collectives became a major form of coordination. Syndicates are based on work and membership is through work. Membership in collectives is voluntary. See Leval (1975).

members of a social subgroup. For Aristotle, it was the man of practical wisdom among the patriarchs. For the syndicalists, it was those groups among the working class who learned by taking part in direct action.

If we compare Sanger's moral theory with Aristotle's, we see that workers could come to have natural authority in the situations relevant to industrial justice. Women of the working classes could come to have natural authority in the situations relevant to birth control. This isn't to say that simply as women or workers they had the wisdom necessary to govern society or self. Their natural authority rested not only on past and present experience per se but on the fact that their experience was that of people in certain positions in the class and gendered society. It was a position that enabled them to take direct action to reveal the present society as they moved toward the future. Because of this, they were in a position to learn, and to discover the moral knowledge in practice. This, at least, is *my reconstruction* of the syndicalist approach.

The outcome of the collective action was supposed to be the creation of a new good and a new social order. But the moral responsibility in question did not belong to statesmen or heads of households.

The natural authority of Aristotle's man of practical wisdom rested on the training and experience of people in certain positions in a class and gendered society. But the man of practical wisdom represented the established, stable public face of his society. In contrast, at the turn of the century in the United States, the men and women of the working class were believed to be in a position to show what was hidden in their society. I would say that the syndicalist idea was that their direct action showed what was hidden in a way that allowed them to move beyond it and make a new world and a new good for all humanity. In the process, the men and women would make their new selves as they made the new society. In a sense, they would invent their practical wisdom as they invented the world that would suit it. Though each person contributed in his or her own way, they could only make their selves and the new world together. Their direct action made a bond among them. They were empowered by those new relationships. In taking the moral step, they made a new "we."

An Individualist Answer

Even as Margaret Sanger's birth control movement matured into the family-planning establishment, so over the next half century, her syndicalist ethics of birth control was gradually supplanted by a universalistic, individualistic ethics. The ethics presupposes a particular understanding of human persons and human action. Clifford Geertz described it as a "Western conception":

the person as a bounded, unique, more or less integrated motivational and cognitive universe, a dynamic center of awareness, emotion, judgment, and action, organized into a distinctive whole and set contrastively both against other such wholes and against its social and natural background. (Geertz, 1984: 126)[12]

This idea of a person and action relies on a dualism of individual organism and environment, and the idea of action as individual choice among options within the social or natural environment. It usually includes the idea that environment acts on the individual, and it has become the dominant model for professionals and policymakers in the United States.

The individualist ethics was not one of eros and soul but of logos and mind. As it was developed by philosophers, the ethics relied upon a division between *public morality* of rights, obligations, and justice and a *private morality* of life plan and choice and value. In both cases, it was individuals who were said to have knowledge—whether knowledge of the public moral principles or knowledge of one's own, personal preferences and good. This division of the public and private is one that makes no sense in the syndicalist scheme of things. This is in part because it reduces the erotic ethics to private choice, rather than common creation; in part because the knowers and doers are claimed to be individuals, not collectivities; and in part because it presupposes the existence of a state which enforces the public morality of rights, obligations, and justice.

The freedom in this ethics of logos and mind is also individual. Individuals are to have the liberty to pursue their own ends according to their own ideas of the good, provided they don't infringe on the liberty of other individuals to do the same. The ideal of freedom as individual liberty is radically different from what I would take to be the syndicalist ideal of freedom, which I take to be collective possibility in the context of the good of the whole. It is also radically different from Aristotle's ideal which concerned not freedom but virtue as the foundation of a good life and the good of the whole. In the individualist perspective, the good life is left very much to private choice of *lifestyle*—within a public framework of moral principles. There is a public ideal of good of course, involving health and education, for example, and (within broad limits) the proper care of children. But a great deal that Aristotle included in the good life is left to private choice.[13]

---

12. Ellen Messer-Davidow (forthcoming) gives an excellent overview discussion of the liberal, individualist approach in contrast to other theoretical analyses of persons and agency.

13. Michael Sandel (1982, 1984) plays down the many institutionalized expressions of the public good in the United States in his attacks on what he calls the procedural republic and the unencumbered self. In Dewey's liberal ethics, the good had an important place in framing the democracy—particularly in terms of giving room for people to develop and exercise the virtues of intelligence. This moral goal was one of his main reasons for promoting participa-

Many feminists have argued that the division between public and private is tied in with gender dominance, and it is an outgrowth of the old division between men's (public) sphere and women's (domestic) sphere.[14] In the philosophical ethics, the division is associated with a distinction between moral autonomy and personal autonomy. The public morality ("our moral scheme") is defined as one of principles concerning rights, obligations, moral permissibility (rightness and wrongness), and principles of justice. The principles are universalizable, and impartial. They are said to be the sorts of principles having to do with *moral autonomy*; i.e., principles that would be chosen when people freely and autonomously give themselves a moral law. In this philosophical ethics, moral autonomy (or governing oneself under a freely chosen moral law) is complemented by *personal autonomy*, which concerns individual freedom to choose personal values and a good life. Together the two kinds of autonomy form the keystone of this philosophical ethics, as the man of practical wisdom formed the keystone of Aristotle's ethics.

The two sorts of autonomy parallel a separation between rightness and goodness. Moral autonomy is part of the theory of the right, dealing with obligation, rightness, rights, liberty, and justice. Personal autonomy is part of the theory of the good. This marks a kind of division between rightness and goodness that Aristotle did not make, convinced as he was that there was one good for mankind. Nor did Sanger's ethics mark the distinction. My own concern is with how the division is enacted.

Put simply, in this ethics an individual's values, ends, pleasures, happiness, and what he or she takes as good are private and subject to individual free choice provided they do not violate the principles of the sphere of rightness and justice (Rawls, 1971; Sandel 1982, 1984). Other moralities, including religion, sexuality, and politics, tend to be construed as individual choices of attitudes, values, or lifestyles, all of them constrained by the genuine moral principles of the theory of the right. Robert Bellah and his associates claim that, in its everyday form, this ideal of personal autonomy and privacy represents the "thinking about the self of educated Americans, almost hegemonic in our universities and much of the middle class" (Bellah et al., 1985: 84).[15]

---

tion in solving moral problems. Damico (1978) gives a helpful, fairly brief overview of Dewey's approach.

14. Despite the extreme, technical precision of the philosophical theory, the public/private division is one of many incoherencies in the individualist ethics. For some of the discussion, see Ardener (1975, 1985); Elshtain (1981); Jaggar (1983); Collier and Yanagisako (1987); and various books on liberalism listed in my bibliography.

15. The principles of the theory of the right aren't simply those a rational person might choose to govern him or herself. They are taken to be the principles of the public morality in the United States, and to rightly serve as the moral basis for public policy—thus the philosophic analysis of abortion as a conflict of rights. This belief underlies the philosophers' claims to be analyzing "our moral concepts," and in fact, developmental psychologist

What does it mean that this individualist perspective seems to be "almost hegemonic" in the thinking about the self? Or perhaps my question is, What does it matter if people think in terms of the individualist perspective? What does individual *thinking* have to do with what people *do* in the United States? What does individual thinking have to do with the "we"?

The answers to these questions may seem self-evident. After all, both democracy and the educational system in the United States appear to operate by means of thinking ("Let man know and trust him"). The "we" is supposed to be supported by consensus (or at least majority opinion), and an agreement on "our" principles and values includes accepting the individualist ethics which gives the framework. But that pleasant story may operate as a way to hide what is most important in the making of the "we" (despite some philosophers' infatuation with conversation and consensus). The story may hide what is most important to the question of how we should live. To find out, it's necessary to look at some ways in which the individualist perspective is enacted. My strategy will be to use cases in which there has been conflict over the individualist perspective itself, using the conflict to show features of the perspective that tend otherwise to be hidden.

The Case of Sex Education

Throughout the twentieth century, sex education has been an arena of conflict in the United States. The progressive view favored educating all and sundry about sexual matters, and over the course of half a century, it slowly made headway (see chapters 3 and 4). After the "sexual revolution" of the 1960s and early 1970s, the progressive's path was easier—made easier still when teen pregnancy was defined as a public problem in the mid 1970s. With public notice of the AIDS epidemic in the late 1980s, the opposition to sex

---

Lawrence Kohlberg dubbed this liberal theory of the right, "the official morality of the United States" (Kohlberg, 1969). Liberal philosophers do, of course, put in time on the theory of the good. John Rawls devotes the second half of his massive *A Theory of Justice* to the good (and the domestic sphere) (Rawls, 1971). Diana Meyers has developed a detailed feminist account of personal autonomy in *Self, Society, and Personal Choice*, one that radically criticizes the usual liberal account for using male models (Meyers, 1989). Robert Bellah and his colleagues wrote the bestselling *Habits of the Heart* to offer practical suggestions on overcoming the unencumbered (or empty) self, advising us to become a community of memory by constructing a narrative to make sense of our lives, and by teaching civic virtue in the colleges and universities (Bellah et al., 1985). However interesting these efforts may be, they do not offer what is necessary to bring together the good and the right: a useable explanation of how our collective action creates and maintains the moral and political order, thus how we might go about changing it. Others have offered new theories of virtue and the good (MacIntyre, 1981), or accounts of maternal or feminine moral thinking (Ruddick, 1989; Noddings, 1984) or of various "women's ways" or "different voices" (Belenky et al., 1986; Gilligan, 1982; Baier, 1985). The difficulty is that though these new versions of ethics are original and illuminating, there has been, so far, no way to implement them within the public morality.

education began to crumble, though many of the differences in the under-standing and practice of sexuality did not magically disappear.

In the United States, "sex education" proper has usually been understood in terms of classroom courses, professional counseling with individuals, or through posters, publications, and media of various sorts. The individualist perspective reigns: each individual intellectually absorbs information, makes up his or her mind, and somehow changes his or her behavior. It is an approach quite different from driver education, which requires hands-on training and a test of practical abilities—though both driving and sex may lead to regrettable accidents.

In the early 1990s in the United States, there are two main approaches to sex education in the schools, captured in two popular schoolroom texts.[16] They are based on different definitions of the problem that needs to be solved, and so they offer different solutions.

"Sex Respect: The Option of True Sexual Freedom" (Williams, 1991) takes premarital sex to be the problem—sex (as heavy petting or inter-course) threatens vulnerable young women and damages the family. The solution is for teens to choose abstinence from heavy petting and inter-course. This permits learning self-control and respect for others. Abstinence allows girls to act in accord with their inner nature. Abstinence teaches boys that sex goes with responsibility and community and gives them a chance to learn what love is. The text does not offer contraceptive information, but it does give a lot of practical advice on how to avoid getting carried away by passion (heavy petting may lead to getting carried away) and how to stand up against peer pressure.

"Values and Choices: Sex in Teen Dating" (Mast, 1986) also suggests that abstinence may be the best choice for dating teens, but it doesn't restrict sex to love and marriage. The significant problem named in this book is not sex, it is pregnancy. Mast offers contraceptive information in case the teens choose not to abstain. It emphasizes communication, and responsible, ratio-nal decisions as well as making an individual life plan.

"Sex Respect" might be classified as taking a traditional perspective, but not quite under the slogan, "Let man learn his duty and obey!" Like the pro-gressive "Values and Choices," it emphasizes *choice* by the teen—which may reflect the fact that "Sex Respect" has to be suitable for adoption in the public schools. But the traditional text makes it explicit that the choice has to do with following the proper route of the proper life plan of how we should live: love, marriage, and family. The progressive text supposes that the teens may

---

16. I'm grateful to my student Stephanie Shinn for bringing a number of good references to my attention. I also thank Leslie Kayan, who works with the Family Planning Council of West-ern Massachusetts doing sex education classes for local public schools, for background infor-mation and for referring us to the two sex education texts.

choose their *lifestyle* from a broader range. Gender stereotypes are also played down in the progressive text.

I said that "Sex Respect" takes a more traditional approach. But there are citizens in the United States who oppose any sex education in the schools. In fact, sex education is one focal point of an ongoing conflict in the United States over how we should live. The battle is being fought by increasingly sophisticated political means. Conservative organizations at the national level, for example Pat Robertson's Christian Coalition, provide local groups with organizing manuals and speakers for community meetings. In 1994, the "progressive" pro-sex-education forces have been led to use a similar strategy to "reclaim the Bible and the family." Planned Parenthood Federation of America has begun providing materials. This transforms the issue by setting it in ways appropriate for national interest-group politics, thus for the ongoing battle between "progressive and traditional civilization."

Experience and the long battle have softened the progressive approach. "Values and Choices" represents a more cautious approach to sex education than some of the earlier "progressive" efforts. This softening may be an outcome of the conflict in the United States as well as a growing sensitivity to the difficult situations of dating teens. The individualist perspective shows more clearly in the earlier book, *Sex and Birth Control: A Guide for the Young*, by E. James Lieberman, M.D., and Ellen Peck, author of an advice column for teens.[17] The book was selected by the American Library Association as one of the "best books of the year" for young adults when it was first published in 1973 (revised in 1982). The introduction was contributed by longtime Planned Parenthood official Mary Calderone, who by 1973 was with the Sex Information and Education Council of the United States (SIECUS).

The authors presented a relativist position on sex and morality, writing that there has never been agreement about what is normal or moral, and that no one can give absolute answers. What's taken to be true at one time or place may be rejected in another. In fact, they write, any discussion of values is subjective because science can't decide certain issues. Because of this, the authors offer "several points of view, leaving the reader to decide what is best for him or her" (Lieberman and Peck, 1982: 202; xii). Despite the talk about moral truth varying with time and place, the authors set the all-important framework, which includes reducing morality to individual value and choice.[18]

---

17. The authors claimed their book offered "a practical presentation on sexual freedom and responsibility," written at the request of high school and college teachers (Lieberman and Peck, 1982: xi).

18. Lieberman and Peck do insist on some universal moral principles. They want sex conduct to be based on "ethics," which includes respect for other people's rights, and not on a compulsory moral code in the old tradition. They counsel tolerance toward homosexuals, and they advise that anything two consenting adults enjoy is all right (Lieberman and Peck, 1982: 215–18).

I brought up the importance of cognitive authority in discussing Aristotle. It is also important here, as part of the framework. The authors separate fact and value, a move that sets science as the authority on objective truth. The separation makes another division between public and private which, though less often marked, is very important. *Fact is public.* In the United States, it is science (or more precisely, scientific professionals and their aides in the service professions, the educational systems, and the media) that is the primary public source of factual knowledge of nature, including human nature. In the Lieberman and Peck version, "science" tells students not only that there is one truth in factual matters, it tells them that there is a diversity of moral values and goods available for individual choice. This view of knowledge is universalistic and egalitarian; with the proper training, anyone can know the true and choose his good. It involves a premise of epistemic equality (anyone can know . . .), but in fact it presupposes that cognitive authority be vested in certain groups—particularly professionals. In his ethics, Aristotle was explicit about the authority of the man of practical wisdom. In the individualist ethics, authority is hidden under a veil of reason, objective truth, equality, tolerance, and freedom.

The authority is not limited to science or to the "fact" side of the "fact-value" separation. This is because the framework of moral and personal autonomy is a given. The authors of the sex education texts recommend *responsible* sex. In the more traditional book, teens are encouraged to be chaste, while in the progressive text they are offered a choice of chastity or satisfying their sexual "needs" while using contraceptives. But both texts are set within the moral framework as it is implemented in the ironclad practice of the public schools: students have life plans which will be disrupted by "irresponsible" behavior, with resulting harm to the future of both student and nation. The statement skitters along the edge of tautology, since what is irresponsible is understood as what disrupts a responsible life plan.

The framework displays the planning motif that is *basic* to the individualist ethics of democratic state and market. In the more technical statement offered by philosopher John Rawls,

> The main idea is that a person's good is determined by what is for him the most rational long-term plan of life given reasonably favorable circumstances. A man is happy when he is more or less successful in the way of carrying out this plan. To put it briefly, the good is the satisfaction of rational desire. We are to suppose, then, that each individual has a rational plan of life drawn up subject to the conditions that confront him. It schedules activities so that various desires can be fulfilled without interference. It is arrived at by rejecting other plans that are either less likely to succeed or do not provide for such an inclusive attainment of aims. Given the alternatives available, a rational plan is one which cannot be improved upon; there is no other plan which, taking everything into account, would be preferable. (Rawls, 1971: 92–93)

Both the progressive and the traditional sex education texts seem to be ways of implementing Rawls' statement. In fact, the public schools seem to be founded upon it.

The individualist ethics of moral and personal autonomy enters into "public policy" as well as individual choice, of course. It serves as the dominant framework for defining and resolving moral problems that are made public. I'll describe one attempt at making a moral problem public to illustrate what I mean.

The Wilde-Stein Club vs. the Maine Ministers

In "Gay Movements and Legal Change," Steven Cohn and James Gallagher reported on the process of implementing homosexual rights in Maine in the mid-1970s. The significant events included: the founding of a gay student club whose members proposed a conference on a University of Maine campus; adoption of a gay rights plank in the state's Democratic party platform; revision of the state's criminal code to decriminalize homosexual activities; and a second conference organized by the gay students' group. These events took place between September, 1973 and June, 1975. Only the first caused controversy and so might be seen, in the context, as an attempt to make a moral problem public.[19]

The club in question was the Wilde-Stein Club, which was given probationary recognition as a campus group in October 1973 and final recognition a year later. As one of their first actions, group members began planning a statewide gay conference to be held on university grounds. The use of facilities was normally granted to recognized campus groups, and after some stalling by the university president, the Board of Trustees approved the use of campus facilities for the conference. The action caused a controversy to erupt (Cohn and Gallagher, 1984: 73–74).

Cohn and Gallagher distinguished three constituencies involved in what they call an "intense debate" over the issue, each with a different definition of the moral problem involved. There were those sensitive to particular problems faced by homosexuals, and they defined the issue in terms of the need for personal self-development and fulfillment, as a part of the common good. There were those who took a civil libertarian approach, and they viewed homosexuals as only one of many groups whose civil rights must not be abridged. The third group was spearheaded by fundamentalist Christian ministers, and they defined the problem in terms of sexual injunctions in the Bible and the moral importance of traditional family and social structures. The

---

19. The sociologists' terms are "public problem" and "social problem," but for my purposes it is important to speak of making moral problems public. See Spector and Kitsuse (1977); Gusfield (1981).

three groups offered different definitions of the moral problem in question, and their solutions differed accordingly. The first two advocated allowing the Wilde-Stein club to operate and hold the conference. The ministers' solution was to disband the club, cancel the conference, and have the legislature punish the University by cutting its budget (Cohn and Gallagher, 1984: 74, 75).

In presenting their cases, all sides used the methods of communication open to them. But there were significant differences in access to both policy-makers and the public. The ministers were able to reach people through their congregations and through their television and radio shows and they also had the ears of a relatively small group of conservative legislators. But as time passed, they were warned off the topic by the television and radio managers, and they came to be seen as "no news" by the newspaper because "everyone expected them to say what they did."

The president and trustees of the university were distinguished and influential people in the city, and the university was in general considered a valuable institution. Their viewpoint came to dominate the media, and even the politically conservative newspaper's coverage and editorials were weighted in support of the university's position. Professionals and experts of various sorts provided explanations on the legal and psychological aspects of the issue. The problem soon came to be defined in terms of the right to free speech and assembly, and the ministers and their associates came to be perceived as threatening the public good rather than defending it. The Wilde-Stein Club held its conference (Cohn and Gallagher, 1984: 81, 83).[20]

The skirmish more or less effectively damaged the opposition to gay liberties. The gay rights plank of the Democratic party platform caused only a little controversy. The revision of the Maine legal code that decriminalized homosexual acts did not cause controversy, in the main because it received very little public discussion, and then only in terms of eliminating "victimless crimes" in accord with recommendations of the model penal code of the American Law Institute. There was no conflict for the media to report. The second Wilde-Stein conference also received little publicity and no opposition.

Forms of Morality

In the midst of the political fray, the issues involved in the Wilde-Stein affair were represented by "progressives" as objective matters of law, fact, and American guarantees of civil liberties. The ministers came to be painted as being ignorant of science, clinging to religious dogma and superstition. I

---

20. The civil liberties definition is one current way of publicly legitimating the "personal self-fulfillment" ethics—it places that ethics under an individual lifestyle rubric that is protected from public interference. I'll discuss other ways of representing the personal self-fulfillment ethics in later chapters.

represented the conflict (with Cohn and Gallagher's help) as a collective action in which one definition of the situation triumphed over others. It was a skirmish over who "we" are and what "our" American values and norms are. In the skirmish, the *authority* of scientists and legal scholars, educators, journalists, and other professionals was *used* at the same moment that it was *enacted*. The individualist perspective was used to argue one side over the other at the same time that it was being enacted as "our perspective."

I want to stress that I am trying to see the collective process of making a "we" and a consensus here, not trying to defend one side over another. The members of the Wilde-Stein Club, and their many supporters, took the stand that "lifestyles" should be open to the public light of day. Protecting the right of the lesbian and gay students to share public goods is a victory for justice and liberal democracy. For philosophic purposes, my question is not with the justice of the outcome. I am trying to show the way the issue was defined and fought.

Under the definition of the individualist ethics, the gay perspective was opened to the light of day. More than that, in Maine, homosexuality itself was legitimated as a free choice of lifestyle (at least for the time being). By the 1990s, progressive thinkers were writing texts for schoolchildren on the gay "lifestyle choice" aimed at educating children as they developed from grades 1 through 12.[21]

The battle over homosexuality continues, for example, in the struggles over avowed gays and lesbians in the U.S. military. The question I'm concerned with doesn't have to do with the righteousness of the battle, but with the terms in which it is defined and fought. Does it really make sense to parse homosexuality as an individual lifestyle choice? Does an abstract morality of values and principles capture what is at issue? Let me return to the case of the Wilde-Stein Club vs. the Maine Ministers.

I believe the ministers' approach to the public morality was deeply different from the individualist approach. As I reconstruct it, they and many members of their flock had known there were homosexuals around, just as they had known there were prostitutes, abortionists, and other "sinners" around. As long as these people were treated as deviant outsiders, as "hardened offenders," the flock and particularly their children were protected from the knowledge of what those lives were. Homosexuality as an option was *hidden*. The homosexuals' knowledge of the world, and their viewpoint on "respectable" folk, was hidden. The "way we should live" that was open to public view was a way the ministers could endorse.

---

21. See the very disapproving discussion of "The Children of the Rainbow" by George F. Will, in his December 6, 1992 *Boston Globe* column. See also the much better tempered and very funny takeoff of a PBS show on teenage dating and sex on the December 5, 1992 "Saturday Night Live." The dating teens are gay.

In the moral passage in question, the club and its conference opened the gay perspective and knowledge to the light of day. More than that, homosexuality itself was legitimated as a "lifestyle choice." This is not a simple change in the realm of private values. *It is a change in the form of the public morality, and it is a change in the form of moral knowledge and action.* It is not only a change in the understanding of how we should privately live (homosexual vs. heterosexual), it is a change in who "we" are—and of course this is evident to gays and lesbians, for in the past, qua homosexuals, they have been excluded from the "we" and their lives and history hidden away. Closeted. It is a change in how the "we" is constituted, a change in who has the authority and the power to generate the "we" and to define the public morality.

The continuing battles over who is to be allowed to march in Saint Patrick's Day parades raise analogous problems. To include Irish gay and lesbian organizations in the march is to acknowledge them as Irish groups in good standing. It acknowledges their way of life as a publicly accepted way, open to anyone's choice, even though the Irish Catholic Church condemns it as sinful. Homosexuals are certainly known to exist among the Catholics— some say that 40% of priests in the United States are gay.[22] However, the view is that the sexual sin must be resisted, and if it cannot be resisted, it must at least be hidden. From one point of view, this looks like hypocrisy. From another, it is a difference in understanding what the public morality is and how it is to be implemented. It is a difference in understanding what *education* is, including sex education. It is a difference in the form and practice of the public morality and the interplay not between public and private, as the individualist perspective would have it, but between *the public and the hidden.* It is a difference in the way life is lived, so that the moral consensus is upheld publicly and the moral responsibility of the virtuous includes hiding their own vice.

The change in moral form to advocating that deviance be "exposed to the public light of day" is relatively recent, one that began to emerge at the end of the 1960s, in the midst of revelations about the Vietnam War and later, the Watergate affair. The faults of respectable public figures and institutions had been hidden—the physical and moral disabilities of Franklin Delano Roosevelt and John F. Kennedy; the dreadful character of sports heroes like Babe Ruth; even the sins of the FBI, CIA, DOE, and the military. So in a sense, the traditionals were fighting not only for the older form of morality but for the older customs of governance.

These are very deep battles, and they have to do with how the "we" is to be made and who is to define it. At issue is a struggle over authority. The ability to define (or redefine) a moral problem grants the power to disable the oppo-

---

22. I was given the 40% estimate by a friend who is a Catholic priest.

sition and define the solution to the problem—thus to some degree, the future of the group. The ability to make a moral problem public, and so to define it, is an ability to define the way "we" should live. It is a way of defining the common good. The battle for the twentieth century has been, in its crucial aspects, a battle waged by making moral problems public and so defining the public morality.

The Wilde-Stein case serves as an example of the transfer of power in defining the public morality, from traditional holders of moral authority (ministers and righteous folk) to others, particularly professionals, bureaucrats, media specialists, legislators, and jurists. The cast of characters involved in the incident is much larger than it appears at first glance. It includes the people Cohn and Gallagher name—the students, the ministers and their congregations, the university officials, the reporters, the legislators, and so on. It also includes activists and reformers like the American Civil Liberties Union and some feminist and gay groups who enter into defining these sorts of issues on a national level, even though they may not have been actively involved in this event. In a more hidden way, the cast of characters includes lawyers and jurists, philosophers, political scientists, and sociologists who develop and teach theories that support one side or the other. The theories include the individualist ethics of the sort I discussed above, when I used the words of Lieberman and Peck and John Rawls. Under those theories, sex is not a moral issue at all when it concerns consenting adults. Freedom of expression is. So in the battle between the Maine Ministers and the Wilde-Stein Club, philosophers and many other professionals entered the cast of characters as partisans. They entered by providing constituencies, but most of all, they entered by providing a moral language, an "extra-local" vocabulary through which local experience was recycled (Smith, 1987).

The Maine Ministers' idea was that the homosexual answer to how to live should be hidden. But in the Wilde-Stein case, the moral viewpoint of the Maine Ministers ended up being hidden because they did not use a moral language that worked effectively in media, legislature, and university.[23] They were unable to make public the moral problem as they defined it. The minister's viewpoint doesn't find favor among most intellectuals in the United States, so to be persuasive here, I'll mention the viewpoint of another group in the cast of characters.

The viewpoint of what Cohn and Gallagher called "the third constituency" was also hidden. Members of that constituency argued that the Club and the conference were necessary for human self-development. This was at root a

---

23. Dorothy Williams, author of the traditional text "Sex Respect" knew how to use an acceptable vocabulary, thus the framework of teen choice rather than a biblical framework (Williams, 1991). By the 1990s, conservatives had switched to the individualist vocabulary for political purposes.

concern with the good of the whole community and its ability to foster a good life and personal fulfillment for each of its members. Under the rights and liberties definition, personal fulfillment was redefined as the freedom to choose an individual lifestyle.[24] There wasn't a place in the problem, as it was defined, for discussing how we should live collectively, and in what sort of community, even though this line of thought might have opened ground for a more straightforward moral confrontation with the ministers. The discussion was precluded by the presupposition that liberty and tolerance for difference in individual lifestyle settled the question of collective life.

The ethics that supported the Wilde-Stein Club's rights used an essential division between public and private. The division refers, on the one hand, to what is subject to regulation under the public morality of the democracy, against what is left open to "free" and personal choice (and so shouldn't be interfered with). If we parse the Wilde-Stein controversy in these terms, we find that the winning side argued that under the public morality, homosexuality is a matter of personal choice of sexual orientation and holding the conference was an issue of free assembly. In the terms within which the issue was set, the outcome is just and morally progressive. The winners certainly granted that the Maine Ministers had the right to their own free choice of values, but they must not insert them as part of the public morality. That is, the ministers' morality (and in fact their religion and science) were encapsulated within the private sphere and could not be used to regulate others who did not freely choose those values or beliefs, even their own children and kin. Even the concern of the third constituency (a concern with moral issues of collective life) was relegated to the private sphere of individual choice. What operated in the public sphere was the morality of individual rights, liberties, choices, and entitlements. This gave the public framework within which the question of how we should live was to be answered.

By the 1990s, conservatives had moved to the individualist framework. The Maine Ministers proved naive in using their biblical approach. At present, the more successful strategy (used in mounting state campaigns) is to oppose legal protection against discrimination for gays and lesbians, on the grounds that homosexuality is not a *minority* classification. This is politically and legally an effective move falling within not only the usual politics and law but within the framework of the individualist ethics.

Summary

In this chapter, I have compared three moral theories in an informal way, and I've begun to consider some of their modes of implementation. I've

---

24. Bellah et al. (1985) are concerned with the "self-development" theme. See also Taylor (1989).

hinted at a way to approach the issue of how we should live and the question of the common good, not as a question philosophers (or other professionals) might answer in the line of duty, but as something that is fought out in making a "we" and a group life. Morality is a process of making both community and character. Some theorists have said that *narrative* is what brings together community and character (Hauerwas, 1981; MacIntyre, 1981). Using that language, I would say that the *narrative* of the civil libertarians and the fundamentalist ministers was quite different, and I'd explain how. But that would still leave open the most important question of how the narratives were enacted in defining a "we," and in what ways they were used, in practice, to set how we do live. And it would leave untouched the issues of who has the cognitive authority. A narrative, after all, isn't just words, it is words in use, and the use must be uncovered. I begin doing so in the next chapter, looking at cases in order to understand what it might mean to be committed to a narrative, or to apply a moral principle, or to enact a moral norm or choose a value, or to define the common good. I understand these as collective actions, not individual actions. Throughout the book, I try to illustrate the dynamic nature of human group life in generating and regenerating the selves of both the virtuous and the "hardened offenders." I believe the cases will help explain some of the ways community and character are joined in action, ways in which history is written and answers are made to the question of how we should live.

3

Making Moral Problems Public

THE MYTH OF PSYCHE AND EROS gives cultural expression to something that people come to know through their relations with particular others, in particular times and places, as their lives unfold. Eros must somehow be represented and tamed in the process of answering the question of how we should live. This domestication is the moral work of both personal and collective life, embodied in moral passages in which both selves and the "we" are generated.

One way of explaining the process of domestication has been to talk of sanction or praise and blame. As I said in chapter 1, the issue is often parsed in terms of a judging observer, passing judgment on an actor, using norms, rules, principles, or what have you. This analysis yields the "timeless view of time" in which crucial asymmetries between judge and actor are ignored and the judge is placed outside of the judgment. It is an analysis from the perspective of the rule makers and rule enforcers. In contrast, I look at praise and blame as a moral passage or process of the collectivity. In this light, to praise or blame is always a *collective action*, even when it appears to involve (or is represented as involving) an individual judge or actor. And it is always a *creative group action*, not the application of preexisting principles to the facts of the past (the crucial move that places the judge himself beyond judgment). Praise and blame are important processes of domestication that work through regenerating and changing the social order. Reputation, respectability, and the authority of the judges are important factors in the processes.

My first case in this chapter concerns praise and blame in a traditional group facing radically new circumstances—young women textile workers in Lawrence, Massachusetts during the 1830s, the beginning of the industrial revolution in the United States. The case concerns what workers did when faced with behavior that endangered their own reputations and respectability.

The textile workers used a time-honored method of ostracizing the alleged offender. They used a method that would be described as authoritarian, rigid, and "heteronomous" from the point of view of progressive society, and they cloaked themselves in the authority of common decency and God's law. I will describe it rather as a generation of the group morality and the moral selves of the women involved. As such, it was a thoroughly creative activity.

The remainder of the cases in this chapter have to do with explicit processes of making moral problems public, i.e., of reform movements. Making a moral problem public is a moral passage in which various things people are doing come to be established as matters of common concern.[1] These moral passages often bring about transformations in the people involved. In a quite straightforward sense, they constitute forces of history.

The first reform movement I discuss is an effort of the Female Moral Reform Society. The moral problem that the Society made public they defined as the widespread seduction of innocent young women by men who were motivated by lust. In the 1990s, the problem would be defined in terms of rape, abuse, and a moral problem that is not seen as a *public* problem at the moment—one that was defined at the turn of the century as "white slavery." The members of the Society defined their problem as an objectively existing one that was caused by certain individuals' behavior, a behavior that had to change. This is the way in which rape and abuse are understood by reformers in the United States today, but the definition, the grounds of authority, and the solutions are now different. The members of the Society acted not only to protect women but to bring Society into accord with God's law and institute the Millenium. Their actions also enacted the moral authority of women and contributed to a change in women's selves.

The method the Society used was quite different from that used in "social purity" campaigns later in the century—campaigns that resulted, for example, in the Comstock laws. The Society subjected the moral problem and its perpetrators to the light of publicity (a strategy shared with the much-later and otherwise quite different Progressives). The purity reformers acted to hide both problem and perpetrators on grounds that discussing them was obscene. They made deviance the dark shadow of the good society, a shadow that could be hidden but not dispelled. In contrast, the millenial society was to have no deviant shadow—a remarkable understanding. The two efforts mark different approaches in the dynamic of public and hidden. They signify differences in the form of moral practice parallel to those I discussed above in the case of the Wilde-Stein Club vs. the Maine Ministers.

A new approach appears with my third case, the physicians' campaign

---

1. Charles Taylor (1989) discusses the public in terms of "matters of common concern." I find the term (and the discussion) useful, but I'm not following his analysis.

against abortion during and after the Civil War. This was a Janus-faced moral passage. In one way it was traditional: an effort to establish the moral authority and power of higher-class men in the face of the new "anarchic" political and economic democracy—and to establish their control over women, in the name of morality and the good of the race. In the other direction, it looked to the great changes of the twentieth century: the physicians claimed authority on the basis of their special, professional knowledge, which was founded in science and the true knowledge of nature. The latter method is a powerful one, and in time, it gave physicians a great authority in moral issues of procreation. In the particular case of the physicians' crusade, the professionals managed to create the public definition of the moral problem of abortion—in Gusfield's terms, they succeeded in "owning" the problem (Gusfield, 1981: 10). Gusfield writes,

> At any time in an historical period there is a recognition that specific public issues are the legitimate province of specific persons, roles, and offices that can command public attention, trust, and influence. They have credibility while others who attempt to capture public attention do not. Owners can make claims and assertions . . . They possess authority in the field. Even if opposed by other groups, they are among those who can gain the public ear. (Gusfield, 1981: 11)

In the 1830s, the Female Moral Reform Society (and in general, "good women") exercised ownership of moral problems of procreation. The physicians' campaign was an early move by professionals to gain control over problems of procreation. As time passed, ownership of many moral problems passed to professionals of other sorts—scientists, social workers, home economists, psychiatrists, criminologists, and even businessmen, politicians, and bureaucrats. These changes created new methods of moral judgment and a change in the way a consensus and a "we" were made. The physicians' campaign was an early event in a process through which the taming of eros came more and more under the authority of professionals.

I close the chapter with a discussion of the social hygiene movement at the beginning of the twentieth century, a movement that brought together progressive physicians and purity crusaders in an alliance as explosive as current collaborations on the moral problems of teen pregnancy, AIDS, and sex education. Eventually, physicians and scientific researchers found they had to ally with reformers for funding and freedom to do their work. In turn, reformers needed alliances with professionals—relying on the authority of science offered one of the few ways to legitimate discussing sex and other procreational issues. But that is how it turned out eventually. In between, there were efforts of a more radical sort, including Margaret Sanger's early work on birth control.

The Mill Girl and the Millenium

Among the marked effects of mechanization in the United States were extensive changes in women's household work. The first machine industry in New England was the textile industry, with spinning machinery introduced in 1789, the power loom in 1814, and by 1830, the full industrialization of spinning and weaving was achieved.

The changes gradually transformed the home. As time went by, "modernization" removed the production of necessary goods, moral and intellectual education, culture, and eventually much of health care out of the home and out of the hands of women who remained in the home. Even in the beginning, the changes transformed the lives of young unmarried women. At the end of the eighteenth century in New England, married women's work included the general work of organizing the household, caring for children, and managing the manufacture of many items necessary to life. Young unmarried women's work was more specialized, and a large part consisted in textile manufacture for the household. The mechanization of textile manufacture freed many of these women to take part in the Second Great Awakening, the Protestant revival that extended from the late 1790s to the 1830s and was the source of many moral reform movements (Cott, 1975).

When the mills came to New England, some of the young, unmarried women went to work there. For example, in July 1936, nearly three-quarters of the work force at the Hamilton Manufacturing Company in Lowell was female—nearly all native born, most of them from rural families, and the large majority between fifteen and thirty years of age. Three-quarters of these women lived in company boarding houses, sleeping four to six to a bedroom. On the job, they worked seventy-two hours a week together. Only one ninth lived at home with their families (Dublin, 1975: 30–31).

Away from their moral guardians at home, the young women took their own measures to preserve their respectability. A Lowell minister described procedures in the boarding houses:

> A girl, suspected of immoralities, or serious improprieties, at once loses caste. Her fellow boarders will at once leave the house, if the keeper does not dismiss the offender. In self-protection, therefore, the patron is obliged to put the offender away. Nor will her former companions walk with her or work with her; till at length, finding herself everywhere talked about, and pointed at, and shunned, she is obliged to relieve her fellow-operatives of a presence which they feel brings disgrace. (Dublin, 1975: 32)

This is an example of a powerful use of moral judgment, displayed more in action than in words.[2]

---

2. Dublin (1975) argues that these same community powers also operated to make the mill worker strikes effective.

On the usual analysis, one would say that the unfortunate girl violated the moral principles of the group (principles governing her actions or her character), or that she violated the existing normative consensus. It looks as though her "traditional society" said, "Let woman learn her duty and obey!" She learned it and disobeyed, and she was legitimately punished by being ostracized, since she was the bad apple. This might, naturally enough, have been the outlook of her fellow boarders, for they were in the midst of enacting moral judgment. But I would say they were defining a moral problem and making a creative solution.

What I find interesting for moral theory is the way moral praise and blame operated as collective action. The group action involved forceful methods of maintaining moral consensus and the "we." The offending woman was blamed, labeled, and ostracized, and the verdict was enforced by moral and economic pressures on the landlady. The woman was driven off, as birds in a flock drive off a crippled member of their kind. Weak members of the group attract predators, after all. So the action was one of self-protection. The goal of the moral action was as much to maintain the respectability and reputation of the mill workers themselves as it was to punish the "offender." The strategy was to make public the moral consensus.

By marking a clear distinction between insiders and outsiders, the mill workers' action *demonstrated* the moral consensus of group members. They enacted it. Consensus here is not the same as a unity of shared moral beliefs among insiders. In fact, it required only a few strong-minded women to carry the day, with the others simply publicly going along, whatever their secret beliefs about the banished sister's actions in particular or her kind of deed in general. The consensus was putting up a united front, making a public persona for the group of young mill workers as a whole ("Mill workers are respectable girls"), and for the women individually as members of the group ("This woman is a decent mill operative"). The process of declaring the woman deviant was also a creative process of constructing the identity of the group, thus of its members. The persona they constructed distinguished these women from other women who lived apart from their families in urban settings, women who might have reputations as deviants. Reputation, identity, and character were intimately connected. The moral consensus was an outcome of their collective action.

The consensus of insiders was created by hiding the dissention and conflict that emerged with the one woman's actions—hiding it by forcing the woman outside. The women as a group faced a moral problem. They acted to solve it. But in acting, they hid the knowledge and possibilities that the offender uncovered in the process of her offense. She learned through a new relationship (I assume), and to keep her knowledge hidden, the mill operatives changed their relationships to her. She was shunned and so she could not explain herself or share what she had learned. It's worth noting that her knowledge would have been hidden even if she had been allowed to repent and rejoin the insiders in the consensus, because she would have disavowed her newly discovered knowledge and affirmed the old ways. Thus the parable of the prodigal son. If freedom has to do with collective possibilities, then the mill workers retained freedom for a good marriage and a respectable place in their communities but lost freedom by casting out not only the offender but the offender's knowledge. This was an outcome of their collective action.

Declaring the woman deviant of course affected her possibilities. She lost the safe home of the boarding house and her job as well. If word got back to her home town, she might also lose the possibility of a good marriage. She gained the possibility of a hidden life, hidden not from her but from the eyes of virtuous women and children. A change in relationship may open doors, but it may also close them.

In their own minds, the mill workers probably believed they were applying the traditional moral law as laid down by God and Man, only in dangerously changed social circumstances. During the 1830s, there were moral reform groups who dealt with similar "immoralities" by redefining the moral problem and acting to blame the man, not the woman. The group I'll discuss is the Female Moral Reform Society of New York. They were enacting moral judgment, praise, and blame but in a different mode. The mill workers judged a particular person and her actions. The Society enacted moral judgment as moral reformers, by making a moral problem public. The context in which they did their work was the changing world of Jacksonian democracy, in a period when increasing urbanization and industrialization were already transforming life. Their efforts took place in the aftermath of the Second Great Awakening, which gave the philosophical and theological background to their reform work.

The First Great Awakening took place roughly between 1730 and 1760. It resulted in a greater pluralism of Protestant denominations, and a new self-understanding on the part of the colonists, that they were a separate people, far from their royal father, the king. Some scholars say that volunteerism began to replace coercion as a new concept of government. In the process, they said, a new idea of the public good came into being—a reciprocity in which government was to help people to fulfill their individual selves and people, when necessary, were to sacrifice themselves for the general welfare. The American Revolution fulfilled religious ideals of the First Great Awakening.[3]

---

3. For material in this paragraph, see McLoughlin (1978: 79, 97). My sentence about fulfill-ment and self-sacrifice is made awkward by my effort to avoid a gendered pronoun. It's by no means clear how women were to be fulfilled under this patriarchal vision of government, and whether their sacrifices were to be duly noticed. Women's sacrifices of course were noticed and appreciated in the hardships of everyday life, given difficulties of childbearing, childrearing, and household management.

In the Second Great Awakening, the old symbols gained new meaning as the United States slowly began its move toward modern state power. The outlook was marked by Millenial optimism, and the belief that personal and collective good are in harmony. There was a new understanding of free will and moral choice. The argument was that moral law implies moral agents, and moral agency implies free agency in this sense: the power to choose wrong as well as right. Philosophically, the view became standard in school and college textbooks for the rest of the century. In the new theology, Christ died for anyone willing to undergo conversion (not merely for the predestined).

The new idea was that conversion is possible by act of will and heart. *If human nature is such that the person can be transformed in a moment, then so can human society.* If turning points in the personal moral passage may take the radical form of conversion, so may turning points in a passage of collective life. Thus human effort may bring about the Millenium—some people thought it might happen in only a few years' time. Thus the importance of voluntary organizations and reform movements—including the abolition movement (McLoughlin, 1978: 116–21).

The New York Female Moral Reform Society was founded in 1834, with the goals of fighting licentiousness and the sexual double standard and reforming New York City's prostitutes. By 1839, there were 445 auxiliaries, and the society was reorganized to become the American Female Reform Society (Smith-Rosenberg, 1971a: 575–77). The Society published *The Advocate of Moral Reform.*[4] In issue after issue, a major theme was played: men initiated adultery and fornication and were the source of America's immorality. The society called for a national union of women who might control male behavior—particularly that of their sons. They represented women as open-hearted and affectionate, trusting the vow of the faithless. Men were labeled "the destroyer," or "murderer of virtue."[5] Their campaign was strikingly successful.

> The editors of the *Advocate* not infrequently received (and printed) letters from rural subscribers reporting painfully how some young woman in their family had suffered social censure and ostracism because of the machinations of some

4. The *Advocate* was a national women's paper with an exclusively female staff. Within three years, it had over sixteen thousand subscribers and was one of the nation's most widely read evangelical papers. The Female Moral Reform Society was a vanguard group, arguing that there were many jobs women could fulfill as well as men. By the 1850s they were urging women to join unions. Lucretia Mott was a founder of the Philadelphia Female Moral Reform Society, and the *Advocate* printed an article by Sarah Grimke, of abolitionist and feminist notoriety, arguing that each woman must reevaluate her role and no longer be satisfied simply with caring for a family (Smith-Rosenberg, 1971a: 580).

5. (Smith-Rosenberg, 1971a: 570–71). Many of the readers lived in rural settings and sometimes the *Advocate* was the only newspaper they received and moral reform their main contact with the world at large. The cause apparently touched their own condition. (Smith-Rosenberg, 1971a: 575–77).

lecher—who emerged from the affair with his respectability unblemished. [The] letter from the *Advocate* was the first time they could express the anguish and anger they felt. (Smith-Rosenberg, 1971a: 578n)

The Society's strategy was to use the power of social ostracism (that women held) to "outlaw such men from society and hold them up to public judgment" (Smith-Rosenberg, 1971a: 573). Women were to organize campaigns against such men in their communities and to cut them socially—a deadly and effective weapon in rural and small-town life, for it damaged the man's reputation and ruined his prospects. Letters from rural subscribers poured into the newspaper, recounting specific instances of seduction in their towns and warning readers to avoid the men they named. A key tactic was to publish names of suspects in the *Advocate* itself.[6]

Through these means, the society made a moral problem public. It had the power to enforce its judgments through its constituency and the *Advocate.* They gained legitimacy from the postulates of the Second Great Awakening. Another powerful source of their authority lay in the responsibility that women had begun to have for moral and religious matters, one that was embodied in the idea of separate women's and men's spheres.[7] The feminine authority was particularly strong in matters of procreation, including sexuality. It concerned temperance in general and it legitimated the movements in which women took part after the Civil War; for example, the many campaigns of the Women's Christian Temperance Union.

Authority to define the moral problem brings with it a certain ability to define the consensus. The reformers of the society proceeded by bringing to light behavior that the "higher law" condemned. We need not, in fact should not, assume a belief consensus on the higher law. However, no matter what cynicism might actually have existed about that higher law in sexual matters, no opponent could argue that seduction and prostitution were permissible. Opponents used a different strategy, arguing that even to speak of sex was obscene, thus forbidden and perhaps itself immoral. The Millenial reformers made deviance public in order to make it disappear. The kingdom of heaven on earth was a society without shadow, all full of light. Their opponents accepted deviance and sin as the way of the world and kept it hidden in the name of a public virtue. The two strategies made for different moral passages of the nation. They affected freedom differently and had different effects on collective possibilities. The Female Moral Reform Society opened possibili-

6. (Smith-Rosenberg, 1971a:5 73). The newspaper also printed names of employment agencies that were suspected fronts for white-slave traffic and warned women against them.

7. See Elshtain (1981), Gordon (1977) for feminist discussions. "Men's sphere" and "women's sphere" are folk concepts (see chapter 6) and can't be identified with the scholarly distinction between public and private.

ties for women (including "fallen women"), but it truncated the freedom of men who seduced women or visited prostitutes. Their opponents hid seduction and prostitution and so also opened collective possibilities—but illegitimate ones. They created deviant social worlds in which knowledge was hidden and a rich, collective life went on in the shadow of the public world. The battle between those who would hide the deviance and those who would make it disappear by bringing it into the light goes on today in the controversies of abortion, AIDS, teen pregnancy, and many others. I discussed it in the case of the Wilde-Stein Club vs. the Maine Ministers.

Over time, the Female Moral Reform Society waged campaigns to make seduction a criminal offense for the male participant, and in 1848 the New York legislature passed such a bill (Smith-Rosenberg, 1971a: 576). With the passage of laws, the moral outlook of the society on seduction became part of the official consensus of the nation. Legislation officially settled, once and for all, who the outsiders were, and in so doing, it prepared the soil for hidden, deviant cultures—the worlds of the hardened offenders. Legislative means came more and more to prominence as secular professionals began to claim ownership of moral problems. I'll begin tracing that change through the emergence of the moral problem of abortion and the part it played in the making of the medical profession.

Making Abortion a Moral Problem

The years before the Civil War laid the groundwork for the modern nation. The period of the young mill workers and their boarding houses was a brief, transitional one.[8] The population of Lowell grew from 17,000 in 1836 to 33,000 in 1850. The number of employees in the mills doubled and the character of the employees changed. In 1836, only 4 percent of Hamilton employees were foreign born. By 1860, over 60 percent were immigrants, three-fourths of them Irish who were driven across the Atlantic by the great potato famine and its devastating impact on small farm holdings. In the transition, the system of unmarried women working changed to a family-labor system—but in 1860, more than half of those families were headed by women.[9] The changes during this period left few people untouched.

American society from the 1830s to the 1860s was marked by advances in political democracy, by a rapid increase in economic, social, and geographic mobil-

---

8. This is not to say boarding houses for women (or men) workers went out of style. In the 1920s, it was customary for young textile mill workers (and sometimes families) to move from town to town according to which mill had orders and was hiring. My aunt and my father did this before their marriages, and they stayed in single-sex boarding houses.

9. (Dublin, 1975: 34–35). The proportion of women-headed families was the same for immigrant and native born, and Dublin suggests that class rather than ethnicity was responsible.

ity, and by uncompromising and morally relentless reform movements. (Smith-Rosenberg, 1971a: 563)

The reform movements included the abolition and temperance movements as well as the work of the New York Female Reform Society.[10]

Through this democratic time, the paradigm of health and human welfare was shared by healer and patient alike. Charles Rosenberg wrote that a "deeply assumed metaphor" lay at the core of the paradigm.

> The body was seen, metaphorically, as a system of dynamic interactions with its environment. Health or disease resulted from a cumulative interaction between constitutional endowment and environmental circumstance. One could not well live without food and air and water; one had to live in a particular climate, subject one's body to a particular style of life and work. Each of these factors implied a necessary and continuing physiological adjustment. The body was always in a state of becoming—and thus always in jeopardy. (Rosenberg, 1979: 5)

The parts of the body were interrelated in a system, so that health and disease tended to be understood as states of a whole organism rather than the later understanding of occupation of a body by specific disease entities. Balance was also required in intake and outgo, and so there was an emphasis on diet and excretion, perspiration and ventilation.

> In addition to the exigencies of everyday life which might destabilize the equilibrium which constituted health, the body also had to pass through several developmental crises inherent in the design of the human organism. Menstruation and menopause in women, teething and puberty in both sexes—all represented points of potential danger, moments of structured instability, as the body established a new internal equilibrium. Seasonal changes in climate constituted another recurring cyclical change which might imply danger to health and require possible medical intervention: thus the ancient practice of administering cathartics in spring and fall to help the body adjust to the changed seasons. (Rosenberg, 1979: 6)

Thus bleeding, emetics, and other such treatments made sense as efforts to regulate secretions and bring balance.

The paradigm of health and illness was joined with an understanding of inheritance quite different from the current one based on contemporary genetics. One inherited a "constitution," in a dynamic process that began with conception and extended through weaning (often at age two). Constitutional weaknesses could dispose a person to later ills and vices. Physicians

---

10. Gusfield (1976) gives a perspicuous discussion of the temperance movement.

widely held this view, but so did most of their competitors. In the years before the Civil War, there was a plethora of alternative medical practitioners in competition with the "regular" physicians, and some popular dissatisfaction with the regulars' often violent methods.[11]

The paradigm encouraged sensible behavior. Temperance and balance were required. To give a child a proper constitution, the couple had to be healthy and happy in intercourse, not drunk or exhausted. Pregnant women had to be properly fed and cheerful, not overworked. They had to abstain from alcohol or other harmful substances. If the mother was weak, a vigorous wetnurse was to be hired to insure the child developed as strong a constitution as possible.[12]

At midcentury, there were two important features to the usual understanding of what we would now call abortion. One was "quickening," the point at which the woman feels the fetus quicken or move. It was the point at which the fetus could be known to have human life, i.e., to be an ensouled being. With no diagnostic tests for early pregnancy, quickening also served to determine pregnancy for medical or moral or legal matters.[13] The second was that of a "stoppage" of the menses, understood as an imbalance of the equilibrium of the system, under the older paradigm that was shared by physicians and folk alike.[14]

Given these understandings, it was not generally believed that abortion (or curing a stoppage) before quickening involved killing an unborn infant. From 1830 until the Civil War, and after, abortion was available by many means. Home manuals offered information. Herbal practitioners and midwives, as well as physicians, could supply abortifacients. Midwives and physicians, at least, had the knowledge to induce abortion by dilating the cervix, introducing an irritant, or rupturing the amniotic sac (Mohr, 1978: 10–11, 14). By midcentury, there were also "commercial" practitioners with clinics to care for postpartum women, and they also advertised their skill at curing stoppages.

---

11. See Rosenberg (1979), Mohr (1978), Ehrenreich and English (1979), and Gordon (1977).

12. See Rosenberg (1976) which has many chapters relevant to these matters.

13. British Parliament passed a law in 1803 making abortion before quickening a criminal offense in England. But the legal position in the United States was different, where the Commonwealth of Massachusetts v. Bangs remained the ruling precedent in most states throughout the first half of the century. In 1812, charges against Isaiah Bangs were dismissed because the indictment did not claim "that the woman was quick with a child at the time." Mohr states that prosecutors took the precedent so much for granted that indictments for abortion prior to quickening were almost never brought (Mohr, 1978: 5–6).

14. The quickening test should not obscure the fact that there were clearly many cases in which physicians knowingly performed what we would call early abortions, either out of mercy for the seduced young girl whose life would be ruined, or as a business serving women who had too many children.

This was the setting for the physicians' campaign against abortion. To define abortion as a public moral problem required a redefinition of the health paradigm, and a redefinition of fetal life. The campaign was part of a general effort to place regular physicians in the position of moral and medical authority in the changing nation. Although it was a movement for power and authority by elite members of an occupation, it was far more than that in intent and in outcome.

The physicians saw that the morality and the security of their traditional communities were being shattered. They feared the anarchy that lay at the heart of the new democracy and the laissez-faire market. The old moral consensus and the old social order were being swept away. They tried to reinstitute the old moral order, with its foundations in the old class and gender orders, by gaining authority for physicians. They were creative in the effort, because they helped to bind science into the institutional form of professions, joining the traditional and the progressive. They aimed at disciplining the members of their profession to raise it to a higher level and they worked to improve medical education.

The American Medical Association, the first *national* association of the profession, was formed in 1847 out of a concern with the problems in medical education (Rothstein, 1972: 114).[15] It was in this context that the antiabortion campaign began, with Horatio Robinson Storer playing a central role. Storer was the son of D. Humphreys Storer, professor of obstetrics and medical jurisprudence at Harvard and a nationally known physician, well connected with the elite physicians working to control health care and their profession (Mohr, 1978: ch. 6).

Horatio Storer began his crusade publicly in May 1857, first locally, then as head of an AMA committee consisting of prestigious physicians. The committee reported at the 1859 AMA meetings. The report found three main causes of the moral problem of abortion: popular ignorance about the personhood of the fetus; carelessness by medical professionals about fetal life; and defects in the law. The solutions were educating the public; disciplining the profession; and convincing legislators to change the laws (Mohr, 1978: 200). The emergence of the moral problem of abortion was in fact a *redefinition* of the situation by Storer and his committees and as such, it required legitimating the problem and establishing ownership.

Storer began his arguments by saying that abortion is murder because the fetus is a human life from conception: "If there be life, then also the exis-

---

15. This association came late, and through the better part of the century, it was the local and state medical societies that fulfilled the most important institutional purposes. Local and state associations had been formed early, and by 1815, nearly all states had them. Their goals were to separate qualified practitioners from others through licensing provisions and, through personal contacts, to create unity, harmony, and voluntary regulation of competition (Shryock, 1967: 31).

tence, however undeveloped, of an intellectual, moral, and spiritual nature, the inalienable attribute of humanity, is implied" (Storer, 1860: 13).[16] This statement flew in the face of the widely held quickening doctrine. Storer used his status as an elite physician to argue against the quickening doctrine, saying that *current medical knowledge* showed fetal development to be continuous from conception, with no discernable change that signified ensoulment. Storer created a medico-legal definition of something that had previously been understood under a folk paradigm which the mass of physicians and clergy shared with ordinary people.

I say the definition is medico-legal because Storer claimed abortion to be murder, a sort of killing "fit to be outlawed by the state." It made an alliance among elite physicians, legislators, and law enforcement bodies as guardians of the moral character of the nation and the common good. The making of the moral problem of abortion was also part of the making of a new moral order, and quite apart from the abortion issue, Storer pressed for legal requirements on reporting births, deaths, and other vital statistics (something the AMA was independently pressing). The medico-legal definition of fetal personhood allowed Storer to separate induced abortion into the categories of criminal and noncriminal (what later came to be called therapeutic abortion). Therapeutic abortion was to be based on proper professional judgment, and physicians were not individually to usurp the power of deciding life and death. The profession, with its base of knowledge, had the office of setting criteria. That is, the cognitive authority was to lie with the profession itself.

In claiming cognitive authority for his profession, Storer also marked a boundary between insiders and outsiders. He was changing the way the moral consensus was formed, and the way the question of how we should live was answered. He listed the offending outsiders as follows: friends and acquaintances; nurses, midwives, and female physicians; husbands; quacks and professed abortionists; druggists; and worst of all, though "extremely rare," physicians in regular standing (Storer, 1860: 55). Storer's list is interesting in light of the fact that all of these listed deviants were either to be brought under professional control or under legal control with physicians having a large say in the legislation. With the aid of the law, nurses and "druggists" were eventually brought under authority of the dominant profession of medicine (Freidson, 1970). Storer himself and many of his elite colleagues were opposed to training women as physicians. With control of medical training, physicians were able to severely limit the number of women in medicine—as well as the numbers of Jews, Irish, Italians, blacks,

---

16. Storer developed his arguments in articles written for the *North American Medico-Chirurgical Review* between January and November, 1859. They were published in 1860 as the book, *Criminal Abortion*, which is what I have used in reconstructing them.

and others. In a time when democratization, immigration, and industrialization threatened the old dominance orders, the modern professions were invented and allied with "science." The effort worked reasonably well until after World War II, when the GI Bill flooded the universities, and anti-Catholicism and anti-Semitism began to be exposed, followed shortly by the Civil Rights Movement and the women's movement.

In all, the physician's antiabortion crusade was a component in a movement of historical scope to give ownership of both medical and moral problems of procreation to professional physicians. What is remarkable in this is that what had previously been a personal matter, even a concern of the home sphere (whether moral or not), had been defined officially in terms in which the physicians understood it.

Storer defended his new definition of abortion as wrongful killing by claiming medical expertise. But he also used science to claim that there were other noxious causes and effects of abortion. In *Criminal Abortion*, he gave many tables full of figures on population and reproduction in Europe and America. He used them to make the case that abortion was widely practiced in the United States, and that it was primarily practiced by native-born, Protestant, married women to limit the number of their offspring—not (as earlier in the century) by young, unmarried women for reasons of shame. Contemporary demographic data indicate Storer was basically correct. The native-born Protestants had passed through a demographic transition, in which the survival rate of children had improved and the birth rate had dropped. Fertility rates of immigrants, particularly Catholics, were high.[17]

From this perspective, the nation had to be maintained by the high moral character of its Anglo-Saxon people. The women had particular responsibility because of their importance in moral matters and in procreation. Storer argued that native-born, Protestant women were becoming corrupt, giving in to sloth, pleasure, and self-indulgence. Women seeking careers and education weakened their reproductive capacity, he claimed, and they would not only have fewer children, but the ones they had would be inferior. Abortion was an instrument in this degradation of the race. Storer wrote,

> there is need of increased vigilance on the part of medical men, lest they themselves become innocent and unintentional abettors of the crime. If, on the other hand, the community were made to understand and to feel that a marriage where the parties shrink from its highest responsibilities, is nothing less than legalized prostitution, many would shrink from their present public con-

---

17. These issues were of concern at midcentury, and of great enough concern by the end of the century for Teddy Roosevelt to speak of "race suicide," i.e., suicide of white, native-born, Protestant "race." They bring out some of the uglier aspects of the "chosen nation." The chosen nation was a Protestant, Anglo-Saxon nation.

fession of cowardly, selfish, and sinful lust. If they were taught by the speech of their medical attendants, that a value attaches to the unborn child, hardly increased by the accident of its birth, they also would be persuaded or compelled to a similar belief in its sanctity, and to a commensurate respect. (Storer, 1860: 101)

Storer recommended breast feeding ("a law entailed on [women] by nature") for family limitation by women. Like Malthus, he argued for abstinence by men until they could afford a wife.[18]

Using their social networks, elite physicians pressured legislators and took part (as expert consultants) in framing the laws. They felt their place was to educate not only the people but the legislators themselves. They did not construe education in a narrow scientific sense. A Michigan physician stated his understanding shortly after the Civil War:

It is not sufficient that the medical profession should set up a standard of morality for themselves . . . but the people are to be *educated up* to it. The profession must become aggressive toward those wrongs and errors which it *only* can properly expose, and successfully oppose. (quoted in Mohr, 1978: 171)

This certainly was Storer's view as well. It is a view on the border of the old and the new. Because elite physicians were white, mainly Protestant men who lived in the higher classes of society, they were already members of social worlds that defined the moral tone of the nation and governed it politically and socially. But the making of the moral problem of abortion also anticipated the direction in which the nation would move. Storer based his authority on science. He presented himself as a trained professional discovering objective conditions and their causes.

The view that was emerging by the turn of the century was that a changing nation required trained experts to guide its social change. As the decades passed, the movement fractured procreation into pieces suited for the professional specialties—childbearing to one, childrearing to another, "sexual dysfunction" to a third, "marital counseling" to a fourth, and on and on. Journals were devoted to marriage and family life, lifted out of the context of a whole life and a whole community. Sex and birth and bonding became matters of health of individuals rather than sacred powers of the community. It was all part of the modernization of the nation, and the general movement of professionals into management of the morality of progressive society.[19] The physician's campaign contributed to this outcome.

---

18. For remarks on Malthus, see Rosenberg (1976) chapters. 1, 2, 3. See also Gordon (1977) and particularly Young (1985).

19. Starr (1982) discusses physician's "cultural authority" in ways analogous to my discussion of cognitive authority (in this chapter and in Addelson, 1983), and he gives a more substantial history of the medical profession.

Sex and Progressive Society

The sexual side of eros was also a battlefield in the war of progressive and traditional society. After the Civil War there was a major movement by traditional, "social purity" activists to hide sex, either in the dark and deviant corridors of vice or the dark and private bedroom of the connubial couple.[20] Social purity legislation ruling contraceptive and abortion information obscene was pushed through the Congress in the mid 1870s. The federal "Comstock law," (named after Anthony Comstock, who agitated for passage) made illegal the mailing of contraceptive or abortion information or the interstate shipment or importing of "any drug, medicine, article, or thing designed, adapted, or intended for preventing conception, or producing abortion, or for any indecent or immoral use" (Kennedy, 1970: 243). In addition to the federal law, a large number of states had "little Comstock laws." The federal legislation dealt with the mails and carriers. State laws covered the practice of medicine or even the use of contraceptives.

In broad outline, the "purity" understanding of morality was in terms of public and hidden, light and shadow, normal and deviant. The innocent were to be shielded from even the *talk* of vice, lest corruption touch them. In contrast, the broad outline of the Female Moral Reform Society's view was that vice that is hidden *corrupts* the innocent, and that it will wither in the light of virtue, allowing humanity to reach the goal of a society without shadow. Interestingly enough, the progressive view was similar in this respect: the healthy society and the healthy person are to be achieved by making the disease public so that it may be prevented or cured, and in this way, humanity may progress toward the goal of a society without a shadow. This underlies the slogan, "Let man know and trust him." In broad outline, the progressive view was in harmony with the optimistic, millenial view. However, it differed radically in that cognitive authority increasingly came to be vested in trained professionals.

But these differences were made clear only with the passage of time. In the movement against abortion, purity reformers and physicians worked together. They also came together in the social hygiene movement early in the twentieth century.

The social hygiene movement was sparked by conservative physicians troubled by discoveries concerning venereal disease, particularly syphilis and

---

20. Earlier in the century, many Americans had shown a scientific interest. Beginning in the 1840s, there were public lectures on "sexual physiology" to audiences segregated by gender. Some of the lectures employed mannequins and models of the female reproductive organs which "could be taken to pieces and shown part by part, externally and internally, all molded and colored to nature" (Frederick Hollick, quoted in Mohr, 1978: 69). Public schools began offering rudimentary teachings in anatomy and physiology. Home medical manuals gave information on anatomy, physiology, midwifery, and as I said above, "abortion," or bringing on the menses.

gonorrhea. Before this time, physicians had not known the long-term consequences of syphilis—arthritis, degenerative nervous disorders, paresis. Once they did, they realized that many victims of syphilis were the innocent wives or children of men infected by prostitutes. Other innocents were said to be afflicted through kisses, towels, or wet nurses. Some hospitals refused to admit patients suffering from venereal disease.[21]

A major mover in this campaign was the eminent New York specialist (in dermatology), Prince A. Morrow. Morrow advocated changing moral standards through education, particularly against the double standard that allowed men to frequent prostitutes and encouraged the practice of prostitution itself. Purity groups worked with him in his effort. However, purity reformers believed that education should be done in the home, while the physicians wanted to use schools and the press, to educate both adults and children (Burnham, 1973: 898).

After Morrow's death in 1913, purity and medical forces joined to form the American Social Hygiene Association. Medical men continued to press for education so that the ill could get treatment, and they posted propaganda in public rest rooms. The medical men were inspired by science and the belief that new knowledge could obliterate human misery if only social conditions permitted (Burnham, 1973: 907–8). The source of the new knowledge, and the treatment, lay with the professionals. In contrast, purity groups counseled moral prophylaxis. It is interesting that they wanted sexual matters left within the home sphere, not moved into the public sphere and the control of male professionals in the name of science. Women were heavily represented in purity leadership as well as rank and file membership (Gordon, 1977; Pivar, 1973).

During World War I, a deep split emerged in the social hygiene coalition over the question of whether army medics should give condoms to soldiers, thus making immoral conduct safe (Burnham, 1973: 900). This split was not simply over the immorality of sex but over the exploitation of women as prostitutes, and the old view that men had sexual desires that had to be satisfied.

Dealing with sexual desire also required a coalition of scientists and other professionals and reformers, one that continued throughout the twentieth century. One strategy involved resolving conflict by moving issues out of the province of moralists to that of "science," or rather, of professional experts and the teachers they trained. Increasingly, science offered an escape valve for the twentieth-century American obsession with sex, but at the cost of

---

21. Prostitution was one of the major social problems before and after the turn of the century (and a social problem in some circles before the Civil War, as we saw with the Female Moral Reform Society). There were regimentation movements to legalize prostitution that were fought and defeated (see Pivar, 1973). The concern with "white slavery" was widespread and the Mann Act was passed in 1911.

granting the "reproductive science" authority to interpret eros for the modern world.

Havelock Ellis was one of the earliest, great pioneers. According to one researcher, Ellis "stands in the same relation to modern sexual theory as Max Weber to modern sociology or Albert Einstein to modern physics" (Robinson, 1976: 3). Ellis was trained as a physician, but he worked (in England) as a researcher and writer. He approached human sexuality as he would that of any animal species—appropriate enough in a post-Darwinian world. However his view of sex was also romantic: sex demanded "mystery." Ellis was able to join science and mystery by several important moves. First, he distinguished sex from reproduction. Then he argued that sex is a necessity for healthy development, for both men and women. Finally, he redefined procreative morality by declaring sex private and reproduction public.

> Sexual union, for a woman as much as for a man, is a physiological fact; it may also be a spiritual fact; but it is not a social act. It is, on the contrary, an act which, beyond all other acts, demands retirement and mystery for its accomplishment. That, indeed, is a general human, almost zoological, fact. Moreover, this demand for mystery is more especially made by woman in virtue of her greater modesty which, we have found reason to believe, has a biological basis. It is not until a child is born or conceived that the community has any right to interest itself in the sexual acts of its members. The sexual act is of no more concern to the community than any other private physiological act. It is an impertinence, if not an outrage, to seek to inquire into it. But the birth of a child is a social act. Not what goes into the womb, but what comes out of it, concerns society. The community is invited to receive a new citizen. It is entitled to demand that citizen shall be worthy of a place in its midst and that he shall be properly introduced by a responsible father and a responsible mother. The whole of sexual morality, as Ellen Key has said, revolves around the child. (Ellis, 1910: 417)[22]

Ellis played out the consequences of the separation of sex and reproduction in his major works.

In 1897, Ellis published the first volume, *Sexual Inversion*, of his great work, *Studies in the Psychology of Sex*. In it, he removed the label of pathology

---

22. I have not read Ellis' *Studies in the Psychology of Sex*, and I took this quotation from Margold (1926: 6). *The Evolution of Modesty* was originally published as *The Psychology of Sex* Vol. II, but that volume was revised and renumbered as the first volume of the series in 1900. The more controversial *Sexual Inversion* was the first volume completed (1897), but it was withdrawn in the English edition before publication (though published in German in 1896). A revised edition was published in English as Vol. II in 1901 (Philadelphia, F.A. Davis). For a biography, see Grosskurth (1980). See also Ellis (1939). For a criticism of Ellis' discussion of the sex act as private, see Margold (1926). Margold writes from a sociological/Deweyian point of view.

from homosexuality.[23] Other volumes of the work disputed traditional views on pathological medical consequences of masturbation; refuted the notion that women lacked sexual emotions and claimed that women's sexual desire and capacity for enjoyment was equal to men's; and argued that sex, even unrelated to procreation, was indispensable to full human development. Abstinence was unhealthy, he said—but he did argue that love was the proper context for sex, even if sex were not related to procreation.[24]

In 1914, Margaret Sanger met Havelock Ellis in England and spent some time with him (see chapter 4). She later wrote that she was transformed by the meetings, and by his raising sex from the smudgy basement into the clean air (Sanger, 1938: 135). Birth control reformers continued to rely on scientists to legitimate their activist work on sex and reproduction. However, the reproductive scientists also had to rely on the reformers. These scientists faced a long struggle to establish themselves as respectable professionals, something that was necessary for their research and university positions, funding, and public outlets for their work.[25]

The difficulties the scientists faced extended even to sexual research on nonhuman animals.[26] George Corner mentioned the problem in his Foreword to a late edition of *Sex and Internal Secretions*, a work which served as "the bible of American reproductive sciences for fifty years." Corner was a

---

23. Ellis took homosexuality to be congenital but not morally or socially or physiologically pathological. He made various analogies to color blindness and his cases included creative and upright homosexuals. His emphasis was on male homosexuality and his discussion of lesbianism is brief and altogether inadequate.

24. Robinson makes the very interesting point that Ellis emphasizes courtship and sexual arousal as the problematic point rather than control of sexual activity, a revolution in viewpoint that is one main mark of the watershed between the traditional and the modern views of sexuality (Robinson, 1976: 16). Though he criticized traditional marriage, Ellis believed love was necessary, and "natural monogamy" was ideal. This made him different, but not altogether different, from the much more traditional social hygiene advocates who worked to make monogamous sex in marriage something natural that could be fulfilling to both man and wife. In the context of the marriage practices of the day, Ellis' proposal has its repressive side so far as women are concerned. See also the remarks in which Ellis attempts to reorganize heterosexual relationships in Robinson (1976).

25. Here is one standard sociological description of what is necessary to a profession: "a systematized body of knowledge that provides the basis for practice and becomes increasingly esoteric, authority to perform a vital social function which is recognized and sanctioned either legally or informally by the community, a code of ethics to govern behavior toward colleagues and clients, and a unique professional culture.... Academic professionalization also involves the separation of specific academic disciplines from larger bodies of knowledge, the creation of academic departments, professional organizations, and specialized journals" (Furner, 1975: 3n).

26. Adele Clarke has written about the ways in which "the reproductive sciences" came to be developed and legitimated—meaning by reproductive sciences, "the study of mammalian reproduction through endocrinology, physiology, and anatomy, undertaken in biological, medical, and agricultural settings" (Clarke, 1990a: 18).

leading reproductive scientist and medical historian. He wrote that when "the bible" was originally published, it

> represented a major break from the so-called Victorian attitude, which in the English-speaking countries had long impeded scientific and sociological investigation of sexual matters and placed taboos on open consideration of human mating and childbearing as if these essential activities were intrinsically indecent. (Corner,1961: xxxi)

The uproar over Alfred Kinsey's sex research in the 1950s is evidence that the translation from obscenity to science took a long time. The wooden and scientistic language used by Masters and Johnson in the late 1960s also shows the constraints.

From early in the century, the reproductive sciences were associated with the birth control, eugenics, and population control movements, with both negative and positive consequences as we shall see in the next chapter. After World War II, family planning and population control movements came together and supplied most of the nongovernmental funding for reproductive scientists. Clarke wrote that today it is often impossible to distinguish reproductive sciences from organizations focused on contraception and population control issues (Clarke, 1990a: 24–29). The family planners and the scientists are linked together in *social worlds*. In rough terms, a social world consists of people who, over a period of time, engage in some sort of collective action together.[27]

Despite the fact that according to the disciplinary definitions, the work of professional philosophers is distinct from the work of scientists and activists, philosophers are also part of these social worlds. Adele Clarke lists some of the social worlds involved in the contemporary reproductive policy arena:

> in the broad arena focused on human reproduction, participants include knowledge producers (several kinds of reproductive scientists, geneticists, social scientists), practicing medical personnel (physicians, nurses, other health care providers, public health personnel), their various professional medical organizations, sponsors (public and private funding agencies), consumers (both as organized collective actors and as individuals), the pharmaceutical and medical industries, policy makers, governmental regulatory bodies, organized religious and political groups, and others. (Clarke, 1990a: 19).

Philosophers are included among the knowledge producers in these social worlds.[28] Many of them supply not only the individualistic moral theories

---

27. For a classic discussion of arenas and social worlds, see Strauss (1978).

28. In one of the later chapters, I'll take up the notion of social worlds in more detail. It will permit a more satisfactory account of the moral responsibility of professionals.

that are the historically transformed progeny of the Havelock Ellis approach, they offer explanations of scientific truth and human nature that support the authority of scientists and other professionals (including themselves). I said in the preface that collective, moral responsibility has to do with the outcomes of collective action (see also chapter 6). Foreseeing outcomes in such cases requires a way to characterize appropriate acting units; i.e., those that could be said to play important parts in the outcomes. The notion of "social worlds" gives a way to characterize acting units that is suitable for moral responsibility. It allows me to place the academic professions in social worlds whose collective actions have significant outcomes having to do with making the moral consensus and regenerating the social order.

It took many years of conflict before the individualistic philosophical ethics I discussed in chapter 2 fully took root. In the fertile soil of the progressive era, there were other seedlings—among them, Margaret Sanger's early birth control movement. I will trace that passage in more detail in the next chapter.

4

Margaret Sanger's Answer:
The Woman of Practical Wisdom

THE PHYSICIANS' CRUSADE against abortion and the social hygiene movement expressed the hope that science, practiced by professionals, could resolve the moral, social, and political problems of the modernizing nation.[1] The idea took hold. Scientists, statesmen, and moralists were intelligent specialists at their posts, guiding the nation for the common good. John Dewey placed his faith in a union of activists, professionals, and governors, all using scientific method.[2] Science was the method of social progress.

Not everyone put their faith in this sort of meliorism, and some even argued that a union of activists, professionals, and governors would simply reproduce the oppression under which the lower classes labored. The anarcho-syndicalists acted on the thesis that the workers were the ones to be trusted in making the new knowledge and the new world. In the end, the pro-

---

1. Archival references are to materials in the Sophia Smith collection, Smith College (MS/SS) and the Library of Congress collection (MS/LC). I thank Dorothy Green for her invaluable help while I was doing the research at Sophia Smith. This chapter was researched long before Chesler (1992) was published. The Chesler book is the one respectful, scholarly biography of Sanger. However, Chesler does not make much of Sanger's early work with the syndicalists, something that is necessary to understand what Sanger's philosophical and political contribution might have been, as well as something that is necessary to understand the family planning movement today (by the contrast). I'm doing some revisionist history here, through a change in emphasis and interpretation.

2. (Dennis Smith, 1988: 13, 8). This was to be the new democracy. It may be true that Dewey's fondness for democracy was less for a political form of government and more for a participatory, democratic society, democracy in his understanding being the idea of community life itself. See Damico (1978). In fact, Damico says that Dewey's commitment to intelligence in his theory of democracy is a commitment to participation and to ideas in action (Damico, 1978: 120). However, there is a large question of whether the professionals' self understandings suited them for democratic participation.

fessionals conquered, not only in the economic and political realms, but in many of the arenas of procreation as well.

In this chapter, I trace in some detail the changes in the birth control movement during Sanger's lifetime. It is, in a way, her moral passage in becoming and remaining a political activist. In the first period, she had a romantic vision of sex and a passion for freedom and a respect for the women of the poor. Through her own experience, and changing times, she came to rely more on professionals and on the higher classes. In the end, birth control was institutionalized as family planning and population control, and Sanger moved on to support research for the contraceptive pill. Although her politics had to change with the times, she never did accommodate herself to the professionalized point of view of the family planning movement.

George Herbert Mead captured the feelings of reformers and radicals of the earlier decades of the century when he wrote,

> Freedom . . . is the expression of the whole self which has become entire through the reconstruction which has taken place. . . . If one is reconstructing one's situation, one's action may be called rebellion. That is the attitude of the reactionary. . . . But Freedom lies definitely in a reconstruction which is not in the nature of a rebellion but in the nature of presenting an order which is more adequate than the order which has been there.[3]

There were serious disagreements over how the reconstruction was to be made. But the belief that the self and the social world changed together was shared among the activists early in the century. In this chapter, I approach changes in the nation through the work Margaret Sanger did in her early fight for birth control.

I'll mark several steps in Sanger's early passage from being a middle-class housewife in Hastings-on-Hudson to finding *room to move* with New York's radical bohemians; to *stepping out* into her own political work with the syndicalist International Workers of the World, including her flight to Europe as a fugitive; to her *stepping outside* with the "direct actions" involving the illegal pamphlet "Family Limitation" and the Brownsville Clinic. Her early career was followed by a turning point in the personal and national passage, marked by the conflict over U.S. entry into World War I and the persecution of the "Reds" that followed. By the early 1920s, the radical movement was shattered. In the circumstances, Sanger began working *with* women and professionals of the respectable classes *for* the women of the poor.

---

3. (Mead, 1938: 663). My quoting this here is anachronistic, and it represents Mead's thought after the progressive era had passed. I believe it does represent the feeling that Addams and Sanger had at the beginnings of their work.

Room to Move

It was through what I might call the problem of the breadwinner that Margaret Sanger began her activism.[4] She moved out of a housewifely role into a social world obsessed with the place of labor under capital—and obsessed with cultural revolution as well.

Margaret Higgins was finishing nursing training at the Manhattan Eye and Ear Clinic when she met William Sanger, an architect, draftsman, and artist. She was young (in her early twenties) and an "incurable romantic." He was a decade older and swept her off her feet. He sat on her doorstep all night in order to walk with her next morning; he sent flowers; he took her to the opera. His circle of friends was impressive: musicians, writers, and artists—as well as the labor organizer Eugene Debs, whom her father Michael Higgins had admired. The two talked of marriage and saving money to go to Paris, where a revolution in art was taking place (Lader, 1955: 28; Sanger, 1938: 56, 57).

They were married in 1902, and domestic life overcame the dreams of going to Paris. The couple eventually moved to Hastings-on-Hudson where they built a home in a small enclave of teachers and professionals. There they had three children, two boys and the baby Peggy. For a time, Margaret was taken up with family matters. As Peggy became a toddler, however, the "tame domesticity of the pretty riverside settlement seemed to be bordering on stagnation" (Sanger, 1938: 66). She was a member of a literary women's club and, with her husband's encouragement, she was writing. But she wanted action for herself. And there was also a question of her disappointment with Bill Sanger's lack of achievement (Lader, 1955: 34).

The Sangers sold their house in 1910 and moved to New York City, to an uptown apartment of "the old fashioned railroad type" with high ceilings, roomy, and bright.[5] Mrs. Sanger, the children's grandmother, was with them to help manage the household and to look after the children (Sanger, 1938: 68). Margaret began earning her own money by nursing. Both Sangers sank themselves in political work.

Margaret later wrote of the Sanger family move to New York:

---

4. I believe that because of her class background as the child of an artisan who was himself a radical, she never was comfortable with the "top down" method of reform of the "meliorist" progressives, though she was forced to change her strategy when the "red tide" was driven back.

5. The description is from Sanger (1938: 68). She gives no date for the move to New York, and her biographers, when they do give one, usually give 1912 as the date of the move. A. Sanger (1969) details their activities that indicate it had to be no later than 1911. Chesler (1992: 55, 56) reports that the Sangers sold their house in Hastings-on-Hudson in 1910 and gives that date for the move to New York.

Headlong we dived into one of the most interesting phases of life the United States has ever seen. Radicalism in manners, art, industry, morals, politics was effervescing, and the lid was about to blow off in the Great War. (Sanger, 1938)

The Sangers moved fully into a relationship with the radicals—from anarchists to socialists to progressives. The political radicals were joined by various intellectuals, writers, and artists—among them Emma Goldman, Alexander Berkman, Lincoln Steffans, Bill Haywood, John Reed, Walter Lippmann, Frances Perkins, Max Eastman, Gertrude Light, Mary Heaton Vorse, as well as labor leaders, poets, journalists, editors, and actors (Dodge Luhan, 1936).

One of the meeting places was Mabel Dodge's salon, which "burst upon New York like a rocket," to use Margaret Sanger's phrase (Sanger,1938: 73). Mabel Dodge was a wealthy woman who had joined the radical social circles and was part of the radical culture. Her apartments were a marvel of white walls and curtains, glinting mirrors in gilded frames, white marble fireplace, delicate French chairs and chaises longues (Dodge Luhan, 1936: 4–5). The guests made a contrast with the elegant rooms. Margaret Sanger described an evening:

> the whole gamut of liberalism had collected in her spacious drawing room before an open fire. Cross-legged on the floor, in the best Bohemian tradition, were Wobblies with uncut hair, unshaven faces, leaning against valuable draperies. Their clothes may have been unkempt, but their eyes were ablaze with interest and intelligence. Each knew his own side of the subject as well as any scholar. You had to inform yourself to be in the liberal movement. Ideas were respected, but you had to back them up with facts. (Sanger, 1938: 73)

She reports that "Just before the argument reached the stage of fist fights," the butler would announce that dinner was served.

Bill Sanger was a member of the Socialist Party Local No. 5, and Margaret joined as well—though she later wrote that her personal feelings drew her toward anarchism and she was reading Kropotkin, Bakunin, and Fourier. Local No. 5 was made up of Italian, Jewish, Russian, German, and Spanish immigrants—plus American intellectuals like the Sangers. The local was "something of rebel in the ranks which, against the wishes of the central authority, had been responsible for bringing Bill Haywood East after his release from prison" (Sanger, 1938: 75). Though he had been a major figure in the Socialist Party, Haywood was under a shadow for espousing the more radical principles of the Industrial Workers of the World (the IWW or Wobblies). Bill Sanger had made the arrangements for him to speak (A. Sanger, 1969: 30).

Bill Sanger plunged into activities that were open to energetic and talented men in the party—he ran as a Socialist candidate for alderman and he was a delegate from Local No. 5 to the 1911 convention of Socialist Locals (A. Sanger, 1969: 31). The place of a woman in such a party was very different. Though the party *supported* women's suffrage, a woman could not vote in elections, much less run for alderman. Within the party, men's and women's work was as clearly distinct as it was in the home.

At·the suggestion of Anita Block, editor of the "Women's Sphere" section of the socialist newspaper, *The Call*, Margaret began writing articles. The first, "To Mothers—Our Duty" was published in March of 1911.[6] In September, they published her "Impressions of the East Side," in which she wrote of the problems she saw as she went about her nursing work: poor women did not want large families but they had only the quack abortionists to turn to.[7] She worked with the Socialist Party's Women's Committee through the summer and fall, and at the end of October she was elected to the committee's paid organizer position, with duties of recruiting women, organizing campaigns on women's issues (including suffrage) and doing outreach to other locals so that they might set up women's meetings. In addition, she organized naturalization classes for immigrant women (A. Sanger, 1969: 34–35).

In early January 1912, Sanger attended a rally supporting the laundry workers' strike. The gathering was chaotic, and she felt helpless, knowing that that she had neither the speaking voice nor the talent to stir such an audience. It was at that rally that she first met Elizabeth Gurley Flynn who had, "at her tongue's end ... the words and phrases they understood" (Sanger, 1938: 79). At the time, Flynn was an organizer for the IWW. Sanger later said that she got most of her "feeling of strength from certain leaders of the radical movements, not from the radicals as a whole"—Elizabeth Gurley Flynn was one of those "certain leaders." Flynn described her own first impression of Sanger at the rally as a "frail appearing, unknown volunteer."[8]

Sanger did speak to a meeting of women workers during the laundry strike, asking them to support a Socialist Party legislative effort to improve hours and wages. One woman worker gave a practical objection to the strategy, saying, "Oh! that stuff! Don't you know that we women might be dead and buried if we waited for politicians and lawmakers to right our wrongs." The remark, in the context of Sanger's other experiences with the laundry workers, apparently capped her growing dissatisfaction with the Socialist

6. Margaret's apprenticeship had begun while they were still living in Hastings-on-Hudson. Some time before they moved, she began giving sex-education talks to a mothers' group. While they were still at Hastings, she wrote these up—with her husband thoughtfully helping with the dishes.

7. (A. Sanger, 1969: 31–33). Published in *The Call*, March 26, 1911; September 3 & 10, 1911.

8. (Hersey, 1938: 100–01; 155).

Party and its legislative strategy for change. She resigned as Women's Committee Organizer, and although she continued to give lectures on sex education at some of the locals, she did not work for the Socialist Party again. She moved away from her husband's party and turned toward active involvement with the IWW.[9]

The laundry workers' strike gave her other food for thought as well. When she interviewed workers in their homes, she found evidence that the thrust of the radical movement was toward solving social problems as the men saw them.

> This was the only time I came in contact with men and women on strike together. I could see the men had two things on their minds: one economic— the two-dollar extra wage and the shorter hours they might win; the other political—the coming of the social revolution. The women really cared for neither of these. Dominating each was the relationship between her husband, her children, and herself. She might complain of being tired and not having enough money, but always she connected both with too many offspring. (Sanger, 1938: 79)[10]

Sanger would build on these women's insights.

In leaving the Socialists for the IWW, Margaret Sanger moved with the times, for the Wobblies were on the rise. Labor historian Melvyn Dubofsky wrote,

> American newspapers, magazines, and commentators had alerted citizens to the "rising tide of socialism" in 1911. But, as the socialist tide receded in 1912, Americans discovered a new and grave menace: the rising tide of syndicalism. Decent citizens seemed to have been left stranded on a lonely beach, where wave after wave of immigrant industrial workers beat in upon them, and where tidal waves of direct action and revolution inundated them. Throughout 1912 and 1913, many Americans wondered whether the IWW tide would recede or whether, instead, it would surge on and submerge forever the America they knew. (Dubofsky, 1969: 258–59)

In one of her autobiographies, Sanger wrote that she inclined, in political philosophy and method, toward the anarchist or syndicalist view, and her

---

9. The laundry worker's remark was reported in *The Call,* January 14, 1912. See A. Sanger, (1969: 35–36) for the story and his references to *The Call* for data on the resignation.

10. I would not question the importance of these early political experiences to Sanger's understanding of birth control politics. But the reader should bear in mind that Sanger wrote her autobiographies in the service of the birth control movement. At the least, that purpose would have influenced the events she selected to relate and what she emphasized in reporting them—and her growing commitment to birth control would have influenced what she remembered, of course.

work at the time and her diaries confirm it. As political philosophy, anarchists and syndicalists held that all forms of government rest on violence and so government is wrong and harmful, as well as unnecessary.[11] The syndicalist hope for the future was for just communities, not a just state, in which syndicates, or worker federations coordinated the economic affairs, without politicians, national legislatures, police, courts, or capitalists.

The differences in views on government and the state in the movement formed the basis of major differences in strategy for social change. Socialists and meliorist progressives took government to be legitimate, the former arguing that the capitalist state must be exchanged for a democratic socialist one; the latter that capitalism must be controlled by progressive legislation and public solution of problems. In the long run of the political battle, socialists and progressives moved toward each other. David DeLeon says of the Socialist Party of America, that by 1912 it could be described as "the left wing of the progressive movement." He goes on with a historical evaluation:

> Its primary function, despite its own definition as a replacement for capitalism, was to assist, during a critical period, in the transition to a different form of liberal society. Many in the party were unhappy with this historical task. (DeLeon, 1978: 106)

Socialists and progressives ran candidates for office and worked for labor legislation. But syndicalists used principles of direct action. Through "direct action," capitalist economy and state were to be nonviolently overcome and replaced by a federation of unions. But direct action was also a way of simultaneously creating relationships among people so that they came to class consciousness and could begin to build the new society. In other words, education took place in relationships created in action. The action showed the social organization of the class society, not in abstract terms but displayed in action and reaction among social worlds. For example, in a strike, the spiraling conflict of workers and management would reveal the connections among capitalists, bankers, governors, and priests in the region (and perhaps beyond). In the direct action of a strike, workers would be empowered not only by learning their own effective power to act but by beginning to make new kinds of relationships in organizing their lives collectively, for example, in the strike relief committees. Direct action, I would say, gave a way to embody eros in the relations of sisterhood and brotherhood of the revolutionary movement.

By learning about and aiding other strikers across the nation, workers would become sensitized to class relations under the capitalist state, and they

---

11. See Goldman (1969).

would gain class consciousness and a commitment to a way of making the common good. The working class would become a "we." Finally, through preparation in the local strikes, the "general strike" would be possible, the strike in which workers would shut down production and paralyze the capitalist system and its government. Doing away with government, capitalism, and the state did not mean doing away with coordination and communication, but it did mean social control by other means: local control and coordination by worker syndicates.

In the great Lawrence textile strike of 1912, Wobblies practiced their peaceable principles of "industrial warfare at the point of production." Their success brought thousands of new members, national publicity, and the belief that revolution was around the corner (Dubofsky, 1969: 260, 263).

The action began to unfold in January 1912, when a "protective labor" bill went into effect in Massachusetts, reducing the maximum number of hours per week, from 56 to 54, for women and young people under 18. On the first payday following, employers in the Lawrence textile mills cut wages accordingly. Workers spontaneously began to walk out, and in a short time the textile industry in Lawrence was effectively shut down (Dubofsky, 1969: 242, 249). The Lawrence strike received wide publicity in the establishment press and, of course, heavy coverage in the radical press. Mary Heaton Vorse described it this way:

> It was a new kind of strike. There had never been any mass picketing in a New England town. Ten thousand workers picketed. It was the spirit of workers that seemed dangerous. They were confident, gay, released, and they sang. They were always marching and singing. The gray tired crowds ebbing and flowing perpetually into the mills had waked and opened their mouths to sing, the different nationalities all speaking one language when they sang together. (Boyer and Morais, 1955: 175)

The strike itself was spontaneous and the major part of the workers was unorganized.[12] But once begun, it became an IWW strike infused with IWW principles and shaped by IWW activists. Unlike the Socialist Party, the IWW was revolutionary—not by advocating overthrowing the government but by advocating "industrial warfare." Although the Wobblies spoke of industrial "warfare," many of them were pacifists, increasing their vulnerability in the later struggles over United States entry into World War I. Bill Haywood advised workers to keep their hands in their pockets, in the double sense of refusing to work and of using nonviolence as a tactic. The Wobblies were

---

12. About 2,500 skilled workers belonged to the United Textile Workers, a craft union. The IWW had been organizing locally, but at the time of the strike, they had only about 300 members (Dubofsky, 1969: 234).

often involved in violence, but it was almost always violence they suffered, at the hands of vigilantes and police, not violence that they dispensed.

Like other unions, the IWW used strikes to gain advantages in wages or work conditions. Unlike the other unions, they took these advantages not as an end but as a temporary melioration, for they believe that united, the workers could effectively shut down the capitalist political and economic system. Unlike other unions, they used the strikes as direct actions through which the workers were to educate themselves to become a self-conscious class.[13]

> Wobblies hoped that simple ideas would lead to action, and that action in turn would transform the strikers' originally simple concepts into more complicated revolutionary principles. In other words, the simple concept that employers mistreated workers would result in a strike, the nature of which would teach the strikers about the realities of class, the viciousness of employers, and the depravity of the capitalist state, and from this the strikers would derive a sense of class consciousness and revolutionary principle. (Dubofsky, 1969: 284)

By means of the strike, workers would gain short-term benefits in the workplace. More importantly, they would change themselves and their understanding so as to create a feeling of solidarity and "class spirit, class respect, and class consciousness" (Dubofsky, 1969: 272).

A second kind of action had to do with making new social forms, not as utopian experiments but to deal with new necessities. At Lawrence, the strikers had no financial reserves, and they were short on food and fuel. Many of the workers lived in drafty, shoddy, wooden tenements.

> The strike committee organized an elaborate system directed by a relief committee composed of representatives of all the nationalities caught up in the struggle. Each ethnic group also had its own special relief committee. These committees investigated the needs of applicants, provided soup kitchens for single men, and furnished food or store orders for families. The committees provided for fuel, shoes, medical assistance, and in some cases, even rent. Although loosely organized and administered by uneducated immigrants, the committees operated with remarkable efficiency. As a result of their effective operation, no worker or his family starved during the strike; none went without the necessities of life; and none, certainly, lived any more poorly than he would have done during ordinary periods of unemployment. (Dubofsky, 1969: 250)

These efforts were designed to make a start on the syndicalist society in which worker federations would coordinate the economic affairs of the soci-

---

13. They also counseled work slowdowns and snafus—Elizabeth Gurley Flynn counseled laundry workers to send back blue denim shirts to men who sent in dress shirts (Sanger, 1938: 80).

ety, without politicians, national legislatures, police, courts, or capitalists. The knowledge for the new society was to grow as workers throughout the country gained consciousness of their powers and organized their day-to-day needs. I would call this freedom, not in the individualist sense of liberty but in the sense of freedom as the creation of collective possibilities. In the collective possibilities, the common good would grow.

Margaret Sanger had her part in the Lawrence strike. Italian socialists in New York had suggested taking strikers' children out of the cold and hunger and danger of Lawrence, and she was asked to head the small committee managing transport of the first group of children. On February 11, 1912, they brought out over a hundred ragged and thinly clothed children, from toddlers to thirteen year olds.[14] When the strike was settled in mid-March, both Bill and Margaret Sanger organized art exhibitions and sales to help finance the children's return (A. Sanger, 1969: 33).

The Sanger family spent the summer of 1912 in the New England countryside, though from time to time, Margaret returned to the city for nursing jobs. Early in the fall, she was called back to care for Sadie Sachs after the second abortion and faced the shock of her death. She marked this as a turning point in her life:

> The Revolution came—but not as it has been pictured nor as history relates that revolutions have come. It began in my very being as I walked home that night after I had closed the eyes and covered with a sheet the body of that little helpless mother whose life had been sacrificed to ignorance. (Sanger, 1931: 50)

Like other women, Sadie Sachs had asked Sanger for the secrets of preventing birth. Sanger later wrote that the only methods she knew to tell the women were withdrawal and condoms, and the women laughed at her thinking that any man could be relied on to use those ways (Sanger, 1931: 51). It was after Sadie Sachs' death that Sanger began her active search for contraceptive methods.[15]

Margaret Sanger was still actively promoting sex education, and she began writing a second series for *The Call*, later published as *What Every Girl Should Know*. The articles discussed social and physiological aspects of reproduction and sexual development in children and adolescents. The last

---

14. The figure of 119 children is given in Sanger (1938: 81). Sanger (1931: 78) says 250 children and Flynn (1973: 137) says 150.

15. Given the importance of "turning points" in autobiographies of the time, and the fact that Sanger wrote her autobiographies with a political purpose, it is difficult to know whether the Sadie Sachs event happened as recorded. There is no question that Sanger lived through similar events and that her experiences nursing on the Lower East Side were a basis for her commitment.

part of the series, on gonorrhea and syphilis, had the distinction of having its publication held up under the Comstock law.[16]

In the winter of 1913, workers in the Paterson, New Jersey silk industry began a strike that was to last for seven months, a strike coordinated by the IWW. In April, Bill Haywood sent Margaret Sanger and Jessie Ashley to Hazelton, Pennsylvania as IWW organizers for the striking workers there. Margaret was arrested twice. She was then sent to work in Paterson, where she spoke to strikers on family limitation, and, with her sister Ethel Byrne, organized the transfer of Paterson children to New York (A. Sanger, 1969: 50).

Measures against the strikers at Paterson were severe. Company owners had hired armed private detectives to patrol the mills and police were arresting strike leaders. Eventually, 1,850 of the strikers, as well as journalist John Reed, were arrested. The IWW continued to counsel nonviolence. Company detectives shot and killed a bystander in April and a strikebreaker killed a striking IWW worker in July (Dubofsky, 1969: 277–78).

At Mabel Dodge's salon, John Reed suggested a pageant that might give the strike publicity, raise funds, and link the labor struggle with Greenwich Village radicals and intellectuals. The organizational meeting was held at the Sangers' apartment, and Margaret was one of the six members of the organizing committee. They had only three weeks in which to stage this major event. In their strikes, IWW members had always encouraged workers to put on shows and stage dances and debates, but this pageant was at the old Madison Square Garden, not in the public halls, streets, and parks of the strikers' neighborhoods. The aim was to dramatize direct action and to raise funds. Twelve hundred strikers were involved in the production, as were key organizers and sympathetic radicals.

Sanger described the pageant as "a fitting conclusion to one period of my life." But that is a cool perspective from later in her career. At the time, she went into a crisis. Political anguish was only one part of her crisis, however. She had begun to feel a dread that her political commitment would separate her from her children.

When the pageant was over, she went away with the children to a rented cottage on the beach near Provincetown, Mass.

> I tried to run away from life, from its turmoil and perplexities. I wanted the quiet of the sea, the loneliness of the dunes, to be alone with myself forever. I wanted to have the children solely to myself, too. I wanted to drive away that descending, foreboding barrier of separation by closer contact with them. I wanted to feed, to bathe, to clothe them myself. I wanted to bind them to me and allow nothing to force us apart. I clutched at them like a drowning woman in a raging current, as if to save myself from its swiftness. (Sanger, 1931: 58)

---

16. The order was rescinded, and later the U.S. Government reprinted her work (without permission) to distribute to servicemen.

"Socialism, anarchism, syndicalism, progressivism—I was tired of them all."[17]

She was not the only one burned out by the events of the year. When the strike collapsed in July, Bill Haywood went to Provincetown as the guest of Jessie Ashley, suffering in spirit and physically ill from ulcers (Flynn, 1973: 169). The IWW itself needed to recover. Although there were to be future IWW successes in the west, it was never again a force in the industrial northeast (Dubofsky, 1969: 283–90).

Stepping Out

Shall we who have heard the cries and seen the agony of dying women respect the law which has caused their deaths? Shall we watch in patience the murdering of 25,000 women each year in the United States from criminal abortions? (Margaret Sanger, Journal, October 19, 1914, MS/SS)

Bill Sanger interpreted Margaret's reaction to the radicals as inevitable— not, however, on political grounds, but as a reaction to a movement that was nothing but a "Saturnalia of Sexualism." Of the IWW leader, he wrote, "while Bill Haywood is up there [in Provincetown], let's get a healthy point of view and not mixed up with sexuality under cover of Revolution."[18]

At Provincetown, Bill Haywood was serving as Margaret's confidant and advisor. He saw that she was "getting ready to kick over the traces." He knew her struggle with the conflict between her political commitment and her devotion to her children—a conflict intensified by her troubles with their father. He also knew that her political disillusion was not simply with the failure of industrial warfare in Paterson. It included the radical movements' inability to take certain "women's issues" seriously. Years later, Margaret wrote that she was despondent after the Paterson debacle and angry about

---

17. (Sanger, 1938: 94). In addition to her desire for a safe harbor, there is a struggle here between political commitment and her commitment as a mother. But see Chesler (1992: chapters 2 & 5) on Sanger's childcare and housekeeping methods. Chesler's book is far and away the most careful and sympathetic study of Sanger, but although she is careful to be light-handed in attributing motives and making judgments, I feel her interpretation of Sanger takes a "middle-class," psychological outlook too much for granted. As a result, she neglects the importance of Sanger's own life in Corning, and the importance of Sanger's personal knowledge of class and gender structures. In the last chapter of this book, I describe a different sort of struggle, between commitment to personal autonomy and development and commitment as a mother. It is one of the individualistic and conservative features of the second wave of the women's movement that personal autonomy (including choice of a career), rather than political commitment, has been named as the one pole of the struggle, though of course many feminists have acted out of political commitment. On the New Left (including women's liberation), the other pole of commitment to the children tended to be ignored—except for occasional offerings of childcare during events.

18. Letter from William Sanger to Margaret Sanger, Sept. 3, 1913, MS/SS. William Sanger was in Boston. See Chesler (1992: chapter 5) for more detail on the problem of "sexuality under cover of Revolution."

the stubborn focus on a man's economic need to support a family, a "shallow principle" for the new civilization, a tunnel vision that ignored woman and the quality of life itself (Sanger, 1938: 85). Haywood suggested that in France she might gather information about contraceptive methods—syndicalist women there had been using family limitation for generations. He himself would be there with Jessie Ashley in the fall and he could help her out (Sanger, 1931: 60–61; 68).

Bill Sanger had left architecture by this time to concentrate on art. He was more than eager to go to Paris—fulfilling the dream that was dreamed during the Sangers' courtship. And so the family sailed for Europe in October 1913. In Paris, Bill found a studio and "came home aglow with news of meeting Henri Matisse and other revolutionary painters" (Sanger, 1931: 74). Meanwhile, Margaret gathered information from French neo-Malthusians, and she purchased contraceptive devices from shops and bookstalls. With Bill Haywood she visited working-class districts and homes and learned from the women the methods they passed down from mother to daughter (Sanger, 1931: 68, 72). But, in a short time she was restless again.

> Bill was happy in his studio, but I could find no peace. Each day I stayed, each person I met, made it worse. A whole year had been given over to this inactive, incoherent brooding . . . I had practically reached the exploding point. I could not contain my ideas. I wanted to get on with what I had to do in the world. (Sanger, 1938: 105)

A year had passed since the tragedy of Sadie Sachs' death.

On December 31,1913, she "left the artist husband ensconced in his studio" and sailed for New York with her three children. It was, in essence, the close of her life as Bill Sanger's wife—and the end of being any man's help-meet. She later wrote to a friend, "Where is the man who can give me what the movement gives?" She arrived in New York to take the first step on her own path. She had decided to "stir up a national campaign."[19]

Margaret Sanger had gone to Paris with the turmoil of her New York life still unsorted. "The whole of life was like a picture puzzle," she wrote later, "and think as I would I could not put it together."[20] Back in New York, her first effort in trying out the waters as a political leader was to publish a monthly magazine, *The Woman Rebel.* She managed to get the first eight-

19. The quote on "Where is the man . . . " is from Lader (1955: 52). Other information in the paragraph is from Sanger (1931: 74) and my general interpretation is from many letters written by William to Margaret, fall 1913–spring 1914; and Margaret's 1914–1915 journals (MS/SS, MS/LC).

20. (Sanger,1931: 74). On these remarks and Sanger's mention of her "sleepwalking stage" (below), see my discussion in chapter 8 on having to proceed without a label for oneself or one's activities.

page issue out by March 1914. In an editorial explaining "Why the Woman Rebel?" she wrote,

> Because I believe that deep down in woman's nature lies slumbering the spirit of revolt.
>
> Because I believe that woman is enslaved by the world machine, by sex conventions, by motherhood and its present necessary child rearing, by wage-slavery, by middle-class morality, by customs, laws and superstitions.
>
> Because I believe that woman's freedom depends upon awakening that spirit of revolt within her against these things which enslave her.

It was not only in women she believed, but in "the offspring of the immigrant":

> Because I believe that on the courage, vision and idealism of the immigrant and the offspring does the industrial revolution depend.
>
> Because I believe that not until wage slavery is abolished can either women's or man's freedom be fully attained.

The first issue of *The Woman Rebel* contained an article titled, "The Prevention of Conception." That article did not give contraceptive information, though it did advocate breaking the law:

> As is well known, a law exists forbidding the imparting of information on this subject, the penalty being several years imprisonment. Is it not time to defy this law? And what fitter place could be found than in the pages of the *The Woman Rebel?*

There was an immediate and spontaneous response. Although the magazine had only a 2,000 circulation (and far fewer reached subscribers because of Post Office interference), labor papers across the country carried news of the publication. In six months, she received over 10,000 requests for contraceptive information (Sanger, 1931: 81).

The clash with the Comstock law came with the first issue.

> One morning after the children were washed and dressed and sent away to their school in the neighborhood I started my day's work by looking over my huge batch of mail. My attention was immediately caught by an unstamped envelope from the New York Post Office. I tore it open. "Dear Madam," I read: "You are hereby notified that the Solicitor of the Post Office Department has decided that *The Woman Rebel* for March 1914 is unmailable under Section 489, Postal Laws and Regulations. (Sanger, 1931: 81)

The letter did not specify which article was obscene, nor would the Post Office Department give any word on which articles they later counted as obscene in the May, July, August, September, and October issues.

It would be a serious misinterpretation to suppose that Margaret Sanger was aiming at a test of the constitutionality of the Comstock laws. Fights for free speech were a major part of IWW strategy, but they were not tests of the legitimate limits of government in restricting free speech. There were no legitimate limits of government in the Wobblies' eyes because government itself was illegitimate, a monopoly on violence, an instrument of oppression. Rather, free-speech fights demonstrated that America's dispossessed could, through direct action, challenge established authority (Dubofsky, 1969: 173–74). They showed that the law was not sacred, and they spread the word. They were also a necessary part of organizing strategy. Free-speech fights were an important part of IWW organizing tactics—local officials regularly passed ordinances forbidding their speaking, and regularly filled their jails with Wobblies. This usually brought national publicity.[21]

In her letter to subscribers after her indictment, Margaret asked whether we should watch in patience the murdering of women from abortions, and whether we should "fold our hands and wait until a body of sleek and well fed politicians get ready to abolish the cause of such slaughter" (Sanger, 1931: 94). But her effort to "stir up a national campaign" was not simply a direct action on a recognized problem. It was an effort to make a moral problem public—a problem that complemented that of industrial injustice. Which moral problem was it?

In part, Sanger was concerned with the problem of abortion, but in a very broad context that suited radical analysis. In an article in the May issue of *The Woman Rebel,* titled "Abortion in the United States," she wrote,

> "Criminal" abortions arise from a perverted sex relationship under the stress of economic necessity, and their greatest frequency is among married women.

She also understood the problem as being defined in terms of what she saw as its solution:

> What a wholesale lot of misery, expense, unhappiness and worry will be avoided when woman shall possess the knowledge of prevention of conception!

It took Margaret years to work out the theoretical underpinnings of the problem to which she would devote her life. At the time of *The Woman Rebel* she herself didn't understand it as she later would. But she did know that it needed a name to distinguish it.

---

21. (Dubofsky, 1969: 173–74). In free-speech fights, Wobblies often received brutal treatment. About 400 were imprisoned in Spokane between November 1909 and March 1910. IWW estimated that as a result of mistreatment, 334 were treated in the emergency hospital a total of 1,600 times (Dubofsky, 1969: 179). As time wore on, they suffered lynchings and beatings by vigilante committees and they suffered persecution around the time of World War I (see below)

A new movement was starting, and the baby had to have a name. It did not belong to Socialism nor was it in the labor field, and it had much more to it than just the prevention of conception . . .

I was not advocating a one-child or two-child system as in France, nor did I wholeheartedly agree with the English neo-Malthusians whose concern was almost entirely with limitation for economic reasons. My idea of control was bigger and freer. I wanted family in it, yet family control did not sound right. (Sanger, 1938: 108)

She and a few friends worked out the name: birth control. "Birth control" named a nest of problems. It included the abortion problem. But in its deepest moral sense, I believe it was the problem of the woman of practical wisdom and through her, the problem of the good life for all human beings and the problem of the future of the human race.

Sanger later explained some of the moral and philosophical intuitions that, though unarticulated at the time, eventually clarified her actions.

It seemed to me the whole question of strikes for higher wages was based on man's economic need of supporting his family, and that this was a shallow principle upon which to found a new civilization. Furthermore, I was enough of a Feminist to resent the fact that woman and her requirements were not being taken into account in reconstructing this new world about which all were talking. They were failing to consider the quality of life itself. (Sanger, 1938: 85)

I believe that in her criticism of this "shallow principle" of man's economic need to support a family, there is the beginning of a theme of unifying public and private, men and women, in enacting the common good. The unity was not to be accomplished under the hierarchy of the citizen patriarch (as Aristotle had it), and not under the rubric of private family as the container of the erotic bond (as the individualist perspective would have it). Nor was it the sort of oppositional, interest-group stand that dominated the second wave of the women's movement in the United States. Rather, eros (as sex and procreation) expressed the common concern that was to be collectively enacted through the virtue of birth control *and* the virtue of industrial justice. Work that supplies the material needs of life is, after all, a procreational issue. At any rate, it seems to me that the envisioned syndicalist society would overcome the division of public and domestic. In the process, the selves of all participants were to grow in the freedom of creating collective possibilities.

The small group of friends who worked out the name "birth control" also founded a society called the National Birth Control League (though nothing much came of it until a little later). They helped solicit support and funds. Socialists, anarchists, and trade unionists helped by taking prepaid subscriptions to *The Woman Rebel* and by running notices in their newspapers. Active feminists weren't interested.[22] When the May issue was suppressed, friends asked her to stop. One "noted woman rebel" advised her to go back and take care of her children.[23] Later, Margaret wrote,

> During what might be called my sleepwalking stage, it was as though I were heading towards a precipice and nothing could awaken me. I had no ear for the objections of family nor the criticism of friends. People were around me, I knew, but I could not see them clearly; I was deaf to their warnings and blind to their signs. (Sanger, 1938: 116)

She was in her apartment with her father, the old rebel Michael Higgins, when the arrest took place.

The conflict between political commitment and the children came to a head when it began to seem certain she would be sentenced to a federal penitentiary. She consulted with friends and with Bill Sanger, who had left Paris to come to her side in the time of trouble. There seemed no political point to her serving time in prison, but the alternative was to become a fugitive. Years later, in an interview with her biographer Lawrence Lader, she said of the hours of struggle on the day before her case was to come to court:

> They were my Gethsemane. How could I do it? How could I leave three adorable children? It sickens me even forty years later to think of that struggle within me. But there was no turning back. I had to fight this through even if it meant leaving children, home, friends, everything I held dear. (Lader, 1955: 60)

At midnight, she caught the train to Canada. During the trip, she wrote a letter to be sent to friends and to the two thousand subscribers of *The Woman Rebel* (Lader, 1955: 60). In it, she announced that she would attempt to nullify the law by direct action—she would give knowledge of birth control to women and men so that by their own direct actions they would disarm the law. She had written her knowledge of birth control into a booklet called "Family Limitation."

---

22. Sanger took revenge by publishing a criticism. In the first issue, she ridiculed feminists espousing the "right to ignore fashions" and the "right to keep her own name." She said they represented a middle-class women's movement, and that "the freedom which the new feminists expound can only be obtained through the greater enslavement of the already enslaved workingwoman . . . "

23. Her family, still in upstate New York, got wind of the legal troubles and held a family council. They concluded that she was having a nervous breakdown, and her father Michael Higgins was sent down to find a way to ease her into a private sanitarium—his first visit to New York City in forty years. He found her rational and determined. He also found that he could not dissuade her by rational argument. She eventually got Michael Higgins to see her point. See Sanger (1931: 90; 1938: 115).

This first version of "Family Limitation" was a small pamphlet of 7 x 9″ paper folded in half to make a booklet. It said only "Limitation" on the outside cover. It contained descriptions of contraceptive methods and even recipes for suppositories and douches and a suggestion for an abortifacient. It counseled that a husband's callous behavior would lead to the wife's nervousness and avoidance of sex. It was so clearly in violation of the law that no printing business could handle it. She found a linotype operator who would set it in secret, after hours.

> After that, there was still the question of printing, binding, and storing, all of which was accomplished by individuals of five nationalities over a period of three months despite the careful watching of Uncle Sam. (Sanger, 1931: 86)

With the help of IWW workers, bundles of copies were sent to organizers in the silk, woolen, and copper industries (Sanger, 1931: 61).

Margaret stayed in Montreal for a short time. Then, on November 3, 1914, she boarded the R.M.S. Virginian and set sail for England. Aboard the ship, she sent out a message that organizers were to open their bundles and release the booklets. A hundred thousand copies of the pamphlet "Family Limitation" were distributed to working men and women across the United States.[24]

Stepping Outside

Sanger set sail under the name "Bertha Watson." On board, she wrote in her journal of her loneliness for her baby Peggy, remembering their trip the year before. But she also wrote philosophically on the intermingled themes of reason and emotion, male and female, machine and human, developing her thought through the days of the voyage. She pondered the relation of reason and emotion to action, writing that judges and juries are there to keep us cold and calculating in our thought, and that the law stands as a piece of paper against human life. She went on to link men's thought and legalistic thought, and she criticized the reasoning processes of liberal men who kept their wives subservient.

On the third day of the voyage, she sent the message to release "Family Limitation." On the fourth, she returned to the theme of reason, and (needing definitions) concluded that reason in the relevant sense is accumulated knowledge of past acts or consequences while emotion urges from within, not fearing the consequences. Together they make the perfect human being. In contrast, the perfect "Anglo Saxon Man" served the machine of modern

---

24. My remarks on the content of her letter, and on "Family Limitation," are based on documents in the Sophia Smith Collection. The documents also offer background to the discussion here.

industrialization: such a man has a splendid mind that is unable to see the class war; he has reasoned his impulses out of existence to don the cold cloak of logic; he is a symbol of the machine he serves (Sanger diary, 1914: MS/LC).

Once in London, Sanger rented a room at the top floor of a bed and breakfast near the British Museum.[25] She was to spend nearly a year abroad, a year in which she broadened her theoretical and strategic understanding of birth control. She spent time with Havelock Ellis. She also met British members of the neo-Malthusian movement, and she worked at one of the Malthusian League clinics, operated by Dr. Johannes Rutgers in the Netherlands. Finally, she met Lorenzo Portet, a passionate Spanish activist and a student of Francisco Ferrer, founder of the "Modern School" movement that had been taken up by anarchists in New York.

Sanger had previously read a little of Ellis's *Psychology of Sex,* but the reading had given her "psychic indigestion." By the end of their first, long-drawn-out teatime, Havelock Ellis had done his work and Margaret Sanger was over the "psychic indigestion."

> He, beyond any other person, has been able to clarify the question of sex and free it from the smudginess connected with it from the beginning of Christianity, raise it from the dark cellar, set it on a higher plane. That has been his great contribution. Like an alchemist, he transmuted the psychic disturbance which had followed my reading of his books into a spiritual essence. (Sanger, 1938: 135)

He gave her a copy of his book on sexual inversions—which had been judged obscene under British law. He also gave her his copy of Ellen Key's book on Karazza to read saying the method was splendid if the man could manage it (Journal, Dec. 22, 1914, MS/LC).[26] When she returned to her chilly room, her feeling was too deep for excitement. "I felt as though I had been exalted into a hitherto undreamed-of world" (Sanger, 1938: 136). The vision of sex that Ellis and Sanger shared was a romantic vision, suited to nineteenth-century roots. As moral problems of sex and birth control came more and more under the cognitive authority of scientists and family planners, the romantic vision was leeched away.

In January 1915, despite the war and the fact that she was traveling under an assumed name, Sanger went to the Netherlands, where the Malthusian

---

25. (Sanger diary, 1914: LC). In the British Museum she was recognized by Edward Carpenter, who shocked her by calling her by name when she was traveling as Bertha Watson (Sanger, 1938: 131).

26. Karazza promoted a sexual method in which intercourse went on for an hour or so without the man's ejaculating. It was a also a method practiced, for example, at the utopian Oneida community in New York, for eugenic purposes as well as those of sexual fulfillment. See Gordon (1977) for an overview.

League had several thousand members and fifty-four operating clinics (primarily among the poor). She trained at the clinic, learning that fitting pessaries was more complicated than she had previously thought. Though she made much of the experience in her autobiographies, her journal entries at the time described it as "another drilling in methods."[27]

In fact, Sanger was still very much the radical. After a brief return to London, Margaret spent most of March and all of April traveling on the Continent, the bulk of the time in Spain with Lorenzo Portet. In December, in London, she had contrasted him with the Italian anarchist Malatesta, describing Portet as "full of vigor, confident, quick to understand" (Dec. 13, 1914 journal, MS/LC). He saw the importance of the "birth control" problem and the "masculine all too masculine" character of Marxist and socialist thought and action. In the spring, she interviewed him (probably in Spain) and drafted an essay giving his biography and a history of the "Modern School" movement founded in Spain by Francisco Ferrer.

> [Ferrer's] idea was to teach the child life through nature, to analyze religions, governments, etc., and to reject that which could not be reasoned. He taught that the regeneration of Spain depends upon education and social organization. . . . Ferrer created a new idea of education in Spain of anti-church, anti-Capitalism, anti-patriotism, anti-militarism and combined these teachings in the Modern School for the promotion of universal peace through economic justice.[28]

For a time Sanger's son Stuart attended the Ferrer school in New York. The school had been organized by Emma Goldman, Alexander Berkman, and others.

Portet was under 24-hour surveillance by the Spanish secret service, and so was Margaret during her visit. He inspired her, and she described him as "what the Americans call a hard-headed businessman." He was also "a spirit that flames in protest at every injustice he meets."[29]

---

27. (Sanger, 1938: 146–48). From the perspective of later years, in her biographies, she described the clinic experience as if it brought on a sudden conversion to the view that medically trained personnel should dispense contraceptives. In fact, she barely mentions the clinic in her 1914–1915 journal, saying little more than, "another drilling in methods" (Feb. 12, 1915; MS/LC). The diary also conflicts with Sanger (1938: 148) in which she says she spent two months in the Netherlands.

28. Emma Goldman published an essay on Ferrer some years earlier (Goldman, 1969). Sanger published a series on the Modern School in Modern School Magazine, May, July, Sept., and Oct., 1916 and Jan. & Feb., 1917.

29. Unpublished essay on Portet and Ferrer, 1915, in MS/LC. Ferrer had been executed by the Spanish government in 1909. The idea of a spirit flaming in protest seems to me to carry some of the same romantic force that the idea of an artist carries as an image of the rebel in the novel I discuss in chapter 8.

When Margaret returned to England, she did some work with suffragists, and she observed their tactics of resistance and hunger strikes. She wrote pamphlets on contraception to send back to subscribers to *The Woman Rebel*, to make up for the issues that could not be completed. Philosophically, she was mulling over Nietzsche's ideas. She objected to his habit of deducing sociological characteristics from personality, but she found some of his language useful. In July 1915, she gave a speech in Fabian Hall in London, saying that the Birth Control Leagues in the United States were formed to

> inject into the working woman a class independence which says to the Master produce your own slaves, keep your religion, your ethics, and your morality for yourselves—I'll have none of it and we refuse to be longer enslaved by it, for we are creating our own and are building up a New Society through which we are creating our own morality and individuality.[30]

Through Lorenzo Portet, she was offered a salaried position as an advisor on English books to French and Spanish publishing houses. She began making plans to bring the children over and to take a house in Versailles. But she began having troubled dreams and premonitions about her daughter Peggy, and the date November 6 began to haunt her (Sanger, 1938: 175). Then she received the news that Bill Sanger had been arrested by Anthony Comstock himself for giving out a copy of "Family Limitations."[31] Margaret Sanger sailed for New York in late September, 1915.

Where the Cause Was Born

Although Margaret Sanger later minimized the importance of *The Woman Rebel* when its radical stance became a detriment, her work on the magazine and the early, radical editions of "Family Limitation" had helped make birth control a recognized moral problem. By the time she returned to the United States, the National Birth Control League, which had been announced in *The Woman Rebel*, had become a reality under the leadership of Mary Ware Dennett, former secretary of the National Suffrage Association—with the help of Anita Block, Jessie Ashley, Lincoln Steffens, and *The Woman Rebel* subscription lists (A. Sanger, 1969: 85). "Family Limitation" had been widely distributed, and there was interest in forming leagues in other parts of the country.

30. My understanding of Sanger's work with Nietzsche is from her journals and a copy of a paper on Nietzsche in MS/SS. This quotation and the information on Fabian Hall I took from Jensen (1981). Jensen's paper is fair and politically perspicuous. I share Jensen's criticisms of secondary literature on Sanger in Jensen (1981: note 1).

31. William Sanger had been tricked into giving one of Margaret's pamphlets to a Comstock agent. When the case finally came to trial (after continual postponements), he was convicted and chose 30 days in jail over paying a fine (Douglas, 1970: 85).

There was publicity in radical publications over William Sanger's arrest and trial and as a result, a flood of requests for contraceptive information. Birth control was becoming a respectable issue. But Margaret Sanger was not considered respectable. She returned to face trial, still an anarchist in her own eyes and those of more proper folk.[32]

Before she was to come to trial the premonition which had haunted her in London was fulfilled. Her daughter Peggy took sick. On November 6, the little girl died of pneumonia.

> The bottom seemed to have fallen out of the very earth itself. A great gulf of loneliness set me apart from the rest of the world. It separated me from everybody and everything—from facts—from sunshine, night and day. The joy in the fullness of life went out of it on that morning, and has never returned. (Sanger, 1931: 126–27)

With Peggy's death, Sanger's public image was changed. The story was publicized in newspapers across the country, along with a poignant photograph of her with her two sons. She became the tragic mother fighting for all mothers.[33] Contributions and letters of support came in. Distinguished lawyers offered their aid. An open letter was sent to President Woodrow Wilson on her behalf—signed by nine internationally known British authors, including H. G. Wells. A fundraising and support dinner was held, with distinguished guests from among the radicals and from among the wealthy of the city. There she spoke her case and many of the guests pledged aid—including Mary Ware Dennett, who changed heart after all of this and offered the help of the NBCL (Douglas, 1970: 90–91).

Sanger had hoped to make a political statement with her trial, as the British Malthusian Annie Besant had done years before in England. But the trial was postponed again, and finally on February 18, 1916, her case was dismissed. She went on a speaking tour across the United States. She recommended the NBCL to people interested in forming local leagues. She talked up birth control clinics, and interest in them, "seemed to spread like a forest fire."

> Taking everything into consideration, my campaign was a great success. I had created a national public opinion in favor of birth control, had won the press to

---

32. Mary Ware Dennett refused her the support of the NBCL, and even ten years later disapproved of what she considered Margaret's lawlessness and "atmosphere of violence" (Douglas, 1970: 88). Margaret herself had planned to wear the anarchist women's costume of black tie and skirt and white shirtwaist at the trial (Gray, 1979: 115).

33. Gray (1979: 116) wrote, "John Reed . . . suggested getting Underwood and Underwood . . . to take a picture of her in plain dark dress with a wide Quaker collar, her hair done up in a simple coil and her two sons beside her. The release of this picture, he felt, would raise a lot of sympathy for her." Gray does not cite her source, however. The photograph is effective and was used recently in Planned Parenthood publicity brochures.

discuss the subject, had inspired the organization of leagues to carry on the work throughout the country, and had aroused the nation to a realization of its great moral duty toward womanhood. (Sanger, 1931: 149)

When she returned from her tour in July, Margaret Sanger was a public figure nationally, not simply in radical circles. Nationally she was identified with the birth control movement. This is not to say she had given up her syndicalist roots. Back in New York, she announced that she intended to open a free birth control clinic—another try at direct action.[34]

She received "an avalanche of letters, telephone calls, and visitors." Among the visitors were three women from the Brownsville section of Brooklyn, whose neighbors had offered to care for their children so that they might bring back the secrets.

> They told of their own hardships, poverty and misery; of their own helplessness, their struggles to make ends meet. One woman said that she had just recovered from an abortion from which she had nearly died; another abortion would "take her off." "Then what will become of my children?" she moaned. They rocked back and forth in their chairs as they related their miseries, every tragic event told so simply as each woman recounted her experience, scarcely able to allow the friend to finish before she took up the story of her own sufferings. (Sanger, 1931: 150–51)

At the end of the hour, Margaret Sanger felt as if she had been through it herself. She couldn't contain herself from doing something.

She, her sister Ethel Byrne, also a trained nurse, and Fania Mindell rented space in Brownsville using a fifty-dollar donation that had come in from California. They set up quarters with the help of a sympathetic landlord and went door to door with handbills printed in English, Yiddish, and Italian (Sanger, 1931: 153):

---

34. The clinic episode as it occurred was a direct action. It is possible that Sanger had some thought of a test of the law—at least, the NBCL under Frederic Blossom's instigation was thinking of a test of the law. Under New York law at the time, legitimate contraception was a medical matter in a very narrow sense. According to Section 1142 of the New York Penal Code, no contraceptive advice could be given by anyone for any reason. However, Section 1145 of the code offered a loophole—physicians could prescribe for cure or prevention of disease. The exception was very narrowly understood by most physicians and lawyers to mean prescription of condoms to protect males from venereal disease (Douglas, 1970: 101); (Sanger, 1931: 152–53). To make a plausible challenge to the law, it was necessary to have a physician prescribe contraceptives to the clinic patients, otherwise it would be treated as a violation of obscenity laws or a charge of practicing medicine without a license (and those were in fact the charges brought). Margaret Sanger had made contacts with women doctors who had indicated interest in setting up a clinic. The clinic was opened with no doctor, since none would volunteer to work there. This, and Sanger's later remarks, indicate to me that she was still operating under the idea of direct action.

MOTHERS:

Can you afford to have a large family?
Do you want any more children?

If not, why do you have them?

DO NOT KILL, DO NOT TAKE LIFE BUT PREVENT

Safe, Harmless Information can be obtained of trained Nurses at

46 AMBOY STREET
near Pitkin Ave.—Brooklyn
Tell your Friends and Neighbors

All Mothers Welcome

A registration fee of 10 cents entitles any mother to this information
(Sanger, 1938: 216)

The clinic opened on October 16, 1916, at 7 a.m., to a long line of waiting women. Fania Mindell took case histories and tended the children of the women who were sent in groups of eight or ten to the rear room. There Margaret or Ethel explained the methods and their importance, and estimated the size of pessary from the woman's previous births and miscarriages. They did not do examinations or fittings. As the days passed, women came from as far as Massachusetts, Pennsylvania, New Jersey, and the far end of Long Island—Yiddish and Italian papers had carried information from the handbill. A few came thinking they might get abortion information (Sanger, 1938: 216–17).

The clinic was open for nine days. On the tenth, the vice squad came, threatening the mothers and taking their names, confiscating the demonstration supplies and the case histories, and arresting Margaret Sanger. She spent the night in a jail cell. By the next afternoon, bail was arranged and she went back to reopen the clinic. Once again the women came for information, and so did the authorities—this time uniformed police, not the vice squad. Sitting in the patrol wagon, she looked out at the crowd that stood passively by:

As I sat in the rear of the car and looked out on that seething mob of humans, I wondered, and asked myself, what had gone out of the race. Something had gone from them which silenced them, made them impotent to defend their rights. I thought of the suffragists in England and pictured the results of a similar arrest there. (Sanger, 1931: 160)

As the patrol wagon pulled away, she heard a shout from a woman wheeling a baby carriage who had come to visit the clinic and had suddenly seen the police. The woman cried out,

"Come back! Come back and save me." The woman looked wild. She ran after the car for a dozen yards or so, when some friends caught her weeping form in their arms and led her back to the sidewalk. That was the last thing I saw as the Black Maria dashed off to the station. (Sanger, 1931: 160)[35]

Ethel Byrne was charged with violating Section 1142 of the Penal Code for practicing medicine without a license. Fania Mindell was charged with having sold an indecent book (*What Every Girl Should Know*) and Margaret Sanger was charged with running a public nuisance and also violating Section 1142 (Douglas, 1970: 108–09).

In the end, Ethel Byrne spent thirty days in the workhouse on Blackwell's Island, waging a hunger strike that made front page news and damaged her health.[36] Fania was found guilty and fined (a decision reversed on appeal). Margaret spent thirty days in a cell at the Queens County Penitentiary on Long Island, among women of various ages and callings.[37] She had reached what would become another turning point. She later wrote,

The years from the termination of my prison sentence in 1917 to 1921 were leaden years; years of constant labor, financial worry, combatting of opposition. (Sanger, 1931: 196)

When Margaret emerged from prison the political scene was much changed.[38] World War I and the Russian Revolution had made the radicals' situation nearly impossible. The United States entered the war in April 1917, with the country still split on the issue. Some citizens took action against others—the American Civil Liberties Bureau (a precurser of the ACLU), listed nearly 500 acts of mob violence against individuals from April 1917 to March 1919. Elizabeth Gurly Flynn wrote,

The victims of mob violence were varied—Christian ministers, Negro and white, advocates of peace on religious, moral, or political grounds; Socialists,

---

35. The reader should recall that this event is described in an autobiography written for political purposes.

36. It was a food and liquid fast both, and it affected Ethel's health so severely that the governor's pardon was accepted, even though it was conditional upon her ceasing to disseminate birth control information (Sanger, 1938: 232). Margaret herself apparently received a harsher sentence because she insisted that she couldn't respect the law (Sanger, 1938: 237).

37. See Sanger (1938: chapter 9). Sanger (1931: xiv) has some of her prison journal entries.

38. The dreariness in Sanger's personal life included an ugly dispute with Frederick Blossom, editor of the *Birth Control Review,* put out under Sanger's auspices. She wrote that the dispute was over the issue of magazine policy on conscription and entering the war. As a result of the policy difference, Blossom moved out with the contents of the office and the account books. When she finally brought suit against him, the Socialist Party censured her. Joan Jensen suggests that Sanger also had an unhappy romance during the time (Jensen, 1981). Between the political and the personal stress, her health weakened and she suffered from depression.

IWW's, members of the Non-Partisan League, which was strong among farmers in the Middle West; friends of Irish Freedom and others. Some individuals, both men and women, who made chance remarks on war, conscription or the sale of bonds were tarred and feathered, beaten sometimes to insensibility, forced to kiss the flag, driven out of town, forced to buy bonds, threatened with lynching. (Flynn, 1973: 229)

German-born Americans were attacked simply because they were German. Legislation was soon passed under which conscientious objectors and those who spoke against the war were imprisoned.

After the Russian Revolution of 1917, some made accusations of "Bolshevism." One way the fear of "Bolshevism" showed itself was in violence against radicals—anarchists, socialists, IWW's, progressive trade unionists. The offices of *The Call* were raided and wrecked, and employees were driven out and beaten (Flynn, 1973: 216). Vigilante and police action against the Wobblies was far worse—beatings, castrations, lynchings.[39] In a mass indictment, ninety-three men presumed to be associated with the IWW were convicted in one Chicago case alone and sentenced to five, ten, and twenty years in prison. Bill Haywood was among those indicted. There were other Wobblie indictments and in the end several hundred were sent to prison. Victor L. Berger—the socialist congressman from Wisconsin who had sponsored a congressional hearing on the Lawrence strike children—was convicted under the Espionage and Sedition Act, as was Eugene V. Debs (Flynn, 1973: 239).

Emma Goldman spent two years in prison for speaking out against the draft, and under the Deportation Act (passed in October, 1918) she was deported just before Christmas, 1919, to spend the rest of her days "nowhere at home." Some of the "aliens" were rounded up in the "Palmer Raids," organized by A. Mitchell Palmer, attorney general, and his assistant J. Edgar Hoover. They took place on January 2, 1920 in seventy cities, with over seven hundred people arrested in New York City alone. Over five hundred foreign-born workers were deported (Flynn, 1973: 256).

Elizabeth Gurley Flynn wrote, "It is hard to recreate a picture of the long years of intense, brutal reaction which lasted from 1917 to 1927" (Flynn, 1973: 265). Her efforts—after her own indictment in the Chicago case in which Bill Haywood was convicted—were devoted to freeing those imprisoned. In the post-war years, she worked with broad-based coalitions for amnesty for political prisoners, and eventually, in defense of Sacco and Vanzetti. She also took part in the newborn American Civil Liberties Bureau. Then, beginning in the 1930s, she became one of the leaders of the Communist Party of the United States of America.

---

39. (Flynn, 1973: chapter 6); (Dubofsky, 1969: part 4); (Boyer and Morais, 1972: chapter 7).

Through her "leaden years" of 1917 to 1921, Margaret stayed with her moral problem of birth control. The Brownsville Clinic episode itself had brought her up short as to the political efficacy of direct action. She later wrote,

> I wanted to reach directly the working women, the factory workers, the women of the labor unions, and the unskilled workers. These were the people to whom my work was directed and for whom I was fighting. I felt that I was the protagonist of the mothers of the child laborers and of the wives of the wage slaves. I knew their lives; I knew their burdens, their sorrows, their problems.
> For their freedom my battle was waged. (Sanger, 1931: 190)

She knew from thousands of letters and hundreds upon hundreds of conversations that there was a spontaneous call from individual women for birth control. But direct action required that they take up the banner in solidarity behind their leader.

> I really expected an active follow-up. I hoped to see those women who themselves had gained the knowledge of contraception, had benefited and developed thereby, to stand behind me, to re-open the Brownsville clinic, to undergo arrest, and if necessary go to jail. I expected a rise of indignation and protest such as the English women had voiced in going to jail and enduring days of hunger. Nothing of this kind happened. American women were not going to use direct action nor were they going to put themselves on record in approving ideas at this controversial stage. (Sanger, 1931: 189–90)

Because they did not act, the working-class women could not change their relationships to each other or to the officials in a way that would create "their own morality and individuality." Nor could they offer Margaret Sanger the protection which an activist must be given by the people of her movement.

> I began to realize how helpless they really were, these mothers. How willing they were to stand beside me in the trial!—but I saw how insignificant their words or presence was in the eyes of the court. They counted for naught. For them to go to jail would place hardship on their children and families, and we would gain nothing by their sacrifice. (Sanger, 1931: 190)

In support of her judgment on the lack of readiness of the working class, Sanger later reported a conversation with Bill Haywood, just before he left for the USSR. She wrote that Haywood saw that workers had been split by the war and could not be depended upon as a force—though he hoped to return and organize them in a sunnier time.[40]

---

40. (Sanger, 1938: 265). However, Haywood wrote her a letter from prison shortly before he left the country saying the world revolution had arrived (Feb. 7, 1919: MS/SS). While this isn't incompatible, the reported conversation on workers not being a force is given in Sanger (1938) and not in Sanger (1931). She makes several conservative reconstructions in Sanger (1938).

In "the leaden years," Sanger gradually moved away from radical politics. Joan Jensen has traced the move through changes in the text of "Family Limitation." Jensen finds no significant changes in the booklet until the tenth edition, published in 1920. In that edition, abortion sections are deleted as is all reference to birth control as a method of direct action. Recommendations that women of the working class join together in self-help have given way to recommendations that they seek the guidance of trained doctors and nurses. By the twelfth edition, birth control was described as a means to end poverty, misery, and ignorance, not as a class weapon (Jensen, 1981).[41]

The change in policy paralleled a change in constituency. Sanger explained the change this way:

> Previously I had scorned the idea of appealing to the club woman. I had no faith in her sincerity, no respect for her courage, and no reason to expect her to help in any way. (Sanger, 1931: 190)

However, if working-class women weren't ready for direct action, they still needed knowledge of birth control. She stated her dilemma:

> I could not advise them without violating the laws, and could not stay out of jail if I persisted in doing so. I was of no use to them in jail. They were powerless to get me out. What then was the solution?
>
> The answer was to make the club women . . . use their power and money and influence to obtain freedom and knowledge for the women of the poor. (Sanger, 1931: 190–91)

The "club women" were freed up for action due to the success of the suffragist movement. The social worlds of the socialists and radicals were decimated, and in what little remained of the radical movement, there was no time for, or interest in, women's issues of birth control. Sanger's peace with the "club women" was an uneasy one, and she continued to look like a radical to them.[42]

---

41. Some of the editions are undated, and Jensen found no copies of editions eight and nine in MS/LC.

42. Chesler (1992) is the one thorough, respectful, scholarly Sanger biography. For reasons that I do not grasp, Sanger has suffered insult and invective from many of her biographers. Kennedy (1970) at times comes off like a woman-hater, leaving one to wonder why he chose Sanger as a subject. Because it is otherwise so valuable and influential, the most damaging to feminist scholarship is Linda Gordon's treatment of Sanger as a bourgeoise early and late (Gordon, 1977). With the exception of A. Sanger (1969) and Chesler (1992), the biographers overlook the importance of the Sangers' early years in New York. Jensen (1981) takes Sanger's politics seriously. But Sanger was also a moral thinker.

I feel that her working-class origins and her reaction to her mothers' plight are crucial in understanding her life and work, though not in any simple, causal way. There has been a tendency to explain her actions in terms of her psychological or personal character rather than

Sanger expanded her arenas through the 1920s. Beginning in 1921, she worked with the American Birth Control League (ABCL), a group with an overwhelmingly native-born, Protestant membership that was devoted to educating the public, physicians, and various officials.[43]

By 1923, she was able to open the Birth Control Clinic Research Bureau in New York. It operated under a physician's license and offered free birth control services. The clients were overwhelmingly first- or second-generation immigrants of the working classes, the large majority of them Jewish or Catholic. Their case histories formed the basis of one of the earliest studies on procreation in America.[44]

The third arena was international. Sanger's thought had always turned in that direction, and she organized the first World Population Conference at Geneva in 1927.

Sanger's work with the "club women" of the ABCL was never comfortable—she had little patience with the regulations necessary for managing such an organization, and she considered the women running the league to be provincial and unsophisticated in strategy and theory. On their side, the "club women" found her individualistic and autocratic, and they felt her radical background and radical methods held back the organization (the latter opinion reinforced by public relations studies in 1930 and 1936). She resigned the presidency of the ABCL in June 1928, keeping the clinic under her control (Kennedy, 1970: 104–05).

During the 1930s, inroads were made judicially on the Comstock obscenity laws, for example in court cases involving James Joyce's *Ulysses* and Marie Stopes' books on contraception. In 1936, the Clinical Research Bureau itself was legally involved in the case of the United States vs. One Package of Japanese Pessaries, in which Judge Augustus Hand's decision granted the medical

---

seeing her as a woman who experienced her formative years under class and gender oppression (and ethic and religious discrimination as well), and who must have found with the syndicalists a turning point that helped her resolve the political and personal paradoxes and come to herself. This approach also explains her "leaden years" after the collapse of the movement—without poking around for some romantic disappointment.

43. There is a conflict between the PPFA booklet, "70 Years of Family Planning in America," which says the ABCL was founded in 1922, and some of the historian's reports which say 1921 (Kennedy, 1970: 94). The national Birth Control League that Mary Dennett headed had ceased to exist by the end of 1919.

44. The ABCL had a large national membership (37,000 in 1927) and was 90 percent Protestant and 75 percent native born (Gordon, 197: 296–97). The Birth Control Clinic Research Bureau in New York's clients were 80 percent working class, nearly all first- or second-generation immigrants, and 40 percent Jewish, 20 percent Protestant, and 26 percent Catholic (Kopp, 1933: 49–59). The ABCL referred clients to the bureau where they received free services. Their case histories were taken, and the material was reported in Kopp (1933). Diaphragms were not manufactured in the United States at the time, and those prescribed by the clinic were contraband—in fact, Margaret's millionaire second husband helped out by smuggling some in.

profession authority as "the sole judge of the propriety of prescription in a given case" (Kennedy, 1970: 250–51).

Shortly after the One Package decision, the American Birth Control League and the Clinical Research Bureau were merged to form the Birth Control Federation of America, under the presidency of Dr. Richard N. Pierson. In 1942, the name was changed to Planned Parenthood Federation of America—over Margaret Sanger's protest. In 1952, the International Planned Parenthood Federation was launched. Sanger herself turned to other interests—one of them the development of the birth control pill.

Margaret Sanger died on September 6, 1966, in the midst of the "radical effervescence" of the 1960s. In the year of her death, President Johnson declared family planning to be one of the four critical health problems in the United States. The following year, the United Nations declaration on population proclaimed family planning to be a basic human right and established a United Nations fund for population activities. The United States Agency for International Development was authorized to provide contraceptives in overseas development programs. In 1970, the United States Congress passed Title X of the Public Health Services Act which authorized support and funding for family planning services and educational programs domestically. Planned Parenthood and its domestic and international service and research arms played important roles in all of these processes.[45]

In 1973, the Supreme Court decisions in Roe vs. Wade and Doe vs. Bolton, struck down restrictive abortion laws in the United States. But by that time, it was clear that the battle of progressive and traditional society had taken on new life and a new meaning.

---

45. The information in this section was compiled from the autobiographies by Sanger (1931) and (1938); the biographies by A. Sanger (1969), Lader (1955), Gordon (1977), and Kennedy (1970); and the biographical sketch in Reed (1978). Both Gordon and Kennedy are so biased against Sanger that their work can be used only with great caution (see Reed's criticism of Kennedy). I used the PPFA booklet, "70 years of Family Planning in America: A Chronology of Major Events" as a selection tool in picking out "major events" in PPFA history from from the One Package Decision to the 1970s. My interpretation, of course, differs considerably from theirs.

5

Autonomy and Life Plan:
The Problem of the "Middle Class"

ONE OF THE MOST IMPORTANT moral passages in the nation's history included the change from Sanger's early ethics of birth control to the individualist, planning ethics espoused by Planned Parenthood and other activists and professionals. The outcome was a change in the moral ideals of freedom, personal autonomy, and the self.

In the beginning, Sanger had seen birth control as a knowledge made and shared by women acting together to become the women of practical wisdom who were needed to build the new world. This changed as times changed. With the success of Roosevelt's New Deal, "planning" had become a catchword for progressive society. In 1942, on the advice of a public relations firm, the Birth Control Federation of American had its name changed to Planned Parenthood Federation of America (Nathanson, 1991: 40). The name "Planned Parenthood" signaled a redefinition of birth control, in rhetoric and practice, a redefinition that divided women into atomized families rather than unifying them in action. Birth control was presented as something that could strengthen the individual family, permit responsible and healthy sex, and allow a family to plan its private future.

The planning approach could not be more different from Sanger's early syndicalist idea. It mirrored the cost-benefit reasoning appropriate to the market, something that became particularly evident in arenas of population control: the common good was to be achieved by aggregation, with each family individually deciding how many children it could afford. The common good was to be achieved by each acting in its own self-interest.[1] After

---

1. In the earlier PPFA efforts, the emphasis was explicitly on individual families rather than individual women, to the degree that they had a policy not to prescribe contraceptives for unmarried women. In earlier accounts of market and democratic politics, the emphasis on

the 1960s, there was a steadily increasing emphasis on individual satisfaction of presently perceived needs and on individual life plans. The syndicalist revolution seemed to require tremendous sacrifice in the name of creating the common good—sacrifices people and families were to make for the future and the good of all children. From the "life plan" perspective, the syndicalist effort might seem irrational in the short run because it seemingly sacrificed the individual. I would describe the syndicalist effort not as sacrifice of self but as the flowering of self in the newly created relationships and commitments. From the syndicalist perspective, the planning approach looked irrational in the long run, and a hopeless illusion in the short run for the large majority of workers.

The change to a planning perspective marked a change in the understanding of responsibility in procreation. The "planning" morality came to be described as "middle class," but I suggest in this chapter that it was an official definition of what was *normal* in the United States (and "progressive society"), not a "middle-class" moral consensus (whatever that might be). The strategy for having it pass as middle class required a "continuing process of education of people as to the meaning of new attitudes," a process that "must stem initially from persons who are trained, who are aware of various aspects of the whole problem."[2] Planned Parenthood was not alone in promoting these things of course, but as time passed it began to play an important role. The process of education toward a planning outlook increasingly took place in the public schools and universities, and in the rationalization of jobs as careers. But it found many other locations as well, as I try to show in this chapter.

The planning perspective provided an explanation of how we should live that was used for defining and resolving social problems as well as personal problems. In both cases, it was meliorative, for after all, like banking, planning a life requires stable institutions and a predictable future. In the 1990s, the promise of a predictable future has been tarnished by an economic and social situation in which even highly skilled, educated, experienced workers cannot find adequate employment, and some have lost their homes and the future they felt they had insured. For half a century, the planning perspec-

---

family was implicit, for male heads of household stood in as individuals for the families they headed. The increasing intrusion of market and state into family affairs has promoted and enabled the atomization and individualization. The outcomes are in some ways liberating, in some ways tremendously destructive.

2. The remarks were made at a 1956 conference on abortion chaired by Planned Parenthood's Mary Calderone (Calderone, 1958: 147–48). The gentleman who made the remarks was not a Planned Parenthood official but Clarence Senior, Chief of Migration Division, Department of Labor, Commonwealth of Puerto Rico, New York City, and a Ph.D. in sociology. However, the strategy is one that has been widely followed not only by Planned Parenthood but by many social movement organizations.

tive seemed to work, so much so that it now seems a betrayal when professional economists announce that people will have to take pot luck and shift from one career line to another, facing ups and downs throughout their work lives. How long the ethics of autonomy and life plan survive the new era remains to be seen.

For the better part of the twentieth century, proponents of a planning perspective presupposed that the truth of the world, and its reality, were to be found out by science. Professionals were repositories of the truth needed to resolve personal or social problems—or to put it another way, the professional explanations were given authority by calling on an objectivist definition of truth and reality. Philosophers took part in the explanatory effort, as did sociologists, physicians, therapists, biologists, and knowledge makers of all sorts.

In this chapter, I discuss some outcomes of these collective efforts. As I do so, I introduce some of the new concepts that fit with a collectivist theory. I also bring out some of the concepts of the individualist perspective, to show how philosophical theory and solution of social problems are linked. In this chapter, I am particularly concerned with outcomes having to do with the race, class, age, and gender orders.

Planning and Personal Autonomy

Until the 1960s, Planned Parenthood was one among many voluntary health service organizations, and it did not carry much organizational clout. However, social problems that came to light during the 1960s gave the group opportunities to expand its influence and strengthen the organization. One strategy was to argue that birth control was a solution to problems of poverty, overpopulation, and rising welfare costs. Birth control came to be defined as a medical technology, and dispensing the technology and educating the populace was placed in the hands of professionals and their paraprofessional aids. According to Constance Nathanson, Planned Parenthood was transformed into "the nucleus of a highly effective lobbying group with powerful political ties."[3] By the 1970s, the organization and its affiliates were playing a major role in making public the problem of teen pregnancy.

Early in that period of growth, in the late 1950s, Lee Rainwater conducted a study for Planned Parenthood. It formed the basis for his book, *And the Poor Get Children* (Rainwater, 1960).[4] A major aim of the study was to uncover attitudes of working-class people so that obstacles to family plan-

---

3. In this paragraph, I am following Nathanson (1991: 41–42). See also Reed (1978).

4. The study was conducted for the Planned Parenthood Federation of America, Inc., by Social Research, Inc. PPFA encouraged Rainwater to expand the original report into a book.

ning could be overcome. Rainwater was explicit about there being a class basis to "planned parenthood" thinking. He wrote,

> The ideas of family planning and planned parenthood embody a particular world view, a particular way of looking at the world and oneself. Planning to become a parent implies that the planner is an adult member of a society who makes a choice and who accepts the responsibility which that choice entails. This kind of planning suggests continuous thought and intention. . . .
>
> Planning means that one looks ahead, orients himself toward the future, and commits himself and others to some course of action. Middle class people are used to doing this, and the ramified consequences of looking ahead and making commitments characterize the middle class way of life in connection not only with the family but also with the worlds of work, education, voluntary association, and the like. Middle class people live in a matrix of commitments toward the future, in terms of personal goals, and to other people in terms of reasonably clear-cut obligations. Planning thus involves a picture of the way things will be in the future and of the way one will be and act then. (Rainwater, 1960: 50)

Rainwater took a planning outlook to be more mature, thus middle-class thinking to be more mature than that of the poor. In fact, following family planning professionals, he made much of maturity—for example the diaphragm (used little by working-class women) was considered a "more 'mature' contraceptive" than the condom (used more by working class and poor among whites and non-whites). Rainwater also wrote that "the poor" "tended to view thinking negatively, to regard thought and planning as painful activities to be engaged in only under the pressure of great necessity" (Rainwater, 1960: 53). He cited other experts who remarked on the fact that middle-class children had elaborate education in this kind of planning while working-class children had relatively little training in these methods of "coping with life."[5]

A decade later, John Rawls published his *A Theory of Justice*, one of the major philosophical works of the second half of the twentieth century. It's

---

5. I want to stress that Rainwater has great sympathy with the people he studied. He went to considerable effort to uncover the "attitudes" on family planning (including sex and contraception) of the working-class people in his sample. He insisted that professionals approach working-class people not in terms of their own technical training and middle-class viewpoints, but in terms of their clients' realities, understandings, anxieties, values, and goals.(Rainwater, 1960: 174). But the point of his research was to give Planned Parenthood clinics a more scientific basis for educational and clinical programs with the working classes, and for technological innovation they would accept. Chapter 9 of his book is titled "Rx for Family Planning in the Working Class." The point is to find effective ways to educate the working classes up to the planning outlook—and he concludes that more research is necessary "before we fully understand the psychosocial forces that contend against birth control programs" (Rainwater, 1960: 179).

instructive to compare Rawls' remarks about the moral theory of the good with Rainwater's straightforward discussion of planning as related to life conditions in the middle class. Rawls wrote:

> The main idea is that a person's good is determined by what is for him the most rational long-term plan of life given reasonably favorable circumstances. A man is happy when he is more or less successful in the way of carrying out this plan. To put it briefly, the good is the satisfaction of rational desire. We are to suppose, then, that each individual has a rational plan of life drawn up subject to the conditions that confront him. It schedules activities so that various desires can be fulfilled without interference. It is arrived at by rejecting other plans that are either less likely to succeed or do not provide for such an inclusive attainment of aims. Given the alternatives available, a rational plan is one which cannot be improved upon; there is no other plan which, taking everything into account, would be preferable. (Rawls, 1971: 92–93)

In this chapter, I suggest that one outcome of Rawls' philosophical work, and the work of many other philosophers, is the regeneration of the class, race, and gender organization in the United States. The definition of their professional responsibility, and the methods they used within philosophy, make it very difficult to see the outcome, and very easy to deny it. The professional organization of the discipline and the philosophical method itself make it difficult for philosophers to see their moral responsibility. More important, perhaps, many philosophers make it difficult for others to understand their own moral responsibility.

What Rainwater described as a mature, middle-class planning outlook has been analyzed as "personal autonomy" by philosophers. Personal autonomy is a sort of freedom, though a different freedom from the syndicalist because of its integration with ideas of capitalist democracy. According to feminist philosopher Diana Meyers, personally autonomous people decide to do what they really want to do, and their conduct expresses their true or authentic selves. On the other hand, heteronomous (or conventional) conduct expresses an "apparent self," one instilled by socialization (Meyers, 1987: 619). The distinction echoes H. G. Wells' contrast between progressive civilization ("Let man know and trust him,") and traditional civilization ("Let man learn his duty and obey").[6] I quote Meyers at some length here to clarify the philosophical notion of personal autonomy, so that it can be recognized in the cases I discuss below.

---

6. Like other philosophers, Meyers distinguishes personal autonomy from moral autonomy. The latter concerns giving oneself a moral law or principle (see chapter 1). Those moral principles set the boundary between what is obligatory and what is permissible. Personal autonomy (Meyers says) falls within the range of the permissible.

In doing what they really want to do within the sphere of moral permissibility, personally autonomous agents control their own lives. They are not other individuals' or their society's playthings. . . . Nor are autonomous people the victims of imperious forces within themselves. . . . There is, then, a quartet of threats to personal autonomy: social pressure, externally applied coercion, internalized cultural imperatives, and individual pathology. The first pair of threats confirm that autonomous agents must live in harmony with their selves. They cannot allow outside forces to displace their own desires and thereby to assume control over their lives. But the second pair, in raising the possibility of alien forces operating within the self, suggests that autonomous agents must live in harmony not merely with their selves but with their "true" selves. To be in control of one's life is, then, to live in harmony with one's true—one's authentic—self. Just as moral autonomy would be unintelligible without criteria of correct judgment, personal autonomy requires a touchstone. That touchstone is the unique, authentic self. (Meyers, 1989: 19–20)[7]

This idea of personal autonomy turns on individual choice and individual life plan. Emotional encounter or bonding with others in a moral transformation doesn't seem to have a place. The individual is the source of choice and plan, but autonomy may be threatened by causal factors acting on the individual from both inside and out. It is an individualist perspective based on an organism/environment dualism.[8]

"Society" enters into this picture in the negative sense of socialization and social pressure, which might include positive and negative sanctions and "extracting duty like a debt," as John Stuart Mill wrote (Mill, 1951: 45). "Society" enters positively in offering education and other cures for the internalized imperatives and pathologies. "Society" may also offer justice and social options.

In this framework, "the poor's" aversion to planning can be seen as an inner obstacle which Rainwater encouraged Planned Parenthood to over-

---

7. Meyers uses three interrelated concepts to construct her analysis of autonomy. Episodic autonomy is one in which a person considers what she wants to do in a particular situation and does it. Programmatic autonomy is a capacity necessary for making a life plan. And the third sort of autonomy is the sort involved in having access to the "authentic self." The unique, authentic self is a process, not a product (she writes). I would interpret it as a lifelong moral passage guided by authenticity as a telos (as we might say Peirce's science is a passage guided by truth as a telos). In that sense, I find "the authentic self" an interesting construct. However, the model of human nature and social life that Meyers uses is an individualist perspective, not a collectivist one, and an organism/environment dualism.

8. I call this idea of autonomy individualistic because the prime source of moral action and "the good life" lies within the individual. In episodic autonomy, moral action is explained in terms of preconditions that exist within the individual and are somehow the "springs" of the person's action and life plan. See Mills (1963) for a well-known criticism of the "springs of action" view.

come by education. Diana Meyers' remark that autonomous people are not "the victims of imperious forces within themselves" indicates she shares the model with therapists who are charged with helping people overcome the inner forces, and of course with educators. It is a "clinical model."[9] It is a medicalized view of moral deviance, and it gives professionals a good deal of authority in defining "our public morality" and the moral selves of young and old. The idea of personal autonomy, together with the associated baggage of inner and outer causes, yields a way of explaining how we should live that can be taught to groups through formal education or to individuals undergoing cure. It contributes to a rationalized, scientific, and moral picture of self and society and supports the cognitive authority of professionals (see my discussion of sex education in chapter 2).

In the quotation above, Meyers mentioned outer conditions as well as inner, and it is part of her *feminist* approach that outer conditions must be modified to allow women to develop their personal autonomy. Rainwater also referred to outer conditions. He not only claimed that middle-class people use a certain kind of planning reasoning, he wrote that "the worlds of work, education, voluntary association, and the like" required a planning outlook (Rainwater, 1960: 50). He didn't, of course, recommend that Planned Parenthood change the living conditions of the poor to match those of the middle class but only that it educate the poor so that (presumably) they could individually move up to the middle-class worlds of work, education, etc. Planned Parenthood was (and is) an organization with a narrowly defined mission, and its survival would be threatened if it extended that mission to changing the economic conditions of the poor. This seems to be one of the ways that checks and balances work in interest-group politics in the United States. Planned Parenthood officials could, however, make policy recommendations. Because they had a claim to ownership of problems of procreation, their recommendations carried weight.

When Sanger and the syndicalists talked about changing outer conditions, they meant changing the social and economic orders as well as the moral order. In the individualist perspective, changing the outer conditions often means nothing more than offering "options" to individuals within the existing order. When she was president of Planned Parenthood Federation of America (1978 to 1991), Faye Wattleton explained the problem of teen

9. The therapeutic version of this ethical outlook is "the clinical perspective" used in psychology, social work, and education. Jane Mercer described it as an individualist framework that values rational life plans and is etiological—the hidden, irrational cause of the behavior is to be uncovered by the professionals, so that they can eliminate it (Mercer, 1973: 1). The approach leads to looking for causes within individuals and offering cures from professionals.

pregnancy in that it required both educating teens and providing options. She wrote,

> Teen pregnancy is both cause and consequence of a host of social ills. The teenagers likeliest to become pregnant are those who can least afford an unwanted child: those who are poor, those who live with one parent, those who have poor grades in school, and those whose parents did not finish high school. As the National Research Council points out, teen mothers face "reduced employment opportunities, unstable marriages (if they occur at all), low incomes, and heightened health and developmental risks to the children ... sustained poverty, frustration, and hopelessness are all too often the long term outcomes." Compounding the tragedy is the fact that children of teenage mothers are more likely to become teen parents themselves. The burden is felt by the entire society: The national costs of health and social service programs for families started by teenagers amount to more than nineteen billion dollars a year. (Wattleton, 1990: 111)

As a remedy, Wattleton wrote that parents must talk with their children about all aspects of sexuality, and that every school district should provide comprehensive sex education beginning with kindergarten, and that there must be school-linked health clinics and available contraceptive information. She also made the policy recommendation that "society must provide all our young people with a decent general education, tangible job opportunities, successful role models, and real hope for the future" (Wattleton, 1990: 111). Education and job opportunities, and clinics and contraceptives would be classed as options, i.e. features of the environment.

I want to stress that I'm not denouncing Wattleton's policy proposals and I'm not making policy proposals of my own here. My concern is with finding ways to see outcomes of her kind of individualist planning approach, and of the theoretical model that grounds her thinking as well as that of many professionals in the United States.

The ground of Wattleton's argument is the individualistic planning ethics— teens require education to be able to make a rational life plan and options to be able to live it out. The association of the planning ethic with the "middle class" is hidden, not given upfront as it is in the Rainwater quote. Wattleton simply presupposes the ethic is "ours," that is, she presupposes a "we."

In his report to Planned Parenthood, Rainwater distinguished a "we" from a "they" in an interesting way. Rainwater named the "we" as "middle-class Americans," whom he said used a planning kind of rationality. There is a serious question of who this middle-class "we" is, but it is clear that the "they" were working-class and poor Americans—the poor who get children.

It is a short step to taking the "we" to be normal Americans, and the "they" to be deviant.[10] In the book, Rainwater's professional audience is identified with the "we." The identification *hides the position of professionals*. It hides their importance in generating and regenerating the social, political, and economic systems, even as speaking of "middle class" and "poor" hides the class structure of capitalism.[11]

The strategy Planned Parenthood wanted and that Rainwater offered was one for educating the "they" up to the individualistic planning ethics of the "we." The same thinking underlay Wattleton's proposal thirty years later, supplemented by policy proposals that "society" should provide options and opportunities. In her philosophical analysis, Meyers follows the Wattleton-Rainwater strategy.

The strategy incorporates the individualist planning ethics. That ethics, and the individualist epistemologies and ontologies that attend it, use accounts of human nature and group life that rely on dualisms between individual and environment, and between mind and body. There are also "causal" presuppositions—blatant in Meyers' talk of external pressures and inner, alien forces, but also present in Rawls' talk of mentally selecting principles that are to order a society or a life. The dualisms and the causal presuppositions are high-level empirical hypotheses that have been much criticized, and intellectual responsibility requires taking the criticisms seriously, not blandly using them. Moral responsibility requires considering the outcomes of implementing the moral theories. For example, philosophers who use armchair methods of analyzing "our moral thinking" contribute to the outcome that the abstract morality attributed to "the middle class" is legitimated as "ours." Philosophers (and sociologists and psychologists) may end up keeping their methods and their theoretical commitments, but they should not use their theories and positions to hide what they are doing.

In this chapter, I move from discussing some of the ways in which moral

---

10. I don't believe that Rainwater took this step himself, and his later book (1970) indicates otherwise. However, Planned Parenthood policymakers did take the step, and it is clear in Wattleton's analysis.

11. In her early work, Sanger wrote about capitalists, workers, and the immigrants, not middle class and poor. In her pre-war social worlds, "class" marked divisions between worker and capitalist; it was the evils of the ruling class that were to be exposed in the syndicalist strikes. In syndicalist terms, "class" marked systemic categories that were directly related to the economic system. They marked divisions through which the nation was ruled and through which life in America could be transformed to classlessness and statelessness. In contrast, "middle class" and "poor" are categories sometimes based on cultural differences and differences in formal education, but usually explained on the basis of family income. They suit images of democracy, individual equal opportunity, upward mobility, and the melting pot. There may have been some hope of integrating the poor into the middle class in a capitalist democracy, but it is a contradiction in terms to speak of eliminating the working class or the capitalist class, because to eliminate either is to eliminate capitalism.

problems have been made public to discussing some ways in which "our" morality has been implemented in "personal life." My concern is with showing how the moral theory, epistemology, and ontology may operate to define reality for the purposes of action. In the two chapters that follow, I write on a more explicitly theoretical level about the collectivist approach I have been using. But in this chapter, my concern is with some of the ways that "our morality" is enacted as ours—not only "our moral concepts" but the whole enacted world of individualism, individual families, and life plans, the "normal" world of the postulated "middle class." I'm concerned here with the question of how culture, or standards and norms, or "our moral scheme" and "our common good" are collectively enacted, in the personal lives and the selves of people.

I use the moral problem of adolescent pregnancy (or "unwed motherhood" as it was once called) as an example.

The Problem of Teen Pregnancy

In the United States, adolescent pregnancy erupted as a public problem in the late 1970s. Planned Parenthood, and its research arm, the Alan Guttmacher Institute, played significant parts in making the moral problem public.[12] Even at its birth, the problem was a factor in the face off between liberals and conservatives, a confrontation that had been growing through the 1960s, not only on issues of the cold war, the Vietnam war, civil rights, youth rebellion, and government intrusion into the market, but over social welfare policies. The solution offered by one side was individual choice grounded in sex education in the schools and aided by contraception and funded abortion. The solution on the other side was choice grounded in moral education in family and church, and abstinence until marriage. The sex education texts I discussed in chapter 2 show these differences.

"The problem" of adolescent pregnancy had different historical roots for the poor (whether white women or women of color) and the "middle class" (particularly the white women). Before it became a public problem, adolescent pregnancy among the white poor was resolved by various means, often through "shotgun marriages" (a method also used in the "middle class.") Other poor, white women might be labeled as incorrigibles, or as corrupt or coming from dissolute families, as well as suffering from the problems Rainwater attributes to the poor in general. Poor and pregnant black teens

---

12. Nathanson (1991) contains far and away the best discussion of the public problem of adolescent pregnancy available, thoroughly researched and theoretically intelligent. I got hold of the book only at the last revision of this chapter. My own work would have been much easier if I had it earlier. Solinger (1992) was also an aid in the last revision, and I thank Philip Green for recommending it to me.

received worse treatment. Even in some "enlightened quarters," they were often classed with adults as suffering from "the black pattern of mating and breeding without responsibility," an accusation made in less bestial terms of the white poor in Rainwaters' remarks above.[13]

By the mid 1960s, "the enlightened" were blaming external, environmental causes for problems among blacks. There was talk of "the culture of poverty" and the deterioration of the male-headed, black family. While this explanation was welcomed in some quarters, it was heavily attacked in others. By the 1960s, the population bomb had exploded in the media, and so the black women could be labeled as a problem not only for burdening the taxpayer but for endangering the Earth by breeding multitudes of babies. Poor white and hispanic women on welfare were also labeled for burdening the taxpayer.[14]

The historical roots of the adolescent pregnancy problem for "nice girls from good families" were quite different. The more immediate context was the "youth rebellion" and the "sexual revolution" of the late 1960s and early 1970s. But a half century of change lay behind that revolution. Social, political, and economic changes in the industrializing nation were all involved, including the increasing importance of the public high schools—and the privacy afforded by movie theaters and automobiles.[15] In the late 1960s, changes in the sexual behavior of "nice white girls from good families" flared up into the public eye. The consequences for the social and moral order were tremendous, and they are still being worked out in the United States today.

In discussing adolescent pregnancy in this chapter, I use cases from that historical cusp of the late 1960s, that cusp between what seemed to be an older, more traditional order and the individualistic, anarchic, seemingly "immoral" new order. From another viewpoint, it was an unfolding of "progressive civilization" and an important moment in implementing the "middle-class" morality of moral and personal autonomy.

In the late 1960s, sociologist Prudence Rains did several field studies, which she discussed in her book, *Becoming an Unwed Mother* (1971). They

---

13. The quotation is from liberal Theodore H. White, in *The Making of the President, 1964,* cited in Solinger(1992: 55).

14. (Solinger, 1992: 83–85); Nathanson (1991) offers many relevant statistics.

15. "Dating," and "going steady" were invented in the 1920s, when high schoolers were almost exclusively "middle class." Dating and going steady replaced the earlier "keeping company" or "courting." The latter were relationships overseen within the public life of the community because they were preludes to marriage and taking one's place in the life (and the survival) of the group. They set the scene for procreative responsibility. In contrast, dating was much more a matter of free, personal choice, much more anchored in pleasure, and not generally considered a prelude to marriage. It was overseen by peers, not by parents and elders (despite chaperones at dances). Kissing was no longer a commitment among respectable girls, and as time passed, even intercourse was no longer a commitment (Modell, 1983).

included a study of mainly white and middle-class young women at "Hawthorne House," a home for unwed mothers, and a study of black, mainly poor young women at "The Project," an experimental day school for pregnant teens. The basic premise in this home for unwed mothers (and for public understanding of white, unwed mothers in general) was that there was a normal life plan for "good girls." The plan ran something like this.

Good Girl Life Plan

Education   Dating   Work   Courtship   Marriage   Sex   Family   Grandchildren

Figure 1.

Figure 1 shows a traditional life plan. It gives the appearance of a rational series of choices that have, as a consequence, the happiness of the person doing the choosing and the common good as well. The life plan offers a traditional explanation of how we should live as well as how we do live, and in this way it constitutes a cultural or social norm. Maintaining the appearance requires a collective effort of hiding and making public. Some deviations could be hidden, and the life plan put back on track—illicit pregnancy could be hidden by early marriage and the cover story of a "seven-month baby," for example. More significantly, deviations that could not be hidden might be labeled as being caused by immoral character or as the result of personal or social pathology (bad girls, bad homes, bad cultures).

By the late 1960s, the more progressive professionals considered sex to be necessary for health, as Havelock Ellis had argued decades earlier. They did not feel chastity was strictly required, particularly among the college-educated "middle class," who could be expected to practice "responsible sex," that is, to be discrete and use contraceptives. The progressive professionals thought in terms of a larger variety of "non-deviant" life plans—besides allowing sex before marriage, they included the options of being a "career girl" who might choose not to have children, or to marry late, or even not to marry at all. Progressive-thinking people expanded the range of life plans, and so the "good girl" chart had several branches. But they share the essential philosophical framework. In the traditional, linear plan, a woman faces the moral choice of good or evil, virtue or vice, and the issue may be seen as one of free will. In the progressive, professional approach, sin was dismissed as unscientific, and free will was parsed as individual autonomy, aided by over-coming (or curing) adverse inner and outer causes. This is Diana Meyers' model. It is also a clinical model. The progressive move involves the medical-ization, rather than the moralization, of deviance, and authority is passed from moral leaders of the community to professionals.

Despite political antagonisms between traditionals and progressives, the underlying models of moral choice are ontologically very similar: an inner cause of action (either virtuous or autonomous, or else vicious or pathologi cal) operates in the context of a life plan (either traditional or rational). In the 1960s, most researchers on unwed mothers shared the model. In *Becoming an Unwed Mother*, Rains complained that most of what was written about unwed mothers was concerned with causes of the illicit pregnancy; i.e., with features that marked unwed mothers as different from other girls, because of personal or social pathology.[16] Faye Wattleton's remarks (quoted above) indi-cate the approach is alive and well in the 1990s.

The individualist model of moral choice is acted upon as if it captured the truth and reality of human nature and social and natural environments. Tak-ing a collectivist approach requires asking how the individualist model is enacted so that it seems to be the truth, so that it seems to work. To show that process, a different set of concepts are needed. Rather than use notions of autonomy or inner and outer forces or "social options," I'll begin by using the interactionist notion of a career, as Prudence Rains used it in her book, *Becoming an Unwed Mother*.

Using the notions of autonomy, or of inner and outer causes, or of "social options," requires one to separate organism and environment. Once this sep-aration occurs, the focus is on the *products* of social interaction. The prod-ucts are themselves a result of processes of social definition, as I indicated in previous chapters. The notion of a career allows us to focus on those processes. "Career" is a sociological term, and so careers in this sense are defined under a sociological paradigm—one that was devised to criticize paradigms based on an individualist perspective.

The concept of a career has been said to link the self and felt identity with the social and institutional (Goffman,1961: 127).[17] In Rains' studies, the

---

16. Rains cites Vincent (1961) as giving a review of the "causal" literature. Discovering these features would presumably show unwed mothers to be suffering from similar pathologies, and that they were susceptible to similar cures. "Nice white girls" were generally taken to suffer from an inner pathology or neurosis—it being a premise that their nice, white communities were normal, not pathological. I mentioned the "tangle of pathology" attributed to the black communities in the text above. However, psychiatric social workers at both Hawthorne House and The Project tried to look to inner cause, with more success among the young white women (see below).

17. This notion of a career is different from my notion of a passage in ways I'll mention below.

career of an unwed mother called into question the kind of person the young woman was, and it involved a turning point in her learning about the world and making a new self. Both processes were shaped by professionals in social agencies. "Career" in this sense is a pattern, a sort of trajectory, a course of events made through interaction of many people (Glaser and Strauss, 1971). It is the product of a collective action.

Using the concept of a career, Rains analyzed unwed motherhood as one of many routes a young woman might follow. She wrote,

> Becoming an unwed mother is the outcome of a particular sequence of events that begins with forays into intimacy and sexuality, results in pregnancy, and terminates in the birth of an illegitimate child. Many girls do not have sexual relations before marriage. Many who do, do not get pregnant. And most girls who get pregnant while unmarried do not end up as unwed mothers. Girls who become unwed mothers, in this sense, share a common career that consists of the steps by which they came to be unwed mothers rather than brides, the clients of abortionists, contraceptively prepared lovers, or virtuous young ladies. (Rains, 1971: 1)

A career covers both a person's movement through an activity (in biographical terms) and the general pattern followed by anyone going through "that sort of thing." The pattern is displayed in the movements from one step to another, so that a career can be described as a pattern of steps (Becker, 1973: 24).

Rains' remarks above yield a different chart. The "good girl" chart (figure 1) seems to represent a rational "life plan ethics" accepted and followed by the "middle class" in the 1960s. The second chart (figure 2, p. 118) sheds light on some ways in which the appearance of middle-class morality was produced, and ways in which the appearance of the deviant, pathological path of "illegitimacy" was produced as well. The terms in boxes indicate "options" (contraception, marriage, abortion, adoption) that may be offered to the young woman to allow her to return to the line of the good girl plan. Contraception, abortion, and adoption were publicly offered options that were private or secret, so that the young woman's "misstep" was hidden and she was publicly represented as a good girl. Marriage is a public step par excellence, but what is hidden by this public step is the *illicit* nature of the conception. Magically, the unwed mother is saved from deviance. Magically, the "good girl" plan is enacted as an answer to how we should live. Magically, the deviant course that leads to going public about the illicit pregnancy and, particularly, to keeping the illegitimate child is defined as a "non-plan."

The dynamic of moral rescue or condemnation in the good girl plan of course seriously affected the girls in question. However, the coverup was also crucial in maintaining the status of the good girls' families by offering a way

Career Of An Unwed Mother

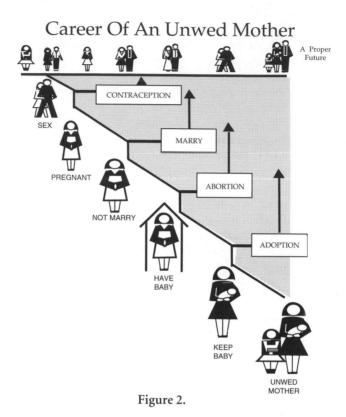

Figure 2.

to avoid the serious risk of their kin becoming déclassé. The dynamic also implemented the appearance of the middle-class planning morality itself. Until the 1970s, keeping a child born out of wedlock was a mark of the lower classes—both white and nonwhite. The complex activities of producing the appearance of "middle-class morality" were in fact ways of generating the age, class, race, and gender orders of the time.

Figure 2 gives a different paradigm of moral action from the usual philosophic or psychological ones. In terms of the careers, what distinguishes unwed mothers from good girls is not the inner or outer causes of the "choices" but simply the shared steps. The steps they follow lead from sex to unwed motherhood, while other young women branched off at one point or another to marry, get an abortion, etc. The "good girl" chart is seen, through figure 2, as constructed from a number of careers—the careers of those who had sex but used contraception and didn't get pregnant; those who got pregnant but married; those who had abortions; those who put the babies up for adoption. It's important to note, however, that figure 2 suits the careers of the white, middle-class women at "Hawthorne House," the maternity home where Rains did fieldwork. Virtually all of those young women took the elevator back to the "good girl" plan by giving the baby up for adoption. The chart for the careers of the poor, black young women of Rains' study at "The Project" would be quite different. (See my discussion below.)

Something like the branching chart of figure 2 also accommodates the approach of people who reject the clinical model of inner pathology and locate the problems in the social environment. They try to cure the environmental pathology by insuring equal opportunity and offering social options (social options are represented by the boxes in the chart, the elevators raising the young woman back up to a proper life plan). Wattleton recommended this in the quotation above—education, jobs, available contraception, legal abortion were some of the options she mentioned. Those options increase navigational points of choice by increasing the number of "elevators" that depart from the deviant, "descending" left-hand fork for the "normal, good girl route." The options may be lifesavers for some individuals—I don't mean to argue that they are not. I also do not mean to say that people are automata who do not make choices. Rather, I want to show the dynamic of hiding and making public that is crucial to the illusion of autonomous choice and the "middle-class" planning outlook.

Hawthorne House

From Civil War times, there were maternity homes to seclude and support unfortunate white girls. Before World War II, the homes tended to be founded and staffed by good, religious-spirited people—the Florence Crittenden Homes are an outstanding example. After the war, they tended to be staffed by professional social workers. Rains did a field study at one such home in the late 1960s—she called it "Hawthorne House" (Rains, 1971).[18] Rains described the effort as a kind of moral rescue. At Hawthorne House, professional social workers took the view that there was a psychological cause to the pregnancy. After taking part in group therapy, most of the girls redefined their moral passages accordingly: they had deviated, they accepted the social workers' explanation of their deviance, and they repented.

From the vantage point of the 1990s, Hawthorne House showed in microcosm the conflicts of the transition from the traditional to the progressive—a traditional nursing home managed by professional social workers. As a traditional institution, it operated on the principle of making the respectable

---

18. I used the Rains studies in Addelson (1991: chapter 5), but I didn't make clear certain differences between my work and the work of the Symbolic Interactionist sociologists. The difference is particularly evident in my use of "moral passage" and Rains' (and other sociologists') use of "moral career" (Rains, 1971: 1; Becker, 1973: 24; Goffman,1961: 127). I discuss moral passages at greater length in the next chapter.

public and hiding the unrespectable. I described this approach with the Maine Ministers in chapter 1 and in various of the social movements of chapter 2, particularly the physicians' crusade and the purity movement. Becoming pregnant was a blatant way of going public about customarily hidden things, and there were many ways of handling it. Historically in the United States, one of the most important ways of hiding it was to marry the girl off.[19] Another traditional way was to label her deviant—a version of the method used by the Hamilton Mill operatives (see chapter 3). And there was also the strategy of sending the girl off to visit a far-distant relative. The maternity homes institutionalized that strategy, and the girls' parents cooperated by footing the bills and tacitly agreeing to give their grandchildren up for adoption. As a traditional institution, Hawthorne House operated to salvage the young women's reputations. Reputation is a major coin in maintaining respectability, and when reputation is damaged, respectability is risked—for the person, the family, the social world. A girl returned to her respectable home with her respectable reputation more or less intact, and her planned-for future still a possibility. Hiding the pregnancy preserved the family's relationships. It was a way of creating the orderly, predictable world necessary for a middle-class life plan.

The time-honored explanation of the girls' behavior was that they were "nice girls who made a mistake and repented." This explanation underpinned the traditional salvage effort and justified keeping up the appearance of a steady voyage along the "nice girl" course. The conflict entered because the social workers were trained to bring people to face emotional and psychological realities and the truth about their underlying motives. The social workers rejected the "nice girl" explanation. They held that becoming an unwed mother was caused by a prior, unhealthy psychological state that showed in irrational, patterned behavior. They took their professional job to be helping the young women break the patterns and stop "acting out" in ways that would put them at risk of getting pregnant again.

Rains wrote that the social workers were concerned that the young women accept responsibility for their behavior and acknowledge the seriousness of

---

19. In middle-class and working-class social worlds, one of the most important ways was marriage—Maris Vinovskis reports that from 1960 to 1965, 65 percent of births conceived out of wedlock were legitimated by marriage (compared to 35 percent by the early 1970s). Even in the early 1970s, about 90 percent of children born out of wedlock were put up for adoption (compared to 90 percent kept by the mothers today) (Harper, 1983: 221–22; Vinovskis, 1981). These overall figures conceal significant differences among different races and classes. Abortion was generally illegal and in some social worlds, even "backstreet" abortionists and pharmacists were difficult to find. When it was forced on their attention, pregnancy was treated as a private crisis by the schools—whose method of dealing with it was often to require the pregnant girl to drop out (permanently, if she kept the child). According to Harper, it was not until 1972 that federal law prohibited public schools from expelling these girls.

the consequences. They argued that if the girls accepted the traditional "mistake" explanation, they would be in *denial.* The point was not repentence but cure. The girls acted irresponsibly to begin with (said the social workers) and cure would allow them to take responsibility for themselves in the future. This does not mean the social workers were opposed to premarital sex. In their eyes, taking responsibility meant being able to choose rationally in the future (Rains, 1971: 63). Translating this to philosophical terms, the girls were to develop autonomy. But it should be clear that autonomy was judged in terms of following a life plan considered rational and normal *by the social workers.* That plan bore suspicious resemblance to the "nice girl" plan above. From Rains' report, nearly all the Hawthorne House girls accepted the benign, helpful posture of the social workers, and they accepted the intrusion of these authorities into areas that are customarily hidden and private.[20]

What happened in the moral passages at Hawthorne House was the redefinition of the past according to the clinical model. Through group therapy and other means, the girls came to accept the social workers' explanation of why they had become pregnant. The girls' circumstances were in each case unique, but most were led to dreams of autonomy. Nearly all of them came to accept the individualist model of learning to handle the irrational "springs of action" so that the future might be rationally planned. That is, both future and past were redefined in a way that supported the "middle-class'" planning perspective that Rainwater identified as "ours." Morality here is not a matter of beliefs or values or principles but a way of defining reality, time, and place, and human knowledge, action, and life. The social workers were instruments of the definition.

The social workers themselves believed in the individualist model.[21] The inadequacy of the model shows here in the fact that though the social workers deplored the secrecy and protection of the traditional homes, Hawthorne House required that secrecy for the "rational life plan" to make sense. The coverup was necessary to allow the girls to return to their communities for a second chance, whatever the social workers' ideas of the real causes of the

---

20. This does not mean that they all accepted the psychotherapeutic explanation. See Rains (1971: 92) and Addelson (1991: 96–98).

21. One remarkable way the social workers' perspective showed was in the way they guided the young women in dealing with the baby. For a large part of accepting and not denying pregnancy, from the staff's point of view, had to do with accepting the baby. Rains says the staff perspective at Hawthorne House was that motherhood was one of life's most momentous experiences and that there are certain natural ways that mothers feel. I would say this "natural" makes the clinical judgment scientific, not a value judgment. Nearly all of the young women gave their babies up for adoption, but even so, the social workers advised them to feed and hold the babies. The staff explained to the young women that motherly concern was shown in the desire to give the baby a better future; i.e., that in many cases giving the baby up was the route of motherly concern. But see the letter from an "unwed mother" that I quote below.

illicit pregnancies. The rational life plan required the traditional means of hiding and making public. Ten years later, by the mid-1970s, "nice girls" could remain in their middle-class communities and keep their babies—but the social changes that brought that outcome undermined the belief in a uniform, inner psychic cause for illicit pregnancy.

Here is a philosophical way of looking at the social workers' dilemma. The individualist perspective (and the clinical model) separated autonomy from reputation and respectability—or perhaps it assumed that reputation and respectability depended on autonomy. The psychiatric social workers were trained to look for inner causes, after all, not to do social analysis. The autonomy they sought as an individual solution to adolescent pregnancy was very like that which Diana Meyers analyzed. But the reputation and respectability necessary for carrying out a rational life plan involve collective action and resources, not merely individual self-respect and the good opinion of other individuals. The traditional maternity home was an essential factor in that collective action.[22] What the maternity homes offered was a wealth of secrecy that allowed individuals, families, and "the class itself" to maintain reputation by judicious concealments and institutionalized denial. The important political and moral dynamics are hidden if reputation and respectability are ignored.

Reputation, respectability, normality, and a plan for the good life are involved in regenerating the dominance orders of the group. I'll argue this by turning to single pregnancy among black women.

The Project

Throughout the twentieth century in the United States, professional explanations of single pregnancy among black women have been different from explanations of single pregnancy among whites. There were vicious, old stories (still alive after World War II, and even today in some locales) about the uncontrollable sexuality and promiscuous childbearing of blacks, with hints that these things were genetically determined—or due to the "lower," more primitive state of blacks which left them closer to "the evolutionary impulse to copulate and breed."[23]

---

22. The maternity home cannot be considered an "option" analogous to those in figure 2. Those "options" (and the ones in Wattleton's policy recommendations) are offered to correct the environment of individuals who are disadvantaged. Perhaps in the thinking of the time, the middle-class unwed mothers Rains studied were not to be considered disadvantaged—that would hardly make sense, given that they came from "good homes." And so the conclusion was that there must be something awry with them individually.

23. See Solinger (1992: 17, 77). The language here is not simply insulting and racist, it carries underneath it the message of evolutionary inferiority. It is in stark contrast to the language of "planning to become a parent," "making a choice," "becoming a responsible adult," characteristics attributed to the white, middle class.

In the case of the white unwed mothers "of good family," the individual woman was labeled as deviant. In the case of the black unwed mothers, blacks themselves, as a "culture" or "race," were labeled as deviant.[24] By labeling here, I do not mean that some professionals, politicians, and bigots just used bad words and had racist attitudes. They did. But labeling is not simply a matter of words. It is a matter of actions, authority, and dominance. And it is only the other side of the bigot's coin to label the environment of the "disadvantaged" as deviant, when the environment of the higher classes is taken as what is normal. Let me argue this by constrasting Rains' study of Hawthorne House with her study of black unwed mothers at the day school she called "The Project."

"The Project" was funded as a pilot school for pregnant teens in a black ghetto of a large Midwestern city. It handled a maximum of about thirty-five teenagers at a time. It was jointly sponsored by the city's boards of mental health and education. The services offered under The Project included a day school for the girls, prenatal care (at public clinics), and counseling. Initially the school was limited to black girls in elementary school. The girls were from low-income backgrounds and many had records of truancy. When Rains did the major part of her study, most of them were about fourteen—many of them old for their grade because they had been "held back."

The Project was designed and run by professionals.[25] The Project social worker was inclined by her training to view illegitimate pregnancy as the result of certain psychological needs and certain patterned ways of handling problems. Like her Hawthorne House colleagues, the social worker tried to help the pregnant girls to understand their motivations, psychological needs, and characteristic patterns of behavior lest their situation recur in the future. However, all members of The Project staff also had to be concerned with the more general problems of being poor and black—problems located outside the particular psychological arrangements of any one family. From this perspective, they tried to help the girls acquire the knowledge and skills necessary to take control of their lives (Rains, 1971: 126).

The passages The Project girls passed through were public in two ways that those of the Hawthorne House girls were not. They were public in the sense that The Project girls continued to live at home, so their pregnancies were

---

24. Solinger reports that in the 1950s, when desegregation of the schools was a major issue, illegitimacy rates among blacks were used to argue that black promiscuity and low moral standards would infect white children if the schools were integrated. There were also ugly discussions about black women having children for financial reasons, to bring income from Aid to Dependent Children (Solinger, 1992: chapter 2).

25. The Project staff included two teachers (one black, one white), a white psychiatric nurse, and a black social worker. The nurse held weekly health information sessions, and the social worker held weekly therapeutic group sessions. Both sessions were held at the school.

widely known and they had to handle questions of respectability and respon-sibility, on the street, and in the kitchen. They were also public in the sense that the girls' doings were known to public officials and recorded in public records. This meant that The Project girls had two damaged reputations to deal with. One was to be rewoven in the everyday life of her home commu-nity. The other was at the mercy of the officials who defined her behavior as deviant—"that type of girl" who was incorrigible.[26]

The social worker at The Project used group therapy, and she had stan-dard, professional views on how group discussions should be handled, what sorts of problems should be discussed, and what the discussion should accomplish—views much like those of the social workers at Hawthorne House. She tried to encourage the girls to express themselves. She tried to develop abstract skills which would allow the girls to take responsibility for the course of their lives—a goal Rainwater endorsed in the Planned Parent-hood strategy for the poor. Her style in running the meetings was one of "moral neutrality," and encouraging the girls to speak of their feelings. Rains says that the style "was simultaneously unbelievable, unbelieved, misunder-stood, and unacceptable to the Project girls" (Rains, 1971: 132). Their objec-tions rested on the fact that she was an adult and, most important, she was in a position of official authority.[27]

The Project girls had every reason to distrust officials and authorities. Because they were underage, statutory rape was an issue, and some of the girls had been to court. They had been grilled about their sexual histories and, as one girl said, officials screamed at them as if they were "some slut dog" (Rains, 1971: 134). Truant officers were intrusive and verbally abusive. The events, translated into the officials' language, went into the girls' records—not only court records but school records, birth records, and wel-fare records. The records made up a public reputation that could seriously affect the girl's "life plans" by giving officials justification to take her baby away from her, send her to reform school, or warn off employers.

Even social workers kept records. The therapeutic privacy that the Hawthorne House girls believed in was much less plausible in a public

---

26. See Gusfield's (1967) classifications of deviants who repent and enemy deviants.

27. According to Rains, there was a mutual understanding between adults and the young peo-ple of The Project girls' home community that certain questions were not to be asked and cer-tain information was not to be volunteered. This was a means of publicly maintaining certain standards of conduct, a way of hiding what in fact goes on and thereby relieving adults of the hopeless responsibility of punishing and correcting the behavior, or else being forced to disre-gard the standards they claimed to uphold. It also allowed the young to respect their elders' avowed principles. This is an important moral principle in action, and it operates in the "mid-dle-class" communities as well. Maintaining norms requires a considerable effort to "look the other way." In this, as in some other matters, The Project girls had a greater depth of under-standing than the Hawthorne House girls, even though they were, on the whole, several years younger. See below, on their insights on sex.

agency which, for all of its humanitarian concerns, was part of a public effort to deal with the publicly defined problems of being poor and black, young and pregnant. In the mid-1960s, neither being middle class and white nor being an illicitly pregnant "nice" girl constituted public problems.

In The Project girls' circumstances, there was no chance of redefining the past through the clinical perspective, with its talk about acting out and denial. The explanation that they were "nice girls who made a mistake" did offer them some protection from shame and blame at school and in the neighborhood. However it did not offer the same protection that it offered the Hawthorne House girls.

In the mid-1960s, in middle-class high school and college dating circles, a reputation as a "nice girl" offered some protection against predatory boys (whether nice or not nice). A nice girl was a respectable girl, and the traditional coverup was effective in protecting the Hawthorne House girls' reputations, and so protecting them (to some degree) from predation.[28] Because of gender differences in procreative responsibility, "respectability" for the girls had particularly to do with sex. But it also carried the more general promise that the girl could be counted on to do what was expected in the "middle-class" life plan appropriate for her age. That plan included her behavior at school (see below). Getting pregnant out of schedule violated this promise.

Social circumstances were different for the poor, black girls and gender relations were rougher. Often the "boys" were not peers but men several years older. One of the girls said, "But even if I say No, especially where I come from, I might as well have said Yes" (Rains, 1971: 160). Their sexual self-understanding was also more straightforward than the Hawthorne House girls'. One of them confessed, "I know me too well. . . . When he's talking, he make you *want* to do it. And even if he don't, you want it because you've had it before" (Rains, 1971: 159). In contrast, all but one of the Hawthorne House girls disavowed sex, and many came to believe they had been "acting out" in getting pregnant.

Unlike the Hawthorne House girls, The Project girls couldn't count on a rosy future of prosperous husband, home, and family. An illegitimate pregnancy jeopardized more than moral respectability. It lessened the chances for continuing in school and possibly attaining a better way of life. Marriage was seen by many Project girls and their parents as more an obstacle than a solution to this other sort of respectability. Going to The Project school did not simply offer an illusion of respectability. It was in fact a way to continue the passage to respectable adult life by continuing in school.

28. In the 1990s a good reputation may be less protection. However, multitudes of newspaper stories seem to indicate that predatory young men in high school are defended among their peers, male and female, by claims that the girl was asking for it, or that she was a whore anyway.

The biggest difference between the Hawthorne House girls' communities and those of The Project girls concerned the baby. Nearly all the Hawthorne House girl gave their babies up for adoption. Nearly all of the black girls kept their babies. The Project social worker regarded it as her professional responsibility to point out the possibility of adoption or foster home placement, but often the girls and their mothers experienced the suggestion as a moral affront. It amounted to nothing less than giving up their own flesh and blood.

For most of the Hawthorne House girls, "moving on" out of the unwed mother passage was publicly moving back to the original position of "respectable girl." All the complex machinery of secrecy was designed to return the girl to her respectable starting place, in the rational life plan of the nice, middle-class girl. For the young black women of The Project, moving on involved passing from "pregnant girl" to "girl with a baby." This is a significant difference, and it returns my discussion to the question of the "we" and the nature of "middle-class" morality.

The Baby

Hawthorne House (and other maternity homes) didn't simply rescue the pregnant girls' respectability. The home offered institutionalized ways of rescuing the respectability of the girls' families. It protected the respectable persona of the "middle class." What would the lower classes do if they discovered that their betters shared all the disorder of their own lives? How could they believe in the standards their betters represented and the predictable, planned future that they claimed was possible? What would happen to the idea of a middle-class morality? What would happen to the orderly, governable community whose members believed planning for the future and individual responsibility was the way we should live—believed it and acted accordingly, investing their time and lives and the lives of their children?

The middle-class way was taken to be the normal way—"our" way. The flip side of the normality was that other ways, particularly ways of the poor or of certain races, classes, or ethnicities came to be seen as deviant. I'll illustrate this through differences in the way babies were involved in The Project and Hawthorne House.

Rains wrote that The Project girls gained strength from their own love and pride in the baby ("I love my baby enough that I don't care what they say" [Rains, 1971: 169]). But also, they gained from other people's love of babies—neighborhood interest focused on baby rather than girl ("They just like babies" [Rains, 1971: 169]). Rains described the situation:

> the Project girls shared a way of life in which motherly responsibilities were usually diffused among a number of persons. The Project girls themselves had

been involved in caring for their younger brothers and sisters and were themselves cared for by a variety of aunts, stepfathers and stepmothers, mothers—persons who for reasons of blood relationship or sense of kinship took interest in them. The Project girls' babies thus did not so much enter the world to an exclusive relation to a single mother, as to a web of persons with a variety of interests and concerns in their welfare. (Rains, 1971: 171)

The relationships through which the selves and the social world itself were realized were different from those of the Hawthorne House girls. At the time Rains did her studies, one well-publicized study described "a tangle of pathology." They were compared with the relationships in the male-headed household consisting of husband, wife, and children, the ideal of the normal "middle-class," nuclear family.[29]

In contrast, in the social worlds of the white, Hawthorne House women, the procreative responsibility of the grandparents and other kin was hidden. Those middle-class grandparents, those grandmothers and grandfathers, gave up their grandchildren for adoption. That painful fact was glossed over by the individualist, "planning" ethics and by the definitions of who gets pregnant.[30] The solution to the middle-class problem sacrificed grandchildren to respectability. I do not mean by this to ridicule "middle-class whites" but rather to point out some of the conditions of their suffering that are hidden under all the talk of autonomy and upward mobility. The sufferings often included leaving kin networks to follow careers. They often included children being deprived of a father's care because his job ate him up. During the 1950s and 1960s, the price included that paid by the housewives suffocating in circumstances Betty Friedan wrote about, and by the men in grey flannel suits who had heart attacks before they reached fifty. In its own way, the life of the higher classes was a bitter one. It must have been particularly bitter for those who had recently moved up into respectable, middle-class status, out of the hardship of immigrant life or the poverty of the Great Depression. Respectability came at a terrible price.

---

29. See Moynihan Report (1965).

30. It was also glossed over by the individualistic way the problem of unwed motherhood (or today, adolescent pregnancy) was defined: as a problem for the individual girl, interfering with her individual, rational life plan. If we believed in social workers' "denial," we might be tempted to believe that this is denial systematized on a grand scale. Framing the issues of sex education and abortion in terms of individual "rational choice" follows the same pattern. The rhetoric may be necessary at some crucial moments of political contest, when whatever works has to be the weapon of choice (as at times this individualist language seemed necessary in the abortion controversy), or it may be necessary to protect people from the state or from other oppressive authorities. But that is something very different from enshrining the rhetoric as the map to moral reality, or as the foundation of how we should live, or for that matter, as the foundation of psychotherapy.

Sometimes, at least, the cost was also high to the "unwed mothers" themselves. Rains' studies didn't trace long-term outcomes of the Hawthorne House method.[31] In 1992, I received a letter from a woman who had read an earlier version of my chapter on the Rains study. I asked her for permission to include her letter in this chapter. She wrote,

> I was at a Florence Crittendon Home in 1968. Your treatment of the subject of white, middle class pregnant teens is very valuable commentary. However, I thought you made it seem that the young women in the homes were successful in returning to their place in society. I have found that not so.
>
> With the hiding of records and documentation, a part of me is denied. I have lived in an extremely unhealthy state in trying to comply with the hiding of my adolescent pregnancy. This cost is high. Fears of losing the daughter I now have overshadow our life together because I know the pain of losing a child.
>
> I always thought that the pressure to give up my first daughter was unnatural, going against the type of procreation you mention. I was asked to rationalize my action about a very emotional and physical event. The confusion caused by that has seemed everlasting.

Beginning in the 1970s, more and more white, young women began keeping their babies (see Nathanson, 1991 for figures). This result of the "sexual revolution," plus the advent of legalized abortion services, more or less put the maternity homes out of business. Deviance among young women began to take on a different definition.

The Uses of Deviance

In describing the problem of outsiders, Howard Becker wrote,

> It is easily observable that different groups judge different things to be deviant. This should alert us to the possibility that the person making the judgment of deviance, the process by which that judgment is arrived at, and the situation in which it is made may all be intimately involved in the phenomenon of deviance. (Becker, 1973: 4)

Becker expanded the understanding of deviance into a collective enactment, not the flaw of an individual or a "hardened offender." As professionals gained authority, there came to be a change in the definition and cure of deviance—even a "medicalization of deviance" (Conrad and Schneider, 1980). This was accompanied by a change in the form of morality, as I mentioned in the case of the Wilde-Stein Club vs. the Maine Ministers (chapter 2).

---

31. For some of that, see Furstenberg et al. (1987).

By the 1980s, the individualist perspective and the ideals of autonomy had come to dominate—something indicated in the fact that both progressive and traditional sex education texts counseled rational, individual choice (see chapter 2). Unwed motherhood became a choice of lifestyle—provided the woman wasn't on welfare. Abortion was declared an individual woman's choice. This is a different method of hiding and making public; for example, the outcomes for (and responsibilities of) prospective grandparents, aunts, uncles, and possible siblings are ignored, and those for the biological father are played down. Some people decry this as a deterioration of family values, and at the other end of the political spectrum, some people talk about "changing attitudes." That talk not only presupposes the same, flawed ontology as the individualist perspective, it hides the importance of the organization of work in a market economy, as well as the ways the individualist perspective is embodied in the institutions of education, politics, health care, law, and a hundred others—as well as in the more informal worlds of leisure, neighborhood, and in some cases, in the home itself.

The individualist perspective also hides some of the important processes through which the social order is regenerated. In the middle-class communities of the 1960s, *the individual* was labeled deviant—and her misstep had to be hidden to maintain family and community respectability. *The black communities* themselves were labeled deviant. That label was glued on even by professionals who deeply wanted to help. The labeling of groups extended also to gender, class, and age as well as race.[32] What we have here is a complex mechanism for regenerating a social, economic, and political order.

The "progressive," professionalized move has a similar outcome, but cloaked in more humane dress. In Faye Wattleton's remarks that I quoted earlier, the poor teens "who can least afford" to have children are judged under the "middle-class" planning ethics, and their communities are judged deviant—not, perhaps, to be blamed for their deviance, not to be punished, but to be cured. The responsibility is "society's."

I must caution the reader that I am not taking a relativist position here— that the poor have their ways and the "middle classes" have theirs. Nor do I mean to be taking the standpoint of the "marginalized" or the "oppressed" in this book.[33] I am concerned with using a collectivist approach to show some

32. See Nathanson (1991) for an excellent discussion. In a review of relevant literature from the 1960s, Meda Chesney-Lind found that sociologists claimed that female adolescents rarely deviated, but when they did, they tended to act out "sexually." The sociologists gave the explanation to explain the preponderance of sexual or sex-role-related offenses (incorrigibility, running away, sex delinquency) in the juvenile courts' female populations. Those "offenses" were cataloged by officials blinded by the double standard (Chesney-Lind, 1973).

33. As my discussion of syndicalism indicates, standpoints are made in social and political action. For me to pretend to take the standpoint of some marginalized or oppressed group in

ways in which a "moral scheme" is generated as "ours," and particularly the role that professionals play in that generation. It is true that the progressive, individualist moral scheme promotes the dominance of certain classes and races, but it is also true that it in many ways promotes the suffering of those dominant classes and races. The substantive question is whether it can give a reasonable answer to the question of how we should live. Many people believe it cannot. In this book, however, I'm writing as a professional philosopher concerned with looking at the collective activities through which the social, moral, and economic orders (and individuals themselves) come to be generated. And how the "dominant," "the oppressed," and "the marginalized" come to be generated. And even how the relativist outcomes come to be generated.

Before leaving this chapter, I want to take a look at the "middle-class," individualist, planning morality in one of its prime institutional locations: the public high schools. The look offers a different perspective on the "we," and a different name for members of the middle class.

Dupers and Greasers

During the twentieth century, as the United States became a modern nation, adolescence came to be seen as a human stage in the status passage from child to adult. The passage became especially risky, not only because the new ways of managing it were experimental but because the traditional controls of family and community were weakened by the social and cultural changes made to accommodate the industrialized economy. Often, controls were transferred from kin, community, and church to professionals and to the young people themselves. The changes in the passage included the change from "keeping company" and courting to dating.

Over the course of the century, a major part of the control of the passage from child to adult was given over to public institutions, particularly the schools. The schools prescribed the official direction and the schedule of the status passage. They supplied the organization through which the passage was controlled—charting and rewarding the normal passages, handling those that got out of line (with the help of outside institutions, as in the passages of the unwed mothers).[34]

---

an academic book like this, *outside of a movement which gives me context and leadership,* would not only be insufferably patronizing, it would be empirically and conceptually mistaken. And, of course, politically mistaken. As I said, standpoints are made in action, and in meaning and outcome they open to the future.

34. In my remarks on status passages here, I rely on theory set out in Glaser and Strauss (1971). See also Nathanson (1991). The Nathanson book is an excellent piece of theory and scholarship, but at times I'm not quite comfortable with her emphasis on *control* of women's sexuality. However, in the context of the usual sociological literature on deviance and social problems, the book offers a *much needed* remedy.

The grand image was, and is, that children would happily cooperate with this institutional plan and be willing subjects in the teaching-learning process that is said to prepare them for adult status. It is not part of the grand picture that the natural state of relations in the school be one of conflict, but in fact it is now and has been so for many years. Conflict of the "blackboard jungle" type has, of course, been defined as a social problem, as have truancy, pregnancy, drug use, gangs, and dropouts. But those conflicts are thought of as problems to be solved so that the schools can get back to normal. Understanding the schools as "socializing forces" requires understanding that the normal state of relations in the schools is one of conflict.[35] In this conflict, some students exercise control by appearing to comply while others exercise control by becoming deviant. Differences of age, gender, class, and race show in the different strategies for exercising control over the passage.

In the mid-1970s, I did field observation and interviews with some young people in Chicago.[36] Then (as now), the high schools were organized on what have been called "middle-class norms," including those Rainwater set out in his "planning perspective." This morality was one of individual responsibility and achievement—students were graded on individual work and collaboration was not usually encouraged and in many circumstances was labeled "cheating." Academic achievement was considered important as a means to career success, but achievement in sports, clubs, and cultural matters was also rewarded.

The very structure of the high school assumed that students should be oriented to long-range goals and deferred rewards—college, an eventual career, or at least a good-paying job after the four years of classroom work. The official assumption was that a life plan was an integral part of the answer to how we should live. The structure of the classroom work required rationality, in the sense of conscious planning and budgeting of time and resources (the schoolroom picture of self-discipline). The ideal student is a paradigm case of Diana Meyers' personally autonomous individual. In the schools, the paradigm is represented as "our way," "the right way," "the way to success," or even "the middle-class way."

Teachers and other officials had their own expectations—proper students were to be clean, polite, and show respect to elders.[37] Officials also con-

---

35. Howard Becker claims that the first ethnography of a contemporary American school, Willard Waller's (1932) classic, makes this point. See Becker's "Studying Urban Schools" in *Doing Things Together* (Becker, 1986).

36. I should say that my interpretation of the struggles in the high schools comes not only from my field research but from my own experience in Providence, Rhode Island as a working-class girl in a "college prep" high school crammed full of "dupers" (I discuss this term later in this chapter); and from my daughters' experience in the Chicago schools from 1967 to 1972.

37. Teachers of course had to adjust their sights to the schools in which they taught. For a discussion of teacher adjustment to ghetto schools see Becker (1970: chapter 11).

demned physical aggression and violence, except where it was rule-governed in male sports. "Respect for property" was enforced. In the crudest sense, this meant that damaging or stealing public or private property was punished. In the most effective sense of control, it meant that those who owned the property (or their designated agents) controlled who used the property, when, and for what purpose.

Some of the conflict that marked the high school passage centered around these "norms." Some students exercised control over their passage by giving the appearance of accepting and following the rules and satisfying the expectations of adult authorities. In a sense, they followed the path of a normal, respectable high school student—but of course, they were also *the ones by whom officials defined* what was normal and respectable. They were the "perceived paradigms." "Normal students" managed by hiding what they knew would infringe the rules—a process in which adults collaborated by providing private space, or by not asking questions. When an obvious offense occurred, adults could define the offender as "a nice kid who made a mistake" as in the Hawthorne House pregnancies. Or they could define the offense as normal, youthful high jinks and cover it up (compare "joyriding" with "auto theft"). If all else failed, they could label and ostracize the individual.

In the late 1960s, in the Chicago high schools, these "paradigm" students were called "dupers"—a term from a student perspective that named them by their practices of control instead of taking them as paradigms of normal student behavior. The name "duper" captured the conflict-management techniques of "normal" students. "Duper" was a name given by student outsiders to those students who were officially treated as "normal high school kids" or "typical students," and it expressed a shrewd and sharp humor. According to student lore, the term "duper" or "dooper" is an acronym for "Dear Old Upton Parker," or "Dear Old Oak Parker," both respectable, middle-class suburbs of Chicago.[38] One of the young women I interviewed described dupers:

> What are dupers? Duper guys usually want to be on the football team, or are on it. They usually get good grades. Duper girls usually got even better grades and did a lot of the guy's homework. When they were in a real tight relationship with a guy, some of the girls would talk about getting married and "We're going to buy a house." But not all of them. Some of them were into just going to college, and a lot of them were into thinking about going to college. If someone wasn't into at least *trying* to go to college, you knew they weren't really a duper.
>
> The main thing for real dupers was to be on all the school clubs—social clubs, Latin clubs, gym club.

---

38. My Hyde Park sources told me it was Oak Park. Steve Buff's sources told him it was Upton Park. Buff (1973) and personal communication

In the Chicago high school terminology, football heroes, cheerleaders, and valedictorians were "super dupers."

Ordinary dupers were part of the crowd, and they might just squeak by so far as grades go. But for the most part, dupers succeeded in learning the material teachers offered, and they appeared to accept the institutional goals and the rules of the high school. They allowed teachers to feel successful by more or less learning the sort of material that was taught in the way the teachers taught it. Dupers dominated school clubs and extracurricular activities, which were duper territory in fact and by definition. It was dupers who "took advantage" of the opportunities and enrichments the high school offered—though dupers formed a pyramid, and many students were dupers only in the sense that they dressed appropriately, behaved themselves, and seemed to accept more active dupers as leaders.

Extracurricular activities gave some dupers a means of managing conflict with authorities. Successful dupers could reason with them, or even protest through the student council, the student newspaper, through private chats, and through duper leaders. Authorities preferred this method.

The duper image was one of "typical high school kids"—we meet them in Archie comics (with the exception of Jughead, who just ran with a duper crowd). Duper student culture and way of dress has often been taken as the teen standard, even by serious researchers. Dupers defined the "we" of adolescence. But dupers also cut class, cheated, lied, drank alcohol, took drugs, stole cars, and got pregnant. They were "dupers" in part because they duped authorities. They were friendly with police, and when caught, they were often treated as nice kids getting into mischief rather than as delinquents to be brought into juvenile court. One of my interviewees reported,

> The dupers were always friendly to the cops. And in the school yearbook, you would see some of the duper kids standing with the school cop, getting their picture taken for the school yearbook with Mike the cop, right, and they would be in the school newspaper. You'd never see greaser kids with the police.

In gaining some control over their passages, dupers followed a strategy of seeming to comply. Greasers followed a strategy of noncompliance.

Within the formal arrangements of the school, leadership tended to be defined in terms of duper forms of leadership, particularly in the clubs. Some leadership qualities were not recognized at all, and some were punished when discovered. One greaser I interviewed had been the warlord of his gang, meeting with the president and vice president of the gang to make executive decisions on whether they should fight some other gang. From my own knowledge of him, he had tremendous leadership ability and sound judgment. On his school record, he was a delinquent, truant, and drug user.

One young woman I interviewed was a leader in getting the dress code changed at her school, but for this she received no commendation and her reward, for a time, was to be sentenced to detention.

I've claimed that dupers were the "normal" high school kids, in the eyes of officials, the media, and even some researchers. They were normal not because they followed the rules but because their behavior and dress set the norm. Their infringements of rule and law were treated as normal missteps rather than as seriously deviant behavior. They were "nice kids," and when caught, they repented. This treatment of dupers made an apparent consensus not only on what was normal for high school students but on what life ought to be—dupers, after all, fit into the plan of the "middle-class" answer to how we should live.

Leaving duper ways nameless, i.e., as "the normal way," hides other "we's" and other answers to how we should live. But other answers existed within the high schools. The students who were called greasers took a stance of rejecting authority, the authority of the school and police. However, they had a positive relation to the adult world and they did indeed prepare for adult work—for the boys, mostly blue collar occupations, and for the girls, blue or pink collar work. The duper plan, with its bias toward white collar life, was not a sensible one for them, nor did it jibe with their ideas of respectability.

Steve Buff wrote that male greasers he interviewed liked sports and repairing cars. They had an early identification with the world of work, and they often had to work while in school, to help the family or support a car. They shopped around to find a job that was not too boring or dead end (Buff, 1970: 68).

Not all working-class students were greasers, and some were dupers. But all of the working-class young people I interviewed had an identification with the world of home, neighborhood, and work. They all held jobs during high school, and nearly all of them contributed part of their earnings to family support. In addition to skills learned on the job, they also learned skills at home and in the neighborhood. The young women I interviewed carried a good share of the women's work burden at home: cleaning, sewing, home decorating, childcare responsibilities. The young men shared in the adult male responsibilities of house repair, yard care, and keeping the neighborhood automobiles running. Often, the identification was not with the official plan of the high school but with the adult world. They were conscious that the schools, in practice, favored "middle-class students," whatever the egalitarian rhetoric. They knew that "normal students" were dupers, and that whether they themselves were labeled deviant or not, they were not "normal."

Superficially, the schools were egalitarian and males and females sat in the same classrooms, did the same required work, and received the same diplomas when they finished. In the late 1960s, gender differences were enforced even in the formal structure. They were marked rigidly in official regulations for sex-segregated toilets, and in the codes governing dress and appearance (girls wore skirts and makeup and could have long hair and wear earrings; boys wore pants and shirts and could not wear makeup, have long hair, or wear earrings). Clothing had to be "neat and appropriate," which for girls meant "not sexually provocative" (according to the official definition of provocation). At dances, couples were heterosexual, though girls could dance with girls.[39] Heavy petting at school functions was punishable. These were official arrangements that students explicitly rebelled against during the late 1960s.

What counted as normal also varied according to gender. In the official arrangements, duper ways defined the norm, but according to gender— duper guy ways were the norm for guys and duper girl ways were the norm for girls. Duper girl classroom relations were normal for girl classroom relations, and so on. Duper girls followed the "nice girl" lifeplan—or rather, appeared to do so. The official view of rationality and planning that marked a proper passage to adulthood had duper ways as the standard—duper ways as they were represented to the officials, that is, not the duper activity that went into maintaining that representation.

To someone who took duper girls as normal, with their neat hairstyles, and their sweaters and skirts, other girls' styles might be judged cheap and sexy—white greaser girls, black girls, hispanic and chicana girls might be judged this way. With duper girls as the norm, differences in these other girls' behaviors might signal sexual looseness—their ways of joking, their going out on school nights, their very identification with the world outside the high school. Impudence or truancy were often interpreted by authorities as indicating sexual promiscuity.[40]

The high schools were not only a locus of race and class conflict, they were (and are) a central institution in regenerating the race and class orders in the United States. They regenerated the gender orders, differentiated according to race and class. But here "race" cannot mean biological race, for race is a

39. Homosexual acts, even when properly hidden, were against Illinois law until the end of the 1960s. This was not something the students I knew rebelled against—even among those who were politically radicalized, homosexuality was stigmatized, whether among men or women. This isn't to say that no one had a gay friend or acquaintance who was accepted on his own as a "real nice guy." Lesbian relationships and inclinations were closeted.

40. There is no reason to believe that greaser girls, in general, were more promiscuous than duper girls, and some reason to believe that the reverse held, given that the double standard was more explicit among greasers and other working-class youth. The waters are muddied further by petting practices—"going all the way" meant intercourse, and higher-class couples had a wide scope of sexual activities short of intercourse, something lower-class couples did not (according to Kinsey and other such research at least). There's also the issue of "going public" through a pregnancy, in situations in which access to abortion differed by class and race.

social and political product. "Class" cannot mean "middle class" vs. "poor." The terms "middle class" and "poor" support the idea that we are all equal and share the same values. And so when the planning ethics is attributed to the middle class, it becomes "ours," and suitable to be used in policy involving all races and classes. The fact that it is the professionals of family planning who are the ones promoting the ethics is hidden. *Using the term "middle class" not only contributes to hiding the relations between working class and capitalist class, it hides the work of the professional classes.* The professionals become conduits for scientific truth, aids to progress, implementers of "our" middle-class values.

Race and class are social products of many institutionalized processes. I do not have a definition of the products. But I do believe that the Chicago high schoolers' term "duper" captures what Rainwater called "a particular world view" that seemed to characterize the "middle-class" way of life. The ethics offered by John Rawls and Diana Meyers also represent a duper world view, not the *world* in which dupers (or "the middle class") actually live but the tale that is told of proper life and the road to success, and the *appearance* that is maintained, at considerable cost to all. The cost may be considered necessary to maintain the American way of life, and particularly the American economic system and its social order. And some professionals may have their reasons for aiding the effort. But moral responsibility in the effort requires being honest and clear about the outcomes. Intellectual responsibility requires a theory and method, an epistemology, an ontology, and an ethics that permits morally relevant outcomes to be seen.

Being morally and intellectually responsible requires a way to make explicit the moral relationship between theory and practice, and between professional practice and larger moral outcomes. In this chapter, I have tried to show some large-scale outcomes of collective work by professionals, including philosophers, sociologists, and other academics. I've suggested that progressive society is not so different from traditional society in its ways of making a "we" and a consensus. I've tried to sensitize readers to a different way of approaching moral theory, epistemology, and ontology. Now I can be more explicit about the alternative moral theory, epistemology, and ontology that I have been using.

6

A Collectivist Perspective

IN THE PREVIOUS THREE CHAPTERS, I have tried to show some of the ways in which "our" moral consensus, and a "we," have been made. In this chapter and the next, I turn more directly to questions of knowledge—or rather to moral and intellectual responsibility of knowledge makers. All professions, including service professions and paraprofessions, require knowledge makers for the "difficult body of knowledge" that justifies their status as professionals rather than workers in some other occupation. So a great deal of what I have to say about moral and intellectual responsibility in this chapter can be applied to a broad range of professions. In the end, I think the discussion may also help clarify responsibility in collective actions in general.

I present a collectivist alternative to what I have been calling the individualist perspective. Some philosophers have labeled the individualist perspective "folk psychology," and they have claimed that it is Cartesian, in the sense that inner thoughts, feelings, and attitudes are the causes of individuals' outer behavior. The folk are said to use this psychology to predict behavior of individuals, and there is a teacup tempest over whether it will be shown to be *false* if it doesn't turn out to agree with some *true*, scientific theory about brain states (Greenwood, 1991). Presumably these brain states would cause the behavior, and for many philosophers generating the tempest, the argument isn't over the individualist, causal model but over materialism and the existence of mental causes.

The closest thing to this "folk psychology" that I've discussed so far is the medicalized version used by the social workers in Rains' studies. In those cases, it appeared as a professional psychology that was being taught to clients (some of whom appeared to be unteachable). I mention the philosophic version because it does bring out some ideas that need to be carefully considered: the reliance on professional *authority* (will science show folk psychology false?) and the philosophical use of notions of *prediction and truth*. There are serious questions whether the notions of prediction and truth, as used here, are coherent. And of course there is the core issue: the focus on individuals rather than on collective action.

I begin presenting a collectivist perspective by looking for an appropriate notion of responsibility, because the worth of the collectivist perspective is not that it yields the one truth but that it gives hope of allowing knowledge makers to be morally and intellectually responsible. Looking for an appropriate notion of responsibility will lead me to discussing collective action and its outcomes.

Responsibility

Prediction and truth are modern ideas that have been associated with science (particularly physical science or natural philosophy) as a mode of knowledge, though by no means are all sciences predictive. It is prediction that requires terms that are clearly defined to select out categories of objects, prediction that requires laws that govern those categories, whether deterministic, probabilistic, or statistical. The scientific ways of prediction gain meaning by being contrasted with other ways of knowing the future— through dreams, oracles, prophesies, visions, intuitions, or divination, astrology, and tarot readings. The contrast isn't simply one of ways of knowing, it is a difference in the ways that space, time, facts, reality, and the knowers themselves are defined. Prediction of the simple, scientific sort requires that reality be captured in certain measurable categories of space and time. Prediction requires that the future will be like the past, and it also supposes that the past is like the present. The world in which prediction works is a world in which retrodiction works. The facts of the past and present are given, there to be found out. The facts of the future will be there, to be discovered. The ideal knower is a judging observer, not a participant in the world being judged. Quantum mechanics and relativity theory raise difficulties for this simple world of prediction. But it is for such a judging observer and such a predictable world that professional ideals of detachment and objectivity were devised.

The individualist perspective offers a moral universe that is the companion of the predictable, scientific world. The emphasis is on the judging observer, rather than the actors. This shows most clearly in the view of time. In the moral case, the actor looks forward to what may seem to be an indeterminate future. The judge looks back to a seemingly determinate past. Out of this past, the judge can presumably discover the preconditions of the action (motives, reasoning, character traits, irrational emotions, impingement by environment). The past seems fixed, and discoverable, something that is crucial for legitimating praise and blame, or for finding a cure. It is a "backward-looking" sense of responsibility. But the future is also predictable (or at least, consists of a range of events that can be assigned probabilities) by the judging observer, using the same terms that are used to categorize the past.

This is a timeless view of time, and it gives the judging observer an authority on the truth of what the actor did. In fact, deciding the past and predicting the future require authority.[1] Backward-looking responsibility *requires* judges and it gives a picture of the world suitable for judges. Even the actor is construed as a judging observer, in both the philosophy of science and in most Anglo-American ethics. The version of "folk psychology" I mentioned above clearly turns the folk into judging observers, as does the ethics of personal autonomy and planning.

That outlook on time, and a past and future that is (in principle) objectively available, gave support to the social workers' authority at Hawthorne House. The perspective required not only professional authority but a thesis of "epistemic equality": anyone may (in principle) know the facts of the past, anyone may find out the preconditions of the action, anyone may be the judging observer (Addelson, 1993). The unwed mothers might, as a practical matter, require the guidance of the social workers to uncover their past motives and their future plans. But given that aid, they could learn and become capable of knowing and judging their past, and planning the future. The professionals unearthed the objective conditions but anyone might know them. The premise of epistemic equality is crucial to the individualist perspective, and it is a main support of the associated ideas of truth and prediction.

This view of time from the standpoint of the judging observer also underlies the standard approach to social problems: in the past, certain people have done certain things, and curing the problem requires changing what people do in the present so that the future will be different. And so stiffer prison sentences and capital punishment are cures for crime (or alternatively, rehabilitation programs and anti-gun laws) with the prediction that crime will lessen thereby. And so sex education, jobs, and schooling opportunities (or alternatively, abstinence and strong family and religious values) are cures that will lower the incidence of teen pregnancy in the future. I presented cases in earlier chapters that showed that making moral problems public involves conflict and cognitive authority. My point here is that it also involves the perspective of the judging observer, in the understanding of time and in the thesis of epistemic equality.

What is perhaps most important is that this view of time that attends the individualistic perspective hides crucial *asymmetries* between acting and

---

1. For an interesting discussion about judgment and authority, see Aubert (1965), particularly page 30.

judging. In acting, the future isn't simply open to a range of alternative actions or consequences that are already categorized, as the planning outlook says. It is open to giving names to actions, to categorizing them anew. The actor faces a future in which truth is still to be enacted and outcomes are still to be named. This was the syndicalist premise. It was denied by the social workers, and it is hidden in the individualist perspective generally, by restricting knowledge to judging observers.[2]

The "juridical" or "backward-looking" notion of responsibility fits the individualistic perspective. The question, "who is responsible for this?" applies to the backward-looking notion because it concerns fixing liability on individuals (whether human beings or corporations or some other group). It is a notion of responsibility with indispensible but limited uses. It isn't suited for asking some of the most important questions about responsibility in collective action. For example, when feminists or other liberationists discuss responsibility for gender, race, class dominance, or oppression, they make their arguments incoherent if they use the juridical notion of responsibility-as-blame. Their success in making their points and finding solutions requires a different understanding of responsibility. And so does success in raising issues about the authority of professionals.

The responsibility of professionals that I am concerned with has to be understood as a responsibility in collective action. It isn't simply a "professional responsibility," if that means responsibilities that attend roles or offices. Professional responsibility in this "role" sense is a personal responsibility. There is also a kind of responsibility that attaches to a profession as a whole, and derivatively to the persons who create the professions in their collective actions. This notion has been worked out in practice as the professions developed.

The overall justification of a given profession (and its monopoly) is that its practitioners can be counted on to serve some public need or public good responsibly.[3] Fulfilling the public need or good does seem to be a collective effort of members of the profession. However, professionals themselves have a major hand in defining the public need and good that they serve. Professionals are, after all, members of occupations that require a market. And they understandably define the good they serve to their own advantage. This is a

---

2. French (1991) contains articles almost exclusively devoted to the backward-looking notion of responsibility. John Ladd is explicit about the different sorts of responsibility, and I have learned a great deal from his work. I must thank Caroline Whitbeck for referring me to Ladd's work and even for giving me copies of many of his papers, and for her continued support. Her work in ontology is very much compatible with my own. I take off from Ladd's account of moral responsibility (see below).

3. Newton (1983) has a very interesting discussion of professions around these sorts of points.

broader way to understand "professional ownership of public problems" (Gusfield, 1981). Serving the "public good and need" usually includes measures that protect the monopoly and authority of the professionals themselves. Let me give an example.

The monopoly that academic professionals hold on higher education and certain important kinds of knowledge making is protected and legitimized through ideals of free inquiry, academic freedom, and through the practical control of the institutes that fund research and the institutions of higher education—and of course through the authority to certify academic and other professionals. The statement on professional ethics of the American Association of University Professors intones that professors have a primary responsibility to see and state the truth as they see it, and their "subsidiary interests" must never compromise their free inquiry. It goes on to say that as teachers they encourage free pursuit of learning in their students, respect the confidential nature of the teacher/student relationship, avoid exploitation or harassment, and protect students' academic freedom; and that they do the same for colleagues. They must also share responsibilities in the governance of their institutions. They must seek to be effective teachers and scholars. They must measure the urgency of their rights and obligations outside against the responsibilities to their subject, students, profession, and institution. And finally, that they have a particular obligation to promote conditions of free inquiry and to further public understanding of academic freedom.[4]

In practice, this statement is useful and may help professors contribute to the common good. However, it presupposes that what is good for the academic professionals is good for the nation—something that must at least be open to question on issues of collective responsibility. It is particularly important to keep the question open since most of the clauses of the AAUP statement on professional responsibility work to defend professional control and freedom.

I believe that a useful understanding of moral responsibility requires a different practice and moral approach, one that is not clearly compatible with professions as organized occupations selling services. John Ladd has warned professionals against simply operating within the rules of their occupations, professions, and organizations because then the institutional goals give the justification for what people do. And as I said, the justification is framed so as to preserve the important place of professionals. Ladd offers a notion of collective responsibility, developed within a circle of concepts that are different from those used in the individualist perspective. They include the concepts of "participation," "joint action," and "outcomes." "Participa-

---

4. Statement adopted in 1966. Reprinted in Windt, et al. (1989: 592).

tion" (in Ladd's terms) involves a kind of action: a joint action. It is a way of engaging in a social process, "a process in which a group of individuals is involved, acting or interacting together, that has a significant outcome of some sort or other." Outcomes are quite different from consequences, as I'll say below (Ladd, 1975).

In Ladd's terms, the basis of participation is responsibility. As a moral attitude, it requires an emphasis on forethought, care, intelligence, and initiative. Responsibility itself he takes to be a relation between a group of actors and a broad state of affairs (or a broad outcome). One example of an outcome is the health and education of one's children, or of the children of the community, or even of the children of Somalia or Bosnia-Herzegovina. The examples make it clear that responsibility may rest more heavily on some people or groups than others, due to their social, political, or personal positions. But the responsibility (Ladd writes), is inclusionary not exclusionary: one person may have more than another, but that does not relieve the other of responsibility (Ladd, 1975: 112, 115).

One main question about this moral theory of responsibility concerns the nature of outcomes. Ladd wants to distinguish outcomes from what are usually called consequences. In ethics, consequences are related to acts in some causal or "becausal" sense (Greenwood, 1991). The most straightforward example is act utilitarianism: the rightness of an act being considered by an individual is determined in terms of its consequences (does it produce a greater surplus of happiness over pain than any alternative act?). I would say that in the paradigm case at least, this model presupposes that the possible consequences lay before one, categorized and in principle predictable (or at least capable of being assigned some probability). The supposition is that in judging a previous act, the consequences and their connection to the act may, in principle, also be objectively found out. And of course it presupposes a definition of the act that is appropriate for discovering consequences. The notion of act and consequences (in this sense) relies on the peculiar view of time and the judging observer that I mentioned above. It is at best suitable for juridical responsibility or for "medicalization" notions that involve rehabilitation or cure of the ailing individual or environment.

But how are outcomes different from consequences? And what are the processes through which they are defined? I believe that acts and outcomes relevant to collective responsibility are not predictable because they are not categorizable in the way prediction requires. They are not categorizable in that way because they are historical.[5] Historical "consequences" cannot be

---

5. I made great efforts to argue this in "Nietzsche and Moral Change" ([Parsons, 1973] Addelson, 1991: chapter 2). That paper has been reprinted in several anthologies, but with one exception; editors eliminated my discussions of science and of utilitarianism because of space limitations. The full text is reprinted in Addelson (1991: chapter 2).

defined beforehand. I mean their definitions are not ready to hand, because their definition is the work of the future—it arises out of the act itself and the definition of act and outcome are revised by the judges and authorities and folk of the future as part of the process of generating group life. Even when the *same* categories seem to be used, *it is a creative, collective act to enact them as the same.* What is described as judging the facts of the case in a juridical account amounts to interpreting the past as a piece of history. Judging that the future will be like the past amounts to interpreting the future as a piece of history, only not yet unfolded.

I can fit Thomas Kuhn's interpretation of scientific discovery into what I've been saying here—though Kuhn might not now follow his interpretation through to its more radical consequences. Kuhn discussed the question "Who discovered oxygen and when was it discovered?"—a question that required a name and date in the answer (Kuhn, 1970: chapter 6). After raising difficulties with attributing the discovery to either Priestly or Lavoisier, he concluded that there is *no answer* of the kind sought. Asking it shows something askew in the image of science. He went on,

> Clearly we need a new vocabulary and concepts for analyzing events like the discovery of oxygen. Though undoubtedly correct, the sentence, "Oxygen was discovered," misleads by suggesting that discovering something is a single simple act assimilable to our usual (and also questionable) concept of seeing. . . . discovering a new sort of phenomenon is necessarily a complex event, one which involves recognizing both *that* something is and *what* it is. . . . But if both observation and conceptualization, fact and assimilation to theory, are inseparably linked in discovery, then discovery is a process and must take time. Only when all the relevant conceptual categories are prepared in advance, in which case the phenomenon would not be of a new sort, can discovering that and discovering what occur effortlessly, together, and in an instant. (Kuhn, 1970: 55)

The discovery of oxygen was an outcome of a collective activity, involving not only Priestly, Lavoisier, and their peers and predecessors, but of those who came later. However, I would take discovery as the model, with a limiting case being "that in which all the relevant categories are prepared in advance"; i.e., those in which "the same" categories are used as were used previously. The limiting case is not commonly called discovery but *prediction*. But as I said above, it is a question of outcomes and it is a creative, collective act to enact the categories as "the same."

Outcomes, then, are socially and historically generated. When I say this, I do not mean that responsibility is subjective or that punishments can't be justified. I mean that judgments are folk judgments, settled in the ways the folk settle them in all the political, moral, economic, and social contexts of their own social orders, by their own authorities. When professionals give the interpretations of outcomes, they do so not as detached, judging observers but as participants in collective activity. *The truth of the judging observer is collectively enacted,* and so are the predictions and plans and consequences. The question is, how to explain the historical generation of outcomes.

A Collectivist Perspective

I've described some ways in which individuals are basic in the individualist perspective. It is the decisions, actions, and motives of individuals that are important; individuals are judged, rewarded, and punished. Individuals have rights, duties, obligations, and entitlements, they reason and carry on dialogues with each other. Individuals sin, and they get sick. Individuals get promotions and earn wages and honors. Individuals have knowledge and beliefs, and individuals learn and take advantage of opportunities. In these and other ways, individuals are basic units for the philosophical ethics—and for many of the institutionalized ways in which our lives are managed in the United States.

In contrast, the perspective I will set out takes action as basic—action in lived time, people collectively enacting a meaningful past and future. I begin building my explanation out of the symbolic interactionist tradition.

Interactionist sociologists trace their roots to pragmatist philosophers John Dewey and George Herbert Mead and to the Chicago sociologists Robert E. Park and W. I. Thomas, as well as to the younger generations that included Herbert Blumer, Everett Hughes, and Anselm Strauss (Strauss and Fischer, 1978). Jane Addams is probably the most important source of inspiration for some of the earlier fathers, but she did not work in an academic tradition and so is not usually listed (but see Deegan, 1988). I've personally worked most closely with Howard Becker, and he has been my teacher, colleague and friend.

Taking collective action to be basic means that people and societies have their existence and meaning in action—the action and experience of making, meeting, and managing situations. The perspective has philosophical roots in John Dewey's paper on the reflex arc experiment. In that classic paper, Dewey refused to accept the dualism of stimulus and response that was becoming influential among American psychologists and instead took the unit of experience to be the act. It is out of the act that stimulus and response, subject and object are generated (Dewey, 1896; Mead, 1938: 65).

In his paper on the reflex arc experiment, Dewey discussed what seems to be the act of an individual: a child sees a candle flame, reaches for it, gets burned, withdraws its hand. The candle flame is a stimulus eliciting the response of reaching; the pain is a second stimulus eliciting withdrawal. As stimulus, the flame is an existing object in the outer world, just as the pain is an existing object (a sensation) in the inner world. It was *this* analysis that Dewey refused with the claim that the act was basic.

Because Dewey is correcting psychologists, the focus of the paper is narrowed. Expanded, the child and the candle would be embedded in a collective action that included the social setting of the laboratory, the experimenters, parents, whatever fuller cast of characters was involved, and I would include the figures and social relations of the institution, the profession, and ultimately the political system.

Over many decades, the interactionists developed the implications of taking the unit of experience to be the act, integrating contributions of George Herbert Mead and many others. In Herbert Blumer's development of the perspective, the keystone is that human beings have selves.[6] That the child has a self means the act of reaching for the flame is a reflexive process: the child takes the flame to be an object in the world with certain possibilities for action. The child indicates the flame to itself—as an object, the flame is a product of the child's disposition to act. In the reflexive process, the flame comes to have meaning *as* an object in the world. It comes to be an object in the world of the child because it is a locus of action for the child, a condensation point.

In indicating the flame as an object, the child acts as a subject. The child also comes to be an object as well as a subject in its world. The child acts and takes itself to be acted upon by those objects that it acts toward—the flame burns and hurts.[7]

In the act, time is constituted as well. The child's situation has an immediate past (not mentioned in the experiment) in which parents, experimenter, etc. were involved in helping the child make a meaning for the situation. The act itself has a lived time, in which the child first reached for a bright object and then learned it was a painful one. The reaching is the past for the drawing back. All of this is within the circuit of the act itself. This is quite different from the stimulus-response approach, in which the candle flame is an object in the world with the power to cause the child to reach, and similarly, the pain is an object in the inner world with power to cause the child to pull back, and the meaning of candle and pain is taken to be given, independent of child (and perhaps even independent of experimenter). The independent meaning relies on the thesis of epistemic equality.

---

6. I am more or less following Blumer's lead here, and he is more or less following Mead's. But my discussion is very much biased by my own understanding and mustn't be taken as an exposition of Blumer—nor should his discussions in Blumer (1969) be taken as exposition of Mead.

7. Living organisms may also have objects in their world that are identified only as "something I know not what." Sometimes we don't know what hit us. That doesn't falsify the account, it only means that the child-candle example is only one sort of case and there are many others.

I've tried to write this in terms of the act of the individual in order to stay with the discussion in Dewey's paper—though even so I had to bring in parents and experimenter. However, the basic unit for the interactionist perspective is not individual action but what I would call collective action. It is within the continual process of collective action that the objects of the human world are generated as condensation points of action—stones, candles, cows, words, families, bureaucracies, nations, and even nature itself. In collective action, the child not only indicates objects in the world for itself, it indicates them for others (and others indicate objects for the child).

Taking the unit to be the act in this way releases meaning and reference from a narrow connection with thought and language. The child in Dewey's discussion may be so young that it still babbles, though it already has a rich experience in collective action and indicating objects. I would even propose that all animals create a world of meaning and objects through collective action. By this, I don't intend the anthropomorphism that all animals have concepts in the way that humans have concepts. On the contrary, I intend to play down the importance of concepts (as mental constructs) in human action. This seems one way to overcome the organism/environment dualism and the mind/body dualism as well.

In the reflex arc experiment, as it was reported by the scientists, the child reaching for the candle is abstracted from the collective action, which includes the laboratory situation, and beyond that, the everyday world of the child. That situation and its meaning are generated through the collective action of the parents, the experimenters, the participants in the university, and the experimenter's professions, as well as the more global situation which enacts the meaning of the child as a child (I mean the collective activities that yield children as certain kinds of public objects).

Today, the stimulus-response analysis is out of favor in many quarters. But Dewey's basic criticism, that the unit is the act, operates against analyses that *are* in favor today in many circles. For example, the usual explanations of human behavior in terms of social structure or roles, assume that those objects (structures, roles) act upon human beings without explaining how they come to be constituted as meaningful objects within the actions of the human beings they are said to affect. For a second example, the "clinical perspective" presupposes that there are inner pathological causes acting on the person that result in pathological outer behavior (an analogy with the way the pain caused the child to withdraw the hand) and the cure is to substitute rational thought and self-knowledge as the inner cause, resulting in rational outer behavior. Yet the teenagers at Hawthorne House were converted to seeing themselves and the world in those terms, even to the point of accepting their own irrational motives as objects. In the outside world, public policy is aimed at providing social options, like candle flames there for the grabbing.

Yet those options are defined as objects within a vast framework of collective action, one that includes whole processes of defining what is normal and what is deviant and thus in need of options. The temporality of living and knowing is submerged in the timeless time of the judging observer. The psychic nature of living selves is lost.

So far, I've given "establishment" examples. But many rebels run the risk of disregarding the psychic nature of living selves as well. For example, some feminists who make much of the oppression of women under patriarchy became embroiled in controversies over whether some women were complicit in their own victimization, seeming to take "patriarchy" as a timeless, social/political structure. In my view, "patriarchy" is a historical reading of past and present. If that reading is to be meaningful, women must be converted to seeing the world in terms of patriarchy—as women were to be converted by Sanger's direct action in opening her clinic, in the process of creating an understanding of birth control. The process requires commitment and action. Patriarchal oppression isn't an object existing in a timeless time laid out for the judging observer. It is discovered, and the discovery is a historical interpretation made in collective action. The meaning and fact of complicity is also to be discovered in collective action, and in action that is specific and local.

I can also use the syndicalist example to try to clarify these points. The capitalist system was enacted in one way in Lawrence before the strike and in quite a different way when the workers walked out. In the course of the direct action of the strike, the capitalist system was enacted anew as an object for participants on both sides—enacted in a way that allowed workers and their allies, and capitalists and their allies to understand past and future in a new way. It is true that Adam Smith described a capitalist system that people self-consciously tried to enact. It is also true that Karl Marx and Friedrich Engels described a capitalist system in quite a different way. Marx and Engels' description was explicitly historical, and it worked more or less well enough to convert people to seeing past and future in its terms.[8]

I'm not saying that capitalism doesn't exist; that would be foolish. I'm saying it does exist and it has existed, but that judgment of existence is a historical one in terms of the enactment of capitalism in collective action, an enactment that includes the participation of theorists like Adam Smith, Marx, and Engels. Giving up the timeless time of the judging observer doesn't drive us to saying that all is illusion and subjectivity, or that one explanation is as good as another. Explanations may be historical and dis-

---

8. Some interpretations of Marx and Engels take the "judging observer," timeless view of time approach to history and that, of course, is incompatible with my approach here. Other interpretations of Marx and Engels seem more compatible.

puted, but some are more responsibly made and some work as a basis for collective action and others don't. Some hold up over time and others don't. I discuss some of these things in the following chapter. The point I want to emphasize here is that the theorist and the experimenter and the therapist must include themselves as participants in the collective actions they are explaining.

I want to give one more example before going on to discuss some important premises of the collectivist standpoint.

In chapter 1, I mentioned Richard Lewontin's idea that organisms do not find the world in which they develop ready-made, they make that world. Lewontin also raises issues concerning the human genome project saying (among other things) that an organism does not "compute itself from its own DNA," and that the importance of gene mapping for therapy of human ills is far from clear (Lewontin, 1992). These are the judgments of one specialist on the work of others. I would add that the human genome project is clearly one in which the psychic nature of living selves is ignored—it is based on a biological determinism of human beings and their natural and social environments. It deals with human beings (and other organisms) as bodies. It is also a project in which the researchers are hidden by presuppositions about truth and the benefits of scientific knowledge. In his discussion of the project, Lewontin introduces the scientists as part of the research by discussing their lobbying for funds, their organization of the project, and their financial involvement in biotechnology (Lewontin, 1992). Apart from these specific issues, there is the general issue of the authority of the researchers in defining what we are, who we are, and how we should live— not in words or empty theories, but in ways that will be implemented in the health care, educational, and legal systems. Using DNA testing in the courts, labeling people deviant by genetic testing is a powerful contribution to the definition of how we should live. My point here is not to say the scientists involved in the genome project are promoting false theories. I'm saying rather that they are abstracting the experimental situation of their research out of the larger collective action that includes themselves. It is not that their work isn't "true," it is that they run a very serious risk of not exercising moral and intellectual responsibility.

Some Premises on Collective Action

I want to expand the basis of the interactionist position by giving a few of the premises that concern the nature of collective action in human social life. I'll use some of the premises offered in Blumer (1969) as a scaffolding, because he is both philosopher and sociologist and a very fine thinker. However, my aim is to explain the position for the purposes of this book, not to explicate Blumer. I might say (wryly), that this is quite in the spirit of Blumer's use of Mead.

First, human social life is generated in collective action that takes place subject to subject, in the sense that participants take each other into account, not simply as objects but as subjects who operate through their own understandings of the situation.

For example, when the women workers at Hamilton Mills ostracized their wayward sister, they assumed that she knew what she was doing in the past and that she had acted out of a corrupt (or reckless) understanding of the situation. They assumed that each of them (and the landladies, etc.) understood what a proper girl was like and that the wayward girl must be ostracized. They also knew what the action of the girl might mean for themselves and their own reputations vis-à-vis people in their larger social worlds. They took into account how others might respond, and they acted so as to change that response—labeling the girl an outsider, a deviant. The mill workers acted as if they shared a consensus, but I am sure that leaders also took differences into account. This was a very large collective action, composed not of discussion, a vote, and a decision, but of multitudes of actions —who to sit with, who to visit, when to smile, what posture to assume in which situation, and so on.

It's necessary to make some clarification of Blumer's premise. For example, people often assume they know what the others understand, projecting something on them—scientists did this in the reflex arc experiment. People sometimes ignore others as if they had no understanding of their own (or none that mattered)—sometimes the "lower orders" of servants and slaves have been treated this way. It involves treating other persons as objects, a moral violation but a social fact. So the depth of the premise varies with the situation.

Second, Blumer also says that each person takes him or herself into account as a subject as well, in the reflexivity of perception and participation. In this way, one is continually generated and regenerated as a person, and as a person of a particular sort.

For example, the black girls of The Project took themselves into account as subjects, most obviously in taking the initiative to enroll in The Project school. But it also showed in their complaints when the social worker asked questions of a sort that adults should not ask of them, or the complaints at being treated like "some slut dog" in court. The process of change in self-understanding from "that kind of girl" to "nice girl who made a mistake" to "girl with a baby" involved taking themselves into account not only as subjects but as objects. They reflected on themselves with considerable self-consciousness. As another example, among Chicago high school students, the very use of the term "duper" shows that students took themselves into account as subjects and objects. The Project girls and the high school students showed a high degree of reflection and "taking themselves into account." Once again, this "taking oneself into account" may take place on a more or less conscious level.

Third, I would say that persons are also generated in action and interaction, and they are generated not only as persons but as particular sorts of persons.

For example, in their complex passages at Hawthorne House, the white unwed mothers were regenerated as respectable, middle-class girls. The black unwed mothers were generated as members of a deviant community by the officials, but as "young girls with babies" by kin and neighbors. The Rains studies show that this "generation as a person" was not simply a question of public persona but a question of self-understanding as well. The "generation as a person" is continuous and continuously changing, as the letter from the Crittenden Home woman, twenty years afterwards, illustrates.

The reality of the young women's "careers" and social options were also generated. In the collective action that had its immediate focus at Hawthorne House, the career of the unwed mother displayed a pattern of steps shared by the girls. Rains' field research showed how the pattern was generated. The pattern suited the timeless time of the judge, but its reality was a *product* of a living process of collective action. The collective action was widespread and involved a very large cast of characters: school officials, recorders of births, neighbors who refrained from public gossip, and so on. Rains' studies illustrate some ways in which the predictable world necessary for the conditions of middle-class life was generated: it was enacted through collective action. The timeless time and the judging observer necessary for the "middle-class" world was enacted through collective action.

In saying "the unit is the act," or "collective action is basic," I am not saying that the patterns Rains uncovered were ephemeral or "not real." Nor am I condemning to illusion the stimulus-response patterns uncovered by the psychologists of the reflex arc experiments. But these "patterns" are products of collective action, generated by collective action. To understand group life, and how a "we" is made, and to begin to ask questions about how we should live requires asking about the process through which the patterns are generated. I should say here that the pattern that Rains calls a career is not what I mean by a moral passage. A career is a product. A passage is a process of remaking the past and generating the future. A passage is a collective action in lived time. The unit is the passage, in the sense that the unit is the act.

If one accepts the above three premises, then it is clear why individuals should not be taken as the basis of an ontology or a philosophical ethics or psychology. Individuals, including persons and their characters, are generated in collective action. The collective action *includes* taking oneself and others into account as *subjects*. This is a *much* more complex process, *and* it results in a much more complex "inner" structure than most philosophical accounts allow. I'll use Rains' study to show this.

The Project girls had to manage the contradiction of two, disparate definitions of their passages, one from officials and the other from their communities. The process of managing it led sometimes to anger and pain. But it also led to a consciousness of the realities of the larger world that was (at the time) beyond the grasp of most of the respectable, middle-class girls. The Project girls' race- and class-consciousness would be integrated into the reflexive "taking oneself into account" and the "taking others into account as subjects." That is, the "taking into account" sometimes required taking systemic relations of dominance into account. Taking oneself and others into account as subjects may require race-, class-, age-, or gender-consciousness (or consciousness of other sorts). It may be that everyone has perceptions of the systemic relations, but they are experienced and expressed quite differently among the insiders and outsiders.[9]

The three premises also shed new light on some of the most respected philosophical accounts of character. Aristotle promoted "a firm and unchangeable character" in his virtuous man, but only the dominant can pretend they have such a thing, because *it requires that others behave toward him in a firm and unchangeable fashion* as the kind of man he believes himself to be. For some, like the poor, black girls of The Project, or the Chicago students I interviewed, it is clear that a double consciousness (or a triple, or quadruple consciousness) is necessary, yielding a more complex and fuller understanding of life.

My belief in reflexivity doesn't mean that I think it is nonsense to speak of "the authentic self," or personal autonomy or consistency of character. Those terms aim at capturing something valuable that people acknowledge in their lives and actions. I'm arguing against the *professional accounts*, based on the individualist perspective, because they demonstrate flawed scholarship and because one outcome is the support of dominant social orders—not only gender, class, race, and age dominance, but all sorts of dominance of "normals" over "deviant" groups.

The patriarchal authority of Aristotle's man of practical wisdom required that others behave "as if" he had a firm and unchangeable character. The man of practical wisdom was a product of collective action. His truth and the truth of his society were collectively enacted.

---

9. Among the interactionists, this new facet of "taking oneself into account" began to emerge in the transformed accounts of deviance in the 1960s (See Lemert, 1951; Becker, 1973). However, the interactionist sociologists have not developed it to the degree that it warrants, a fact that not only limits the power of the theory but also involves them in the contradiction of not applying their own theory to themselves. I'll say more of this below, and in chapter 7.

In "progressive society," science is a product of collective action, and many people act "as if" science itself had a firm and unchangeable character, "as if" it produced truth and the route to the common good. Enactments are an integral part of human life, and my point is only that they shouldn't be taken at face value. For example, acting "as if" people were individuals having inherent rights, liberties, and entitlements is useful and very humane today—the United Nations Declaration of Human Rights is a useful and humane instrument in some attempts to ease human suffering. It is well worth enacting in some contexts. But that doesn't mean it offers a satisfactory account of who and what "we" are, or of how we should live. And it may not be an account that helps people to be morally responsible.

One of the hallmarks of progressive society today is that we are supposed to act "as if" science itself had a firm and unchangeable character, "as if" it produced truth and the route to the common good—though individuals might go astray or technology might be misused. Over the course of the twentieth century, this premise has been enacted as the truth for the United States, so much so that those who object can be publicly ridiculed. The premise is in the throes of being enacted in "developing" nations—something which can offer us enlightenment on the enactment process, since the struggles for power are quite clear.

I made my remarks on a "firm and unchangeable character" to suggest that it is not only the selves of the participants that are generated and regenerated in collective action but the social order itself. For example, in the case of Rains' unwed mothers, not only were the moral careers of the young women generated, the authority of the social workers and the social orders of the society were regenerated as well. Because the social workers used the individualist clinical perspective in this work, the young women of Hawthorne House seemed to be generated as autonomous individuals of the middle class—that was the story. But in fact, what happened was far more complex.

Rains' studies illustrate how "middle-class" was generated as normal and "poor and black" was generated as deviant. This collective action involved a vast cast of characters, including many kinds of officials. The method was far more complex than the simple method of ostracism used by the Hamilton Mill workers. But it too required defining some groups as "normal insiders," and others as outsiders. The philosophy seemed to be humane—the black communities were to be cured of their poverty and disorganization and given the opportunity to live the "normal" life. But as in the case of the mill workers, defining the outsiders was necessary to the proper self identity of the insiders, and for the dominance of the class and race. "This is what we are not," the definition says. This isn't to say that individual poor blacks were not sometimes welcomed into the "middle class" with open arms. It is to say that their welcome usually required that they wear the apparel of appropriate selves and carry the umbrella of appropriate life plans so that others might interact with them as if they were middle class (and perhaps as if they were white as well). The same was true of whites from the lower classes. In the language of the Chicago high school students, what was needed was to act like a duper.

The authority of the social workers and other professionals was also regenerated at both Hawthorne House and The Project—just as the authority of Aristotle's man of practical wisdom was regenerated in the interactions that established his firm and unchangeable character. The social workers entered the cast of characters as professional authorities. Their action with the girls and their families, (and with officials outside) both exercised and sustained their authority. Their definitions of the girls' passages were accepted as official definitions by the white girls, their families, and by the officials and their records. The black girls and their kin might not accept them, but that was dismissed as one more mark of their need for a cure.

Many of the high school students who didn't become dupers were forcedly brought to the cure of suspension, expulsion, and punishment of one kind or another. It is clear that collective action takes place subject to subject, but this does not mean that all subjects contribute equally to the definition of what is going on. Power and authority are very often integral to the collective action, as are subterfuge and manipulation.

Anselm Strauss wrote about the "trajectory" of an action, which includes the way the course of the action is managed, often through conflict and negotiation (Strauss, 1993).[10] The Chicago students had a variety of ways of managing their passages—as I said, being a duper and being a greaser were two different ways. In the high school case, there was an official explanation of the passage in terms of progress along a life plan. The explanation was one powerful tool used by officials in managing the course of the action. But this doesn't mean that the official definition of the high school passage was the truth, or even that it was the definition that was ultimately enacted as truth. The school officials gave one definition of what happened at the high schools, but it wasn't what greasers and their kin and neighbors enacted as truth in their lives, and it wasn't even quite what dupers enacted.

Official explanations of what is going on are rooted in "hierarchies of credibility" (Becker, 1970). Local hierarchies are usually supported by extra-

---

10. The trajectory refers both to the process over time (illness, dying) and also to the interactions (Strauss, 1993: chapter 2). For example, the interactions of patient, medical staff, hospital administration, family, friends, clergy, insurance companies, and others may contribute to the evolution of the course of an illness, as well as the medically or socially defined disease entity itself. The point is that the trajectory of an action will be shaped in important ways by interactions of concerned participants.

local texts and other factors—the professional social workers and educators had their professional bodies of knowledge to back them up. Often, official explanations presuppose some political, biological, or psychological theory, or a moral or religious theory, and so scholars (including scientists) enter the cast of characters. Scholars are important participants in the social worlds, even though they are not personally present. The "official explanations" not only can't be accepted at face value, they are part of what has to be explained. Official explanations are an essential part of social control—which is why Dorothy Smith's "sociology for women" has the aim of uncovering the extra-local definitions and texts through which local life is "recycled" (Smith, 1987).[11]

What I have been describing as consciousness, character, and the social order, are outcomes of collective action. Some of the outcomes involved generating the authority of professionals. Some involved the beginnings of class- or race-consciousness. My hope is that using the collectivist perspective may help professionals to have a consciousness—not a class-consciousness per se but one suited to professionals as authorities. It is the kind of consciousness I have so far called moral and intellectual responsibility. But there is a potentially sticky problem here.

I set off on my discussion of a collectivist perspective when I was faced with a problem of how outcomes are to be defined, taking outcomes to be an alternative to consequences. But so far, I have proceeded by giving examples of outcomes. That might show that outcomes are different from consequences—they aren't causally or "becausally" related to action, and they aren't predictable in the scientific sense. But the examples were described by professionals—myself and the historians and sociologists who researched the original cases. Does this mean that professionals give the facts, or the true descriptions of outcomes (hoist on my own petard so to speak)? It doesn't, but explaining why requires talking about the sort of concept formation and the kind of truth that goes along with a collectivist perspective. I do that in chapter 6 which focuses on intellectual responsibility. In closing this chapter, I'll say something more about outcomes.

Outcomes

In writing about the collectivist perspective, I have been trying to show how human social life is an outcome of what people do together. If the unit is

---

11. The need to understand official explanations is also why Gusfield writes about professional *ownership* of public problems—the cause of a particular one-car accident on a local road is said to be a drunken driver, which is a definition worked out at a national level by activists, media personnel, police, auto manufacturers, elected officials, bureaucrats, and various other professionals (Gusfield, 1981).

the collective act, then the meaning of the outcome arises within that collective act. There may be one official meaning that carries the day, or there may be different meanings for different groups of participants, at the present. And of course the meaning may change over time, as the collective act forms a past for future collective acts.

Organizations and institutions are among the outcomes of people's participation in collective action. They can be described as outcomes of collective action over time, and organizations include collective actions which themselves have outcomes. I discussed "patriarchy" and "capitalism" above as historical interpretations that are collectively understood and enacted. The historical interpretation of an outcome that is an organization or institution can be indicated by what Howard Becker has called a "folk concept."

Becker wrote that folk concepts are shorthand terms people use to organize the way they do things together (Becker, 1970: 92; 1982). Folk concepts may have associated narratives. They convey a conception of a distinctive way of organizing what people do, including characteristic activities, typical settings, casts of characters, typical problems. The folk term suggests that all these things hang together in a neat pattern. The term may carry legitimations for doing that sort of thing; e.g., in many social worlds in the United States, "profession," "social service agency," "university," and "marriage" provide important legitimations, as does "science." On the other hand, the term may legitimate treating people and activities as deviant; e.g., in some social worlds in the United States, "quack," "amateur," "lesbian," "drug dealer," "pregnant teen," and "abortionist" are such terms. In all the cases I described in the previous chapters, the key terms in making moral problems public and in charting personal moral passages were folk concepts.

Folk concepts are used by the folk to point to what they do and to coordinate what they do together (in the sense that even a war requires coordinating both sides). "Corporation," or "family," or "profession" are complex folk terms that link moral, legal, and social activities.

Folk concepts pick out activities that "the folk" take to be the same, in the sense that people interact together in making "that sort of thing" happen. Whether people are now doing "the same thing" as before depends on how the narratives are used in explaining what is going on, not on abstract criteria or rules, or structures. This isn't to say that if the folk think they are doing the same thing, then they are. Using a folk concept is making a historical interpretation in action (something that simply cannot be understood as "consensus"). Historical interpretations are always open to revision. The test, after all, lies in the future.

Folk concepts are used in knowing "how to go on" together. Which folk concepts are appropriate is decided in the collective action (not by consensus but by a variety of dynamics, including hierarchies of authority). Narratives deemed appropriate for that folk concept help people to "read" or "reread" the situation and understand the outcomes.

So far as responsibility goes, participating in organizations and institutions (or alternatively, acting under the folk concepts) is one way people are enabled to behave responsibly. Institutions are ways that people act collectively to bring about broad outcomes, for example, the care and education of children, or the health of the nation. As those examples indicate, the institutions are marked by hierarchies of authority and the outcomes are often defined in authoritative terms. Moral responsibility may call for contrary ways of uncovering outcomes.

Margaret Sanger began her birth control crusade because she took the outcome of the Socialist party emphasis on men and industrial justice to be the neglect of the problem of woman and the child. So she defined the problem and solution differently—within a new narrative, if you will, provided you don't separate narrative from its embodiment in collective action. The Maine Ministers took the outcome of the Wilde-Stein affair to be the corruption of their communities. Here I am connecting my remark that outcomes of collective action are historical events, defined in action, with the interactionist remarks that social problems are defined in the course of discovering and resolving them.

I mentioned above that research professionals described the outcomes of the activities I discussed in earlier chapters. Let me use Prudence Rains as an example. Rains' report was a professional's interpretation of Hawthorne House and The Project. Using her report, I described some of the outcomes of the collective activity. There is a question that sociologists and philosophers might raise as to whether Rains' report is *true*. I discuss that problem in chapter 7, where I take up intellectual responsibility. Here I'm interested in moral responsibility, and I want to ask whether Rains' work contributed to helping others be morally responsible—this rather than asking the more complex question of whether Rains herself acted in a morally responsible way. I believe that Rains' work does aid others because it allows readers to see a process through which the "nice girl" character and story was enacted as the norm. And her work aids professionals because it allows some of them to see their part in enacting norms even when they want to change them. I'll try to convince my readers of this through the full chart that represents the "career of the unwed mother."

This chart doesn't represent a folk narrative. It gives a way to see how the folk narrative is enacted—the folk narrative including the nice girl/that kind of girl story. As proponents of progressive society, social workers taught their young clients a different story, the individualistic, psychoanalytic story. That story had no collective way of being enacted, and it depended on the folk narrative in ways I discussed in chapter 5.

Career Of An Unwed Mother

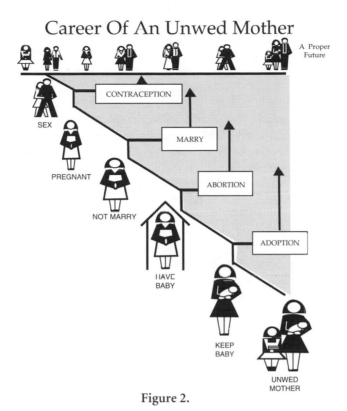

Figure 2.

The chart itself is neither folk narrative nor psychotherapeutic story but a representation by Prudence Rains, the sociologist. It sheds some light on outcomes. It sensitizes readers to the very complicated ways that "becoming a nice girl" may be collectively enacted, so that the outcomes of marriage, career, or family come to be created.

The situation of moral jeopardy, from which the young women began their passages, relates to their moral responsibility in their communities and the society at large. Their responsibility was bound up with character and community, even with the good of the community and its future.[12] From the perspective of character: somehow in passing from childhood to womanhood, a girl had to come to be the kind of woman she should be. She had to

---

12. Stanley Hauerwas has a book called A *Community* of *Character* (1981), in which he links narrative, community, and character the narrative in this case being the Bible, as the book of the Christian community, thus, I suppose, a book in use. I found Hauerwas' work helpful to my own, but despite our sympathies we have large political and theoretical differences. Overcoming them requires taking collective action and hierarchies of authority seriously.

change her early, childish ways to ways suitable to the adult world. But as the Rains studies (and the chart) show, this was a collective action, not simply an individual one. The outcomes included generating the girl's character and (to a degree) the future of her family, community, and class. To reduce all of this complexity to talk of "socialization" is to miss what is essentially human in the process.

The young women risked reputation, self-respect, and respectability—even as reputation, self-respect, and respectability were in the process of being made. From the point of view of character, this was part of a process of making what is called gender identity. It was also a part of the process of becoming a respectable woman in the community with a good future before her, one who could be relied on to carry through her part, and make a sound life plan. On the other hand, if her passage was one of becoming "that kind of girl," she was treated as someone who had ruined her chances for a proper life for herself and her children. These are two quite different outcomes, and which one the young woman faced depended heavily on how various narratives were enacted to explain what she had done—even to make what she had done happen according to the narrative, through the magic of collective action.

From the point of view of community, there are interesting complexities in the different lines of passage. Some lines are public in the sense that they represent the public norms, the public narratives, the "rules." They represent the consensus upheld in a straightforward way. A young woman may uphold the consensus by making only limited forays, or by "going all the way" but not getting pregnant, or by getting pregnant but getting married quickly, or by taking some of the other routes. What is important is that the deviant activity is hidden but the outcomes are public and acceptable. The means of a coverup may be ready to hand.

At the time Rains did her studies, abortion was illegal and hidden. What is hidden upholds the consensus by being hidden. Labeling the "hardened offenders" as deviant doesn't upset the consensus, it upholds it. And that is because their passages and their worlds are officially written in the narrative of authorities. But once again, I have discussed these outcomes in a professional's terms. Rains was a participant in the collective action at Hawthorne House and The Project not only while she was doing her work there but afterwards, when she wrote it up and published it. But she was a special kind of participant. She took part in the collective actions at Hawthorne House and The Project, but the meaning the interactions had for her was sometimes different from the meaning either staff members or the girls intended to give. Rains wrote about "double participation" in gathering data:

> The participant-observer is a double participant in conversation—doing the work of an ordinary participant and doing the provisional theoretical work necessary to acquire material which may become relevant. (Rains, 1971: 186)

The "double participation" also requires a sensitivity to what is not said. Ordinary participants often do something like double participation as well, but for Rains, it was explicitly part of her set of research tools. Her construction of the career of the unwed mother was the reconstruction of a professional participant-observer.[13]

As a professional sociologist, Rains wasn't simply an individual trying to understand the people at Hawthorne House and The Project. Her work at those locations was part of the collective activity of her profession. In that larger sense, her participation was double. One outcome of the collective activity in her profession was to undermine the collective action that supported the authority of the social workers and the narrative of the "nice girl" norm—undermine it only to a small degree, perhaps, but undermine nonetheless. The moral responsibility involved in Rains' part in the collective, sociological work can't be explained away by citing her professional training and norms, nor by saying her report gave the truth and falsified the folk account (or the social workers' account). Both of those explanations ignore Rains' double participation in society as it concerned the good of the whole and the answers to how we should live. This is an issue of intellectual responsibility as well as moral responsibility, and it calls for a new understanding of truth and scientific concept formation, one appropriate to a collectivist perspective.

---

13. We are all participant-observers in the sense that we all build analyses and stories of what is going on. Rains referred to Harold Garfinkel (1967) on the "retrospective-prospective possibilities on an event":

> Persons in conversation tolerate a great deal of (necessary) ambiguity and vague talk, making the assumption that what is being talked about will come to make sense. In employing this wait-and-see attitude they come to provisional understandings of what the conversation has been, is, and will be about, but these understandings have less to do with what the conversation was in fact about and more to do with a negotiation process by which persons arrive at a retrospective agreement as to what the conversation was about in terms of what it in fact became. (Rains, 1971: 186)

Garfinkel's remarks may help clarify my discussion of historical interpretation (above). My point here is that Rains was a professional participant-observer, and her interpretations were legitimated by means within the profession, and they were given authority through being published. I say something more about this in chapter 7. It is an important point, and a reason that Dorothy Smith requires that sociologists relocate their research in making a sociology for women.

7

The Knowers and the Known

SOME COLLECTIVE ACTIONS are of special importance to scholars, scientists, and other researchers, actions in which we take part "in the line of duty," so to speak. This fact was implicit in my discussion of the reflex arc experiment—if the unit is the act, then in understanding the experiment, the experimenters and the laboratory situation must be included in the scientific explanation, not hidden by abstracting child and candle out of the larger, collective action. Prudence Rains pointed in this direction when she described her double participation: she took part in the actions at Hawthorne House and The Project, but there was a systematic difference in the meaning of the collective actions for herself and the other participants. The difference was systematic because she entered the collective action in two ways: as participant and as sociological observer (Rains, 1971: 186).[1]

In Rains' double participation, there were two discernably different collective actions going on. There was the action of the participants (with all its outcomes for past and future). This was part of the ongoing personal and everyday collective lives of the subjects. Second, there was the collective activity that she took part in as a professional researcher, activity that constituted her discipline and the institutions of science.

The collective activities of folk and professionals meet in the *local* research setting (and elsewhere, of course). In local settings, whether laboratory or field, professionals "interrogate nature," or they "interrogate their subjects"

---

1. Double participation that involves systematic difference in meaning is a mark of many occupations, of course. Professionals of all sorts, including nurses, administrators, managers, teachers, business people, and media people, practice it as part of their work definition, and people generally practice it as part of the parent-child relationship. It is at the core of diplomatic and undercover activity as well as the social lives of many novelists.

in the sites they have chosen. They assume a right to know. If I use the language of rights, I might say everyone has a right to know. What is different about the professionals is that they assume the right to know in their own terms, according to methods and concepts developed in their own disciplines. The professionals define the nature of the subjects and the activity, and they define what is to be included as environment and what is to be ignored and hidden. So the "double participation" is extensive. The important question is how to do it responsibly.

The unquestioned right to know in terms of one's disciplinary concepts and methods is at the foundation of the cognitive authority of scientists and other professionals. It places them in the *local* sites of laboratory and field, not as participants but as "judging observers" who are themselves to be unjudged. The outcomes of their work extend beyond the boundaries of their disciplines, professions, and institutions. This is because the institutions in which professionals make and transmit knowledge are instruments of governance. In the broadest sense, the double participation of scientists and other researchers is a participation in the local activity as hidden agents of governance. Except in special circumstances, whether any particular professional wills it or not, the participation is in support of the existing social, political, and economic orders—loyalty to these things is embedded in the institutional folk concepts of profession and university.

The double participation may be self-consciously used in an effort for change, of course. For example, although she does not explicitly say so in her book, Prudence Rains chose her research sites with a political purpose: to show the repressive nature of the gender structure, the authority of social workers, and differences in the official treatment of middle-class, white girls vs. poor, black ones. Her work was embedded in the movement of the 1960s, in which the universities were involved so that new outcomes of academic work were possible. To the degree that Rains' work contributed to change, it did so in the context of that movement. The movement constituted special circumstances which (for a time) changed the relationship of university with the larger economic and political worlds, as well as the local worlds of city and neighborhood. Academic professionals could participate in new ways. New social worlds were created that dissolved old boundaries. These changes were changes in the double participation. This is a difficult topic, and I'll return to it below. My point here is that whether the professional work is consciously or unconsciously political, it involves a double participation as long as it remains within the institutions. The need is to take account of the double participation so that the knowledge work may be done with intellectual and moral responsibility. This is a requirement for the most conservative laboratory scientist as well as the most radical member of the social science and humanities disciplines.

Over the past century in the United States, the dominant definitions of truth and knowledge have operated to hide the double participation and the cognitive authority. In this chapter, I offer an alternative explanation of the experts' knowledge. My point isn't to give the "real" structure of society nor to give an account that is "more true" or "less false." Because the concern is with responsibility, the point of my discussion is to sensitize readers and researchers to the situations in which knowledge is made and cognitive authority is exercised. It is to encourage professionals to exercise practical wisdom in our work. This is my own effort at the feminist task of making a new problematic of knowledge. I begin with a look at some ways in which "the problem of double participation" has been raised by philosophers only to be hidden again.

Peter Winch's Conundrum

In the mid-1950s, Peter Winch set out a certain conundrum. In his first statement of the problem, he initially framed it in terms of a contrast between natural science and social science.

> The concepts and the criteria according to which the sociologist judges that in two situations, the same thing has happened, or the same action performed, must be understood in relation to the rules governing sociological investigations. But here we run against a difficulty; for whereas in the case of the natural scientist we have to deal with only one set of rules, namely those governing the scientist's investigation itself, here what the sociologist is studying, as well as his study of it, is a human activity and is therefore carried on according to rules. And it is these rules, rather than those which govern the sociologist's investigation, which specify what is to count as "doing the same kind of thing" in relation to that kind of activity. (Winch, 1958: 86–87)

There are two different kinds of points that might be made here. One concerns the validity of social science knowledge when measured by criteria that are said to apply in the natural sciences. The other concerns the double participation of social scientists as makers of knowledge to be used in governance. Traditionally, philosophers and social scientists have tended to focus on the first, ignoring the second. But the two are intertwined.

The conundrum holds not only for anthropologists studying "exotic natives" but for social scientists in their home societies. In the case of exotic natives, the problem concerns the contribution professionals make (for good or ill) in modernization or development. In the case of the natives at home, it concerns the part experts play in defining and resolving social problems and other matters of governance. For example, according to one "old school" sociologist, scientists had the responsibility of identifying those social problems that are "detrimental to the well-being of human societies."[2] Joseph Gusfield has written that this "enlightenment orientation" has been widely accepted in conventional sociology—the orientation rests on the presumption that science can provide neutral theories and facts that give the foundation for public policy (Gusfield, 1984: 48).

Gusfield himself has been a major critic of the enlightenment orientation. That "orientation" not only legitimated the use of sociological knowledge in Western nations, it also supported (and still supports) elites and serves the political purposes of imperialism in non-Western nations. Winch's puzzle, if taken seriously, delegitimates that use. This is particularly so because it was not only social science knowledge that Winch questioned. In his later writings, Winch argued that there were analogous problems for knowledge of the natural world (Winch, 1964). The folk classify natural occurances through their own language and "rules." Reclassifying it in terms of biochemistry or astrophysics may have some use to someone, but it does not serve to show that the folk beliefs are false, superstitious, or what have you. It means that the biochemists and the folk are talking about two different things. Appreciating this criticism requires a change in the progressive world view and practice. It requires taking even natural scientists as participant observers rather than judging observers.[3]

The dominant reaction to Winch's conundrum has been to take it as a challenge to the abstract ideas of truth and knowledge that legitimated the authority of social and natural scientists, and philosophers—and it is indeed a serious challenge. Among abstract theorists, it became the problem of relativism vs. objectivism. According to this definition, relativism is roughly the thesis that knowledge is relative to a conceptual scheme, or a paradigm, or a culture, or an epistemological framework, or something of the sort. Relativism in this sense came to birth as the dark twin of objectivism, with its claim that there is one valid framework for reaching the one truth, thus one genuine knowledge.[4] In its most simple-minded (and inconsistent) form, relativism is the thesis that there is not one truth but many.

---

2. See Spector and Kitsuse (1977) for a detailed review of the sociology of social problems. For a brief, very perspicuous discussion see Gusfield (1984).

3. Most of the critics classified as "postmodernist" or "feminist" have acknowledged this (for example Rorty, 1979, 1991; Harding, 1986, 1991). But in my opinion, the authors most cited have not faced the issues of responsibility and cognitive authority as I feel they need to be faced.

4. For some sources see Winch (1958); Kuhn (1970); Bernstein (1983); Jarvie (1984); Hollis and Lukes (1982); Overing (1985). This list gives a very small selection of books from a vast literature. Nearly all of the authors in the list left behind the abstract ideas of truth and moved toward knowledge as involving some sort of activity or institutions. Gusfield (1981) dumps truth in favor of irony and Rorty (1979) dumps truth in favor of conversational consensus.

The old ideas of truth and knowledge were *objectivist and universalizing*, for the supposition was that there is one knowledge and one truth for all human beings. As such, the old ideas made a "we" of all people. The usual forms of relativism are *totalizing*, because they make a "we" of collectivities of people. They do this by defining truth and morality relative to a conceptual scheme, culture, belief, value, framework, or what have you. All members of a given "community" are assumed to share the scheme. I began raising difficulties with this idea in chapter 1, with the problem of the hardened offenders.

The totalizing approach leads to a philosophic situation in which it is possible to point out the problem of objectivism and relativism but not possible to solve it. For example, Richard Rorty tries to escape the problem by claiming that ethnocentrism must be accepted, along with partisan embrace of one's own conceptual scheme (Rorty, 1986, 1989). This is not only totalizing, it leaves truth and morality in bondage to language and belief and the mental actions of consent and conversational consensus. Politically, Rorty's "ethnocentrism" amounts to promoting a conservative effort that supports elites within "the Western democracies," and the dominance of those democracies over other nations.[5]

It is in the nature of the feminist enterprise to reject objectivism and the enlightenment orientation, with its judging observer standing at a neutral or Archimedean point. However, the very premises of their politics have caught some feminists between the Scylla of objectivism and the Charybdis of relativism. Feminist academics have declared a commitment to respecting women's experience, in particularly the experience of women of a variety of ethnic groups, cultures, or what have you. If this commitment is understood to mean that each group's beliefs are valid in some sense (true, less false, correct, justified, etc.), then it seems to lead to relativism. On the other hand, feminist academics have also declared a commitment to opposing dominance and the oppression of women (and others) where it occurs. This is the requirement that feminist academic work must be "liberatory." In some lights, the liberatory requirement appears to be universalizing: it seems to allow feminist academics to decide that a particular culture is or isn't oppressive to women, whether or not those women think so. And in some cases, feminist academics do so.[6]

---

5. The inability of US politicians and intellectuals to grasp Islamic objections to the secular state is one symptom of this. So is the blind labeling of some killings as "terrorist" and others as "war casualties." This "ethnocentrism" is very dangerous.

6. For a good, brief discussion of the feminist premises and this dilemma see Tong (1993) and references there. I discussed the problem from another direction in chapter 6, in the example of patriarchy and complicity in one's own oppression.

My own solution has been to focus on discovering the ways that truth has been enacted in collective action, and how the appearance of a unified culture or value scheme is politically created in action. This means that the way out of the feminist dilemma of judging other women oppressed lies in political action and conversion in action—whether conversion of the academic feminists or conversion of the other women is to be decided in the field, not the classroom. On both sides, of course, there is a serious question of responsibility.

Objectivism: A Theory for Knowledge Makers

Objectivism wasn't simply an abstract, philosophical theory of truth. It was embedded in the definition of what science is, and in the norms that were alleged to make science a trustworthy source of useable knowledge of how we should live. There were "norms" to guarantee scientific neutrality. "The norm of universalism" was an analog to the "epistemic equality" I mentioned in chapter 5. It required that scientists ignore particularistic factors (like race, gender, nationality, religion) when they evaluated knowledge claims (Merton, 1949). The norm is deeply embedded in the individualism of liberal democratic theory and ethics, in which social and historical context are reduced to a minimum. In that paradigm of a liberal theory of justice, John Rawls relied on the norm of universalism in constructing his "original position." The "rulemakers" were required to put aside their knowledge of what their personal talents and status would be in the well-ordered community in order to select its principles of justice (Rawls, 1971).

To be objective, knowledge claims were supposed to be evaluated rationally, not accepted or rejected on the basis of status or authority. The norm of universalism specified that it made no difference who discovered or stated the truth, because scientific knowledge was not relative to personal idiosyncrasy, status, or political or cultural context. This is a thesis embedded in the individualist perspective: in science, it is individuals who know. It is complemented by universalism: what the individuals know is the one world, the one nature that all living beings face. When the individuals genuinely know, they grasp the one truth, or they observe the facts that anyone properly equipped would also observe. Scientists constitute one paradigm of the judging observer.[7]

Philosophers worked out details of the objectivist epistemology, but in a nontechnical form, it has been widely embodied in public practice. At root, it

---

7. Elizabeth Fee (1983) has recommended preserving some features of scientific objectivity (the useful ones) and dumping harmful ones. I share her opinions on harmful features, but it may be that preserving the "useful" ones would keep us too much to the old idea of knowledge.

was a theory for *knowledge makers,* a normative theory that seemed to tell how knowledge makers ought to reason to reach knowledge of the true or the good or the right. The fact that it was a theory about knowledge makers was hidden by the democratic claim of epistemic equality—it didn't matter who made the knowledge because we were all interchangeable individuals. Given the thesis of epistemic equality, the epistemology wasn't obviously a theory of knowers or a theory about knowledge makers. It seemed to be a theory about *knowledge itself.* This was particularly true for epistemology of science. The question, "Who are the knowledge makers?" seemed irrelevant; they were in fact scientists, but they could in principle be any of "us." The relationship between the scientists' activity and activities of "the folk" was defined by a theory about knowledge itself.

The philosophers included themselves among the knowledge makers as well.[8] Philosophers were to "underwrite or debunk claims to knowledge made by science, morality, art or religion"; and as a positive contribution to the underwriting, philosophers were to construct a "permanent, neutral framework for inquiry" (Rorty, 1979: 1, 9). This is the enlightenment orientation as it emerged among Anglo-American philosophers who assigned themselves the important task of articulating the foundations of knowledge and of the sciences.

What philosophers in fact underwrote was the cognitive authority of the scientists. Even philosophers couldn't insist that existing scientific knowledge is a body of true theories and laws. Rather, following scientific method was supposed to yield "the best knowledge of the day." Relying on scientific method left science (with the aid of philosophers) as the source of its own authority. Scientists were both users of the method and judges of which method was scientific. This is in fact the idea of a profession. The professional body of knowledge is said to be always open to revision. And yet, at any moment, scientists and the people of progressive civilization must act *as if* the knowledge scientists produce is true. They must act *as if* the professionals are indeed custodians of the one truth. This is a normative requirement, of course, a hidden political thesis about scientific (and professional) knowledge and method. It requires enacting truth, both in the scientific community and in the larger society. Legitimated by these "norms," science operates as an instrument for enacting truth. Philosophers have built theories that legitimate that instrument. But enacting truth is a matter of collective action,

---

8. In the disciplinary understanding among Anglo-American philosophers, their work included evaluating methods of inquiry or strategies of reasoning, analyzing what knowledge is and how it differs from mere opinion or false belief, and refuting skeptical arguments that no knowledge of reality is possible (Stich, 1990: chapter 1). Stich himself opts for normative epistemology, though he claims to be pluralist, in the sense that there are a number of such epistemologies.

not a matter of norms and not a cognitive exercise. It is the collective action that needs to be understood.

Folk Terms

In *The Structure of Scientific Revolutions,* Thomas Kuhn wrote about scientific revolution to a new paradigm (Kuhn, 1970). His idea seems to me (though perhaps not to Kuhn) a description of how truth is enacted *within* a scientific discipline in times of radical change. His "normal science" also seems to me to describe how scientific truth is enacted within a discipline in everyday circumstances. His scientific revolutions essentially involved internal conflict gone public, and his normal science involved conflict hidden by the dominance of some social worlds over others. Because of this, there is reason to claim that scientific knowledge in Kuhn's description requires communities, not merely individuals, though community in a thin sense that isn't a great deal of help in understanding the actual, living collective action (see Nelson, 1990, 1993; Addelson, 1993).

Kuhn did not attempt to explain what science was. He simply used the term to refer to historical cases that were customarily (or canonically) called science. That is, he was using a more or less technical term that was given its meaning within the discipline of history of science (and some other disciplines). In this use, the history of science is a history of progress in knowledge. Kuhn did not dispute the progress; rather he rejected the idea that progress came through accumulation of knowledge in normal science because he saw that scientific revolutions were necessary to scientific progress. The implications of *The Structure of Scientific Revolutions* may have been more revolutionary than Kuhn himself took them to be. But however revolutionary the implications, Kuhn did not give much of a basis for looking into the relations between the activities of scientists and the activities of the folk.[9] His work hid the double participation.

Because I am directly concerned with the relationship between the scientists' activities and those of the folk, I need a different understanding of science. Rather than talk about a difference in rules or paradigms, I will take "science" to be a folk concept.

As I said in chapter 6, for the folk, grasping folk concepts *is not a mental grasping of rules or ideas* but an ability to take part in folk activities. Knowing folk concepts requires *knowing how* to take part in the activity in question. Scientists know how to take part in many activities of science through their professional training and their "on-the-job" experience. The professional

---

9. Kuhn (1970) did give a push to understanding science as an activity, and some topics, like his discussion of textbooks, do reach into the relations between science and the folk.

training emphasizes science as the repository of a body of knowledge and scientists as knowledge makers. The on-the-job training involves scientists as disseminators of knowledge and as politicians. In disseminating knowledge, scientists take part in much larger social worlds. I mentioned this at the end of chapter 3 in my discussion of reproductive science (see Clarke, 1990a). But it is true of all the disciplines of science, and those of the humanities as well. The social worlds include the publishers of journals and texts as well as the science writers and reporters in the popular media. They include the worlds involved in politics of grant-getting and the politics of advising congressmen and presidents (whether in person or through the books and popular media). They include the relations between the funding agencies and the market (for example, between the National Institutes of Health and the pharmaceutical industry). They include the social worlds involved in the politics of world markets and banks and development. They include, of course, the politics inside and outside the enormously powerful institutions of higher education and the research institutes. In their collective actions, scientists know how to take part in activities in local, national, and international arenas.

Folk terms let people organize what they do together, but they are also instruments of truth, enacting truth being one important way of organizing what people do together.[10] Scientists and other research professionals not only enact truth within their disciplines, they enact it in the larger social worlds in which they take part, by redefining folk activities. This sort of enactment of truth is easy to see in the cases I gave in earlier chapters. The physicians of the crusade gave official definitions of pregnancy, fetal personhood, and the moral character of women, midwives, and physicians. That truth was enacted through collective action that included legislators passing laws and police and court officials enforcing them. It continued to be amplified and enacted throughout the twentieth century; for example, in the control of the profession over training and practice, and in the whole conquest of procreation by physicians and other medical professionals. The physician's campaign involved public, political conflict, but the most significant ways of enacting truth do not. They take place in the universities, where service professionals are trained in the bodies of knowledge that legitimate their professions, and in the places where these professionals practice. And they take place in the activities I mentioned above, on the local, national, and international levels.

---

10. When Richard Rorty and others promote "conversational consensus," they are promoting a way of enacting truth. It is a way that is simultaneously very naive and shrewdly political. It ignores issues of power and authority at the same time that it reinforces the social and political orders of the Western democracies as well as the dominance of Western ways in the world. I must stress that "Western ways" is a totalizing concept that itself ignores the social and political orders, but that is a main theme of this book.

The individualist perspective and the old theory of knowledge, truth and science supported the authority of professionals and allowed them not only to define scientific truth but to make major contributions to the definition of how we should live. Those old perspectives have been so thoroughly criticized within the academic disciplines, by multitudes of conservative, moderate, and radical scholars, that it is no longer intellectually responsible to continue to use them as a support of professional authority and dominance. Nor, of course, is it intellectually responsible to criticize the old foundations and then continue to make authoritative pronouncements using the machinery of power that the old theories helped create and uphold. The old theory of truth, knowledge, and science legitimated the massive practice of bad faith. It was an obstruction to intellectual responsibility and moral responsibility as well.

What is most needed at this juncture is a new understanding of the knowledge that the professional authorities produce, the knowledge that at present plays such a part in answering how we should live. The new understanding must allow professionals to begin to be both intellectually and morally responsible. Most of all, it must allow a responsible understanding of how the activity of the scientists and the activity of the folk are related. To make a start, I'll return to Peter Winch's puzzle.

The conundrum that Peter Winch presented, of the folk rules vs. the social scientists' rules, was primarily a problem in *concept formation*. It was transformed into a problem of relativism and objectivism by those who presupposed an "enlightenment orientation" toward knowledge and truth. The problem of concept formation has been a major theme of the previous chapters of this book, in the questions of official definitions, labels, defining social problems, and so on. The focus in those chapters was on concept formation as a folk activity in which professionals were participants. My approach in this chapter is from within the research professions, and it concerns concept formation as an issue of methodology and theory. I'll begin with Herbert Blumer's notion of sensitizing concepts and Barney Glaser and Anselm Strauss' notion of "discovery of grounded theories."

Concept Formation and the Knowledge Makers

One way to look for a new understanding of knowledge is to try out an alternative to the old understanding of the *language* of science. A different account of scientific language makes a change in the account of knowledge work within research disciplines. Herbert Blumer offered a useful new account with his notion of *sensitizing concepts*. The point of sensitizing concepts is not to categorize phenomena in order to be able to test statements about them as to their truth or falsity. I would say that the point is to sensitize researchers (and perhaps the folk), to social processes. In this way, knowledge is not contained in theories, language, textbooks, or journal articles. In my understanding, which is different in important ways from Blumer's, it means that knowledge is *embodied in sensitized people*. Knowledge (even knowledge in the sciences) is something that people have and act upon.

Blumer himself seemed to accept the old perspective on knowledge and truth for the natural sciences. His notion of sensitizing concepts was one element in his effort to mark out a different territory for the social sciences. He contrasted sensitizing concepts with what he took to be the ideal in mathematics, logic, philosophy, and the natural sciences. Concepts in those sciences, he wrote, must clearly distinguish their instances—how would we confirm or disconfirm a law if we weren't sure whether some particular event was governed by that law or not? Definitive concepts give what is common to the instances—they answer the cry, "define your terms!" Sensitizing concepts are not appropriate for such theories, and in fact, they are not appropriate when confirmation, verification, or falsification are the primary interests.[11]

With sensitizing concepts, Blumer says, "we seem forced to reach what is common by accepting and using what is distinctive to the given empirical instance." This, he said, is due not to the immaturity of sociology but to the nature of the empirical world which is its object of study. That empirical world, after all, is a continuous process in which people interpret what they and others are doing, a world continually made and remade in interaction. The sensitizing concepts guide the user in approaching empirical instances (Blumer, 1969: 148).[12]

Sensitizing concepts are not defined in terms of observation, but they are suited to an empirical science, i.e., a sociology, that gives knowledge of human life. Blumer wrote,

> the empirical social world consists of ongoing group life and one has to get close to this life to know what is going on in it. If one is going to respect the social world, one's problems, guiding conceptions, data, schemes of relationship, and ideas of interpretation have to be faithful to that empirical world. (Blumer, 1969: 38)

Blumer dubbed the researchers' "rules" for capturing the empirical social world, "sensitizing concepts," or "sensitizing instruments."

---

11. In light of philosophical criticisms, definitive concepts may only be important for what are called "instantial theories," theories whose validity is explained primarily in terms of confirmation or falsification of a law in terms of its instances. Few interesting scientific theories are of this sort. Some have considered B. F. Skinner's stimulus-response theories to be instantial. However, it may be that they are better interpreted along grounded theory lines.

12. Like Winch (1958) (though not Winch [1964]), Blumer seems to accept the idealized, objectivist picture of the natural sciences. But see Latour and Woolgar (1986) on scientific practice and the construction of facts and knowledge in the natural sciences.

Sensitizing concepts are developed to investigate a world in which participants are continually creating and changing and reinterpreting the meanings
of their activities. Sensitizing concepts are developed to trace the processes of
human interaction, not capture its products.

I want to stress the fact that "sensitizing concepts" are not and cannot be
the neutral, objective concepts that the "enlightenment orientation"
required. In part, this is because they are not entirely separable from the folk
concepts. For example, even second- or third-order concepts like family,
class, gender, race, and age are socially, politically, and economically generated in the activities of the folk. But those folk concepts are very much
affected by the knowledge-making activities of the professionals who, in fact,
participate in the generation and regeneration of the social order.

Sensitizing concepts are not suited for the old work that was claimed for
scientists—that of accumulating a stock of certified knowledge. The question
is, what are they suited for?

One thing sensitizing concepts are suited for is what Anselm Strauss and
Barney Glaser call "the discovery of grounded theories." According to Glaser
and Strauss, confirmation and falsification are not prime criteria for sociological theories. Rather, the discovery of empirically sound concepts through
analysis is. Glaser and Strauss frame their proposals for both qualitative and
quantitative sociology, but I'll speak in terms of qualitative work here
because it is what I'm familiar with (Glaser and Strauss, 1967).

Developing rich and complex concepts with which to discuss a field study
is the focus of grounded theories. That is, "theories" in this sense are not
some abstract scheme, nor are they sets of lawlike statements from which
observation statements are to be derived. Grounding theories consists in discovering an integrated network of concepts that fit the empirical case under
study in the process of doing the field study itself.

The process includes comparing the study that is under way with other
studies. In this way, sensitizing concepts that are appropriate in other studies
may be used in the present study. I say "used" rather than "applied" because
the concept has to "earn its way" into the present study through the complex
process of interpreting data. Equally important, the sensitizing concept itself
will be amplified and deepened through the comparative use. This would
disqualify the concept as definitive, because it would be classified as vague or
ambiguous, changing meaning from case to case. It would be impossible to
falsify the theories of which these concepts were a part. The point of sensitizing concepts is not confirmation or falsification of theories, however; the
point is the discovery of a fruitful network of concepts.

What is the network of concepts fruitful for? This is a question that must
in large part be illuminated by sensitized researchers and their critics, as they
participate in the creation of the collective life. Outcomes of the work must

be taken into account. But to say something more about that, I have to push the Blumer-Strauss analysis to suit my use of it.

Blumer wrote about sensitizing concepts as an issue of methodology in sociology. I need something broader to take account of the double participation as an issue of responsibility. I also need to bridge the gap between the researchers doing the intellectual and professionally defined work and the researchers as significant moral and political actors. To do so, I'll have to emphasize sensitized researchers as well as sensitizing concepts. On my understanding, the researcher is more a living, sensitized, embodied being than a detached, rational mind formulating abstract hypotheses and theories to test them against observations. The old view was that the researcher came to the research situation with a set of theoretical propositions to be tested. The new view is that the researcher comes *knowing how* to approach the situation in terms of the professional perspective. The researcher is socially embodied. The moral and intellectual questions concern the adequacy of the professional perspective, the sensitizing process, and the sensitizing concepts involved.

This approach integrates work in the social studies of science with accounts of truth, knowledge, and science.[13] I believe it also allows the best interpretation of Thomas Kuhn's discussion of paradigms in the work of natural scientists (in *The Structure of Scientific Revolutions*, at least). Kuhn's researchers know how to approach a research situation because they have been trained under a paradigm, and if they don't know how, no amount of "knowing that" will let them approach it adequately. "Paradigms" are poorly represented as sets of propositions, and it is only archaic methods that lead scholars to represent them that way. Paradigms are better represented as practices, or as collective ways of knowing/doing. The fact that scholarly (including scientific) research is written up for journals, talked through at conferences, and embalmed in textbooks does not mean that scientific knowledge is essentially propositional knowledge, either in the social or the natural sciences. As with Wittgenstein's "language games," the scientist working under a paradigm *knows how* to go on.

As he describes them in *The Structure of Scientific Revolutions*, Kuhnian paradigms are not sets of propositions that are believed by some aggregate of individuals in a discipline. To take them as such is to turn them into abstract products, a funny, disorganized, contradictory kind of "theory."Then the force of Kuhn's breakthrough is lost, and the result is a cacophony of theoretical babble about the incommensurability of languages and theories.

In one of its meanings, Kuhn does define a paradigm in terms of a text; for example, Newton's *Opticks*. However, this text must be understood as a text

---

13. Latour (1987); Traweek (1988); Clarke and Fujimura (1992), and many others.

in use. Its meaning lies in the creative ways masters use it in training sensi-tized researchers, as well as in the work researchers do and the work their fol-lowers do for generation upon generation. If we followed through on the process of this sort of research, the connections between the scientific com-munity and the larger society would also be discovered—connections that the narrow focus of the Kuhn analysis hides. Unfortunately, scholars (and particularly philosophers) have usually analyzed paradigms in abstraction from their use—even those who, like Kuhn, accept the intimate connections between meaning and use. My discussion of sensitized researchers and dou-ble participation is, *in those terms*, an effort to *expand* the notion of use so that it allows researchers to be responsible. However, the danger is that "those terms" may mislead more than help.

The most effective way that paradigms are grasped is through transferring the knowledge of how to do the work to apprentices (or newcomers) so that they too know how to do the work under the paradigm; i.e., so that they become *sensitized* to the subject matter of the field. Once they reach this point, the work they produce will be credible to others in their disciplines. When the newcomers have the training, they also have the latent capacity to know how to make a scientific revolution to a new paradigm; i.e., to a new way of making knowledge in the discipline. A rare outsider trained in a related discipline may know how, but today, laypeople do not know how, even though they may (in the abstract) say the words of a solution.

At this point, I have bumped up against the limits of the interactionist approach. The ideas of sensitizing concepts and discovery of grounded theo-ries are brilliant contributions but in the end, they do not quite take account of the fact that the research situation is a collective act and that the unit of meaning is within that act. They also leave out the direct, emotional nature of the knowing that accompanies the turning point, the gestalt switch.[14] And of course they leave out the commitments to making past and future—those being attributed to folk not the researcher. The lack is due to the social orga-nization of knowledge making in the professions. For the interactionist approach to work, the researchers would have to be sensitized not only by concepts that capture the folk activity per se (as Blumer suggests). They

---

14. I'm talking here about folk knowledge in action. But the mention of a gestalt switch brings up another question I have. As I said above, the idea of sensitizing concepts in many ways fits with Kuhn's description of science. But as Blumer and others developed the notion of sensitizing concepts, particularly in terms of grounded theory, Kuhn's idea of scientific rev-olution is ignored—the necessary creative moment in science when there is a turning point and a gestalt switch to a new perspective. Sensitizing concepts and discovery of grounded the-ory may not quite involve "accumulation" in the old sense. But they are meliorist. They do seem to rely on consensus. Most of all, they do not integrate the fundamental premise that doing sociology is collective activity. This leads me to the question of the professionals' responsibility in the vast collective action for which we generally lack folk concepts.

would need sensitizing concepts to capture the relationship of their own research activity to the folk activity. They would need sensitizing concepts that captured the collective activity of their own profession in relation to the vast collectivities of the folk. In their studies, they would have to include themselves and the collective intrusion and authority of their professions. The interactionist sociology does not offer sensitizing concepts to do this work. It does offer concepts and research useful to understanding the importance of the activities of professionals.[15] But these are concepts for the participant-observer. They are not reflexive. As these sociologists report, with great sensitivity, on the professional authority they uncover, they rely on their own professional authority and the place that is set for them in the social order. I do so myself in writing this book. How could we do otherwise?[16]

Some Positive Examples

At this point, I'll give a few examples of some work by authors who are making a serious effort to be morally and intellectually responsible.

In *The Dialectical Biologist*, Richard Levins and R.C. Lewontin offer criticisms of research efforts (e.g., the human genome project) and theory within biology, but they also criticize the practices within the institution of science:

> The demand for objectivity, the separation of observation and reporting from the researchers' wishes, which is so essential for the development of science, becomes the demand for separation of thinking from feeling. This promotes moral detachment in scientists which, reinforced by specialization and bureaucratization, allows them to work on all sorts of dangerous and harmful projects with indifference to the human consequences. The idealized egalitarianism of a community of scholars has shown itself to be a rigid hierarchy of scientific authorities integrated into the general class structure of the society and modeled on the corporation. And where the pursuit of truth has survived, it has become increasingly narrow, revealing a growing contradiction between the sophistication of science [in the small within the laboratory] and the irrationality of the scientific enterprise as a whole. (Levins and Lewontin, 1985: 225–26)

The authors write as natives here, out of personal knowledge of the collective work in which they were trained and the institutions in which they earn their daily bread. I like the paragraph because it links the abstract method

---

15. See for example, Gusfield (1981); Freidson (1970, 1986); and especially Nathanson (1991).

16. This is a problem that many sociologists I know struggle with. See the feminist essays in Fonow and Cook (1991), especially chapters 1 and 8; and Smith (1987; 1990a, b). For a postmodern approach, see Schneider (1991) and references from Schneider. See also Stewart (1993).

and theory of science with the person of the researcher, with the way science is done in the United States as a collective activity, and with moral issues and outcomes. The authors are sensitized in ways many academic researchers in the United States are not, a fact that contributes to their being dissenting scientists.

To a degree, Levins and Lewontin rely on sensitizing concepts out of their interpretation of Marxism. That, plus their own first-hand experience, allows them to link the abstract claims about the universality of science with the collective action through which science comes to have the appearance of universality.

> Science entered the Third World as a form of intellectual domination. After the troops depart, the investments remain; after direct ownership is removed, managerial skills, patents, textbooks, and journals remain, repeating the message that only by adopting their ways can we progress, only by going to their universities can we learn; only by emulating their universities can we teach. (Levins and Lewontin, 1985: 227)

I'm not quoting this analysis to say that it is the truth and the certified knowledge. I'm saying that it is the kind of reflection that raises questions about professionals' moral and intellectual responsibility. I particularly like Levins and Lewontin as examples because their being sensitized to the double participation has led them to propose a different biological theory, one that seems to me intellectually more responsible. I say that wearing my sociological and philosophical hats, and recognizing the moribund epistemology and ontology that lies at the foundation of the biological theories they criticize.

Feminist scholars have often insisted that science must deal with the relation between the researcher and the researched. One anthology of feminist articles is entitled, *Beyond Methodology: Feminist Scholarship as Lived Research.* In a paper reprinted in that anthology, Joan Acker, Kate Barry, and Johanna Esseveld set some criteria for adequate research. They write that the active voice of the subject should be heard. They go on,

> the theoretical reconstruction must be able to account for the investigator as well as those who are investigated. The interpretation must locate the researcher in the social structure and also provide a reconstruction of the social relations that produce this research situation and the enterprise of research itself. For example . . . what makes it possible to raise this research problem at this time, in this place, in this society? (Acker, et al., 1991: 145–46).

The reconstruction (they write) should "reveal the underlying social relations that eventuate in the daily lives we are studying." Revealing the underlying relations requires changing the relation between researcher and researched, as Dorothy Smith and others have often argued. I believe that in the end, it requires changing the professions so that professionals may take their moral responsibility seriously.

In the United States, feminist research and teaching in the academy grew out of the mass movements of the 1960s and 1970s. From the beginning, feminists worked at changing their disciplines and the academic professions, not simply to introduce new academic topics and new programs of women's studies, but to change the way classes were taught and research presented. They also insisted that women's experience, including their own, be brought into the picture. As feminists in the movement, they were sensitized differently from traditional academics because of their experience in political action and because of their experience as women, including their relationship with other women. At that time, feminist researchers also developed a network of sensitizing concepts that allowed bridging academy and world. They distinguished sex from gender and insisted that gender be taken seriously as a category of analysis; they introduced notions of patriarchy, male domination, and women's oppression; and they used the notion of liberation, sometimes even insisting that to be feminist, the work had to be liberatory. I have questions about the adequacy of many of those concepts (as I do about Marxist ones) but the important point here is that the feminists used them to sensitize researchers, teachers, and students in ways important to understanding double participation.

I said that I have reservations about the categories of domination and oppression and the idea that feminist academic work must be liberatory. My reservations derive from the fact that professionals do their work in institutions that are institutions of governance willy-nilly, and that includes feminists and Marxists, as well as the crustiest, unreflective, "nonpolitical types." The notions of domination, oppression, and liberation are created in the heat of collective action. I mean that they are folk concepts in a serious sense suited for movements; for example, the women's movement of the 1970s or the syndicalist movement I discussed in chapters 2 and 4. Their meaning has to be discovered in action—folk action is the basis of the creation, not academic theory. So the important question for feminists in the United States at the moment has to do with the relation between researcher and those in whose name the researcher allegedly does liberatory work (and not primarily the relation between researcher and researched). That relation can't be cooked up out of some abstract theory. It must be made in action, with real people, in face-to-face collective work.

In the last section of this chapter, I'll mull over that issue by tracing through some of the history of the professions in which scientists and other academic knowledge makers work.

Autonomy, Loyalty, and How We Should Live

In the United States, the academic professions were born and the modern departmental structure of colleges and universities was made after the Civil War, as the nation modernized. The view among some of the elite was that what the nation needed for leadership was not the old-style gentlemen who shared social and moral values in a stable society (as the gentlemen of the physicians' crusade did) but trained experts who could guide social change. At the turn of the century, the progressive belief was that the nation needed intelligent specialists to advise the statesmen. The intelligent specialists became professionals, and in fact, the elaboration of the professions was claimed to be a central feature of a civilized society.[17]

One of the important features of the professional organization of knowledge has been the autonomy of those who made knowledge. In general, professionals were supposed to be free of lay control (except through laws and licensing) for they were supposed to be subject to self-policing according to their codes of ethics. At any rate, lay people were supposed to trust the professionals' special knowledge—the motto was *credat emptor*, not *caveat emptor*, as Everett Hughes remarked (1984: 376). Within academic disciplines, researchers were said to be autonomous in the sense that they were supposed to be free to do research on any topic, subject to the criteria set within their disciplines. For example, even today, the code of ethics of the American Association of University Professors states that these professionals have a particular obligation to promote conditions of free inquiry and to further public understanding of academic freedom (see chapter 6). This has been an intrinsic part of the search for knowledge.

What free inquiry or autonomy amounted to had to be worked out in practice. Mary Furner has claimed that within the social sciences, autonomy gradually came to be defined in a way that limited freedom to dissent and prevented academic professionals from advocating controversial social policies (Furner, 1975). She traced the process through academic freedom cases around the turn of the century. Labor agitation and socialist politics threatened the wealthy, conservative board members of the private and public universities. Left-leaning faculty members faced losing their jobs, and some in fact were fired. In the academic freedom cases that followed, autonomy came to be defined in terms of objectivity—freedom in the sense of not being pressured to tailor work to suit powerful, interested parties. According to Furner, the trade-off was that the professionals were to avoid advocating "controversial" views.[18]

---

17. Herbert Spencer made the remark on the elaboration of the professions. See discussions in Hughes (1984).

18. The above four paragraphs are paraphrased from Addelson and Potter (1991).

Perhaps Furner states the compromise a little too strongly. However, it does seem that there was a conservative damper on academic advocacy in the United States until the 1960s, and even today, the damper operates by withholding rewards—thus the stress on academic freedom in the AAUP statement. But there does seem to be a rather blatant incoherence in the compromise. If it is scientists' responsibility to produce truth (or at least, "the best knowledge of the day"), then surely they must sometimes advocate "controversial views." Isn't that what Galileo did? Isn't that the engine of progressive civilization? Isn't that why nations need trained professionals and "experts at their posts"? This way of framing the difficulty makes it a surface problem that might be explained away. But it opens a window to something more serious. My own belief is that the incoherence lies deeper, in the folk concept of a profession itself. For that folk concept simultaneously casts professionals as authoritative participants in the society and as detached and disinterested observers standing above the controversies.

In claiming to produce knowledge, the traditional professionals put themselves in competition with activists. In previous chapters, the activists I discussed claimed that the opposition's solutions were false or had disastrous consequences, and that their own way was the correct route to rationality, goodness, or truth—in short, the proper road to the future. Sanger, for example, used two different methods of arguing for her truth. One was an oppositional method in which she used syndicalist methods to learn how the liberal ways were both systemic and wrong (unjust, immoral, oppressive, deceptive, etc.). The second method Sanger used was that of friendly criticism from within. She accepted the syndicalist politics and she accepted the problem of industrial justice (or labor under capital). She saw that the politics had to be extended to include the problem of woman and the child, with all the active learning that was necessary to pose and resolve that problem.

Sanger's work, and that of the other syndicalists, was judged in the heat of the action. People argued out the coherence of the theories and strategies in word, print, and most of all in deed. They judged their usefulness, accuracy, and truth, and whatever other evaluations they believed to be appropriate. They put their lives behind their judgments by joining the actions—or refusing to join, as the case might be. Some of them lost their lives, some lost their livelihoods.

These perfectly proper activist ways of enacting truth, and the perfectly proper methods, were incorporated into the folk concept of the scholarly ways. But they were incorporated side by side with the ideas of objectivity and detachment—ideas necessary for political survival of the professions and the academy. And thus the incoherence.

This incoherence was there at the heart of the early understanding of the place of scholars and professionals. In progressive era terms, scholars are supposed to play a part in governance by giving statesmen expert advice. And scholars and other professionals do play a large role today, not simply as advisors to governors but as makers and transmitters of the knowledge used to benefit some groups of people and to label others. As I said above, they are agents of governance. But we scholars do not play a part on an equal footing with other activists. The tension in the role comes from the way it is legitimated. Scholars, particularly scientists, are supposed to be detached from the fray. We are said to give the best knowledge of the day, or to be experts sensitized to nature and the social order. The heart of the incoherence lies in the fact that we scholars are supposed to be at once detached and engaged, at once observers and activists, at once knowledge makers and expert advisors.

For traditional scholars, objectivity has required simultaneously being politically neutral and being loyal "to the nation." Understanding of what counts as loyalty has changed over the century. For many years, being a "Red" meant being disloyal—thus the purges of the teens and twenties and during the McCarthy years. That cruder understanding has been fought down—for the moment at least. But assuming that experts are to advise the governors presupposes loyalty, even if it is that of "the loyal opposition." The loyal opposition, after all, stays within the political and economic frameworks, and the institutional frameworks of the professions.

The academic professions survived by simultaneously being loyal and appearing to be objective. "Objectivity" was carefully worked out in practice. Objectivity was based not only on the individualist perspective on knowledge, but also on the social organization of the professions and higher education itself. In the end, politics, economics, and science could be distinguished because the occupations of politician, businessman, and scientist were distinguished. It was a division of work and a division of role, not a division of fact and value, and not a question of truth and reality.

My point here is that since the turn of the century in the United States, "objective knowledge" has been defined to suit the way that professionals participate in the myriad folk activities of nation and world. The collapse of the enlightenment orientation has had virtually no effect on the production of knowledge by professionals. In the humanities and qualitative social sciences, there has been a flurry of writings about relativism, constructivism, postmodernism, and the like. But the new products have a status quite like the earlier, "objective" knowledge. Gusfield may declare truth to be dead and that his research only produces "an ironic sense of alternatives" (Gusfield, 1981). But students still study his books in college, scholars still quote them, and groups concerned with drunk driving still invite him to speak as an expert. It is a difference without a difference.

When Richard Rorty disavowed the enlightenment orientation, he wrote that he (and "we") have no choice but to be ethnocentric, no place to stand but within the relatively decent free, progressive political culture characteristic of the North Atlantic democracies. *He* was recommending loyalty, but loyalty hidden under a sophisticated and rationally argued philosophical position (Rorty, 1986, 1989).

The loyalty can be hidden because the very folk concepts of the professions incorporate that "relatively decent" political *and* economic culture. And yet, as Everett Hughes wrote,

> There is more than one way of being ethnocentric. One can think so exclusively in the terms of his own social world that he simply has no set of concepts for comparing one social world with another. He can believe so deeply in the ways and ideas of his own world that he has no point of reference for discussing those of other peoples, times, and places. Or he can be so engrossed in his own world that he lacks curiosity about any other; others simply do not concern him. (Hughes, 1984: 475)

To a large degree, the academic professions are incubators for ethnocentrism. Partha Chatterjee wrote about attempts to avoid Eurocentrism by an act of choice:

> None of us engaged in the academic practices of the social sciences can make such a choice, [Eurocentrism] is in fact the very condition of our intellectual discourse—in the ways it is framed through disciplinary practices in the universities and in the international academic community—that forces us to speak the language of European philosophy. (Chatterjee and Taylor, 1990: 120)

Eurocentrism is the condition of the discourse in the natural sciences as well, though it is more deeply hidden. "Eurocentrism" does not exist only in language. It exists in the folk concept of the sciences and the social organization of knowledge, and it is by no means only Eurocentrism. The emphasis on words—dialogue, conversation, discourse—is one that grows out of class practices, particularly those of academics, politicians, and elites of various sorts. It is also a "gender-centrism," with an emphasis on what was once called "men's sphere." The fact that men and women now take part in the practices, and the fact that professionals in non-European societies institute them, does not affect the "centrisms." And that of course is Chatterjee's point.

Within the United States, we academic professionals tend to be dupers extraordinaire, though dupers who have forgotten the double participation we recognized in high school and who now tend to identify with the official standpoints we profess. For most successful academics (I mean those of us who have achieved certification and a job), the individualistic, planning outlook that is embodied in the schools seems to have worked out in our lives.

That perspective is embodied in the folk concepts making up the institutions in which we work. So most of us are loyal willy-nilly, most of us believe in the relatively decent morality of the North Atlantic Democracies, quite in harmony with the universalizing, dominating nature of the politics and economics that attend it.

When I write these things about loyalty, I am referring to the conservative nature of academia, particularly among the prestigious and influential. I certainly don't mean that individual academics are never disloyal, intentionally and with purpose. Of course some of us are. I also don't mean to say that individual academics are never accused of producing disloyal or partisan or otherwise biased knowledge—of course we are. But in the first case, we are publicly accused as activists or traitors. In the second, we are usually accused within the professional ranks themselves, as part of the professional self-policing operation. In both cases, we are labeled as deviant, and the cases are used to set the boundaries of normal, objective, academic knowledge making. This labeling, this creation of insiders and outsiders, serves to hide the question that is important. That central question is: What is the participatory perspective of the knowledge makers? What is the "double participation" in which the professional knowledge makers really take part? How may we best uncover the outcomes of this double participation?

These are questions that concern responsibility. But they are also questions that concern freedom. Academic freedom in terms of autonomy or objectivity offers a good weapon to use in some necessary battles. But at root, the freedom that has appeared in the century-long process of professionalization is a freedom for collective possibilities. At the turn of the century, scholars were as creative as the syndicalist workers, and a good deal more successful. When they organized into professions, and when they organized the university departments, they created collective possibilities for themselves and generations of scholarly progeny. They created them in such a way that the possibilities could be regenerated, decade after decade, through the renewed creative possibilities for the nation. And they of course systematically excluded other possibilities and made other ways deviant and "outside," not "our" ways.

To claim, with the progressives, that experts are needed to advise governors, is to say what the broader participation of academic professionals ought to be. The claim legitimates the double participation and names it. Some feminist scholars (and other rebels) have renamed the double participation. Rather than pretending detachment and neutrality while being loyal *to* the status quo, they embrace partisanship and the liberation of women (or others) *from* the status quo. In doing so, they rely on academic freedom and the authority and institutional resources due to their professional jobs. They increased "freedom" in the sense of creating collective possibilities. The question is what the possibilities are and who they are created for. Women's studies has found a place among the disciplines, and women researchers have found a place in the academy with access to the usual means of exercising cognitive authority. But whether that increases freedom for women is another question.

During the 1970s in the United States, when there was a mass women's movement, it flooded into the academy and many women professionals gave expression to the liberatory concepts, theories, and actions of the activists—and they were often activists themselves. The professionals were, to a certain degree, sensitized, living, embodied instruments of the liberatory movement. Their work was liberatory, but only to the degree that the movement was. Today there is no mass, liberatory women's movement in the United States. For the most part, feminist professionals exercise their authority in the same channels that traditional professionals do—and that of course includes acting as policy advisors on defining social problems. The outcomes of the work must be understood, and the double participation of feminist academics must be carefully considered.

It is not only the old traditionals but the old rebels who have to ask searching questions about moral responsibility. I believe that Joan Acker, Kate Barry, and Johanna Esseveld were asking those questions in the remarks I quoted above, and Dorothy Smith has been committed to asking them. There are no simple answers (they would agree). But there are also no simple justifications, either in terms of "experts at their posts" or in terms of serving women (or minorities or the working class) by making liberatory theory.

Today, at the end of the twentieth century, what is the place of academic professionals? What ought it to be? What is scholarly freedom today, and what collective possibilities are in the offing, and for whom? What sort of knowledge should the authoritative knowledge makers make, and for whom? What are we sensitized to, and whom do we serve? How can we understand the outcomes of our work? What is it to do morally and intellectually responsible work?

There are no answers to these questions if we stick to definitions of responsibilities under the old folk concept of the academic professions (which is, despite doubts and historical transformations, still the one in practice). The question of responsibility must be answered by asking, What is our freedom? What might our collective possibilities become? What moral passage might we embark upon? These are open questions that have to be answered in practice, as we professional knowledge makers do our work reflexively so that we may in the end do it responsibly. But the process cannot begin without an intimate knowledge of who the "we's" ought to be, and who is to make the collective possibilities, and for whom.

That, of course, is the question of how we should live.

8

Self and Social Order

IN THE PREVIOUS CHAPTERS, I have considered the questions of how
we should live from something of a public perspective—reformers making
moral problems public, professionals exercising cognitive authority, philosophers and sociologists writing moral theory.[1] It may seem to some readers
that a collectivist moral theory, whatever use it has for these "public" matters, hides what is most important about genuine morality. After all, the self
seems to be central in questions of how we should live, and in moral questions of freedom. Autonomy, creativity, and personal development and fulfillment seem to be what is morally fundamental, and all of them seem to
involve the self.

By emphasizing the collective processes of creating selves and worlds, it
may seem that I have obliterated the most intimate concerns of morality, the
vivid features of each person's felt and lived experience. It may seem that, in
the name of human collective creativity, I have disregarded the source of creativity in the inner individual. I think these are serious questions, even
though they carry the odor of the old dualisms. In facing them, I rely on
work done by other feminist theorists in ethics and psychology and on the
work of a long-ago feminist novelist. I believe that my own work offers a
complement and corrective to theirs.

Many feminists have criticized the notion of an autonomous self, a notion
that has dominated psychology, philosophy, and education in the United
States. They disputed the "masculinist" idea that moral development
requires a process of separating oneself from others. They argued against

---

1. I wrote the first draft of this chapter as a paper in the fall of 1976, and I benefitted from
Shawn Pyne's criticisms and from comments by members of my "Philosophy and Women"
class that term.

defining maturation in terms of increasing separation. They refused the emphasis on development of an individual self through separation rather than on development of selves in relationship.[2]

Feminist philosopher Caroline Whitbeck described the "masculinist" separation process as requiring an oppositional "self-other" relationship. Its philosophical foundation lay in the individualist ontology I have described in the previous chapters. Whitbeck suggested an ontology in which the moral world has its foundation in *relations* among people, not in autonomous individuals. Institutions, rules, roles, and professions are constructed upon that foundation. She wrote of the "self-others" relation, rather than the oppositional, "self-other" relation. It is real, empirically existing others that the self relates to and it is in those relations that the self comes to be a self. She saw a paradigm in the mother-child relationship, in which both mother and child care for each other.[3] That "caring" paradigm expresses a normative element in the ontology.

Jean Baker Miller developed a psychological theory that suits the philosophical ontology of self-others. There is an "interacting sense of self," that is present even in infants. Miller wrote,

> from the moment of birth, this internal representation is of a self that is in active interchange with other selves. Moreover, this interaction has one central characteristic, and that is that people are attending to the infant—most importantly, attending to the infant's core of being, which means the infant's emotions—and the infant is responding in the same way, that is, to the other person's emotions. The earliest mental representation of the self, then, is of a self whose core—which is emotional—is attended to by the other(s) and in turn begins to attend to the emotions of the other(s). Part of this internal image of oneself includes feeling the other's emotions and acting on them as they are in interplay with one's own emotions. This means that the beginnings of the concept of self are not those of a static and lone self being ministered to by another . . . but rather of a self inseparable from dynamic interaction. (Jordan et al., 1991: 14)

Miller wrote that development of the self doesn't involve increasing separation. Rather, maintaining relationships is always the important thing, as is doing for others. But one maintains them with an increasingly developed sense of one's own capacities. The relationships with others become more complex. The premise is that one person develops as the others develop, and so everyone develops in the relationship. According to Miller, women use this

---

2. See the good review of the femininist theorists in Tong (1993).

3. Whitbeck offers self-others as an alternative ontology. In Whitbeck (1983, 1984), she takes a paradigm to be the mother-child relation.

premise in practice. And so her psychology also has a normative element, though attached to an empirical assertion.

I've claimed throughout these chapters that not only is the self created in relationships but that the social order is created in relationships as well. In fact, there is a serious difficulty (often noted) in taking the normative step of using the mother-child relationship (or some other caring relationship) as a paradigm. As I said in chapter 1, the mother-child relationship is generated and understood within particular social structures, and the relationship in turn regenerates social structures (generation and regeneration being creative processes, of course).

It may be true that people and other living things develop always in relationship, but *the nature of development depends on the nature of the relationships*. In the central sense, relationships are always with particular others. But the nature of the relationships must be seen in light of the social order itself. This means that Miller's work on development of the self in relationship needs to be integrated with work that can show the nature of relationships as they are generated and regenerated in collective action. Miller's understanding of the self is that it is active and interactive. Explanations of the nature of the self's relationships in terms of social environments (or structures) acting on the self wouldn't be appropriate. However, under the collectivist perspective, the social order itself is understood in terms of action and interaction. And so there seems to be some compatibility between Miller's psychology of the development of a human self and the collectivist perspective on social life and morality. The question is how to show it.

In this chapter, I try to illuminate the compatibility by discussing the moral development of a fictional character, Edna Pontellier, hero of Kate Chopin's *The Awakening*. I present the story in a way that (I hope) shows both that the social order is generated and regenerated in collective action, and that the self develops in relationship with others.

Kate Chopin's story has very often been taken to be the tale of a woman striving for autonomy and freedom in a world that oppresses and represses women. I interpret that striving not as an attempt at separation but as a struggle for freedom and self-overcoming within relationship. As Jean Baker Miller says, it is not because of relationships per se that women are oppressed, rather the problem has to do with the nature of the relationships. In seeing Edna Pontellier's moral passage as a collectively created, I examine the *nature* of her relationships in the patriarchal, bourgeois world of New Orleans at the end of the nineteenth century. It was because of the nature of the relationships that she rebelled and began her passage. In the end, it was because of the nature of the relationships that she could not succeed.

The crux of Edna's triumph and tragedy is a distorted, warped understanding of women and the mother-child relationship, one that was in fact operative at the close of the nineteenth century among the higher classes in the United States. It was a fragmented and truncated understanding of eros, of procreation—one that Margaret Sanger fought to overcome. Edna Pontellier's passage is a struggle for moral self-overcoming (I use Nietzsche's term, though not his analysis). Her self must develop in relationship with others, but she can find these others only on the margins of respectable society. She strives to see the face of eros, and to a degree she succeeds. But the dynamic, collective action of her society is to preserve the truncated vision. Most of all, the preservation operates through the collective possibilities open to her husband, Léonce Pontellier, for preserving the class position of his family. They are also collective possibilities for preserving the respectability of the bourgeoisie in turn-of-the-century New Orleans.

Edna's story lets me show the dynamic creation of deviants and the regeneration of self and social order. And so it also allows me to hint that a social order may be shown to be humanly oppressive through a single person's passage as well as through revolutionary, collective passages like those of the syndicalists. And it allows me to hint that one may come to glimpse a moral truth and reveal the face of eros, even when eros is truncated and deformed in the official understanding and enactment.

The Awakening

Kate Chopin was born in St. Louis in 1851. She began writing after her husband's death, to support herself and her six children, and she lived out her life in the Midwest and South. She died in 1904, as the modern world was dawning in the United States.

Chopin published *The Awakening* in 1899. There are two intertwined themes I draw out of the novel. One concerns the nature of the relationships, including ways available to members of the respectable upper classes to maintain their own class positions, and, in the process, to regenerate the dominant position of their class itself. They also include ways that were available for regenerating the patriarchal order. The other theme concerns a woman's moral passage as she develops her self in relationship. In the end, Edna Pontellier's effort fails, not simply due to the nature of the relationships available to her but most of all because those people with whom she is in relationship do not have the vision and courage to take the moral step.

Superficially, Edna's passage might be read as that of a woman coming to moral or personal autonomy in the liberal sense. Early in the novel, Chopin writes,

> Mrs. Pontellier was beginning to realize her position in the universe as a human being, and to recognize her relations as an individual to the world

186

within and about her. This may seem like a ponderous weight of wisdom to descend upon the soul of a young woman of twenty-eight—perhaps more wisdom than the Holy Ghost is usually pleased to vouchsafe to any woman. (Chopin, 1976: 14)

But Edna's search did not lead to a higher level of moral reasoning, nor to a life plan that captured her idea of the good. Rather, it was a passage to the discovery of moral truth—a local truth about her own social world and an archetypal truth about relationship and life. Edna faced the truth without being able to resolve it or to name it. The novel unfolds Edna's route to the final paradox.

The particular conflict of the novel lies in Edna's attempts to make the voyage of self-overcoming as they clash with her husband Léonce's attempts to maintain a family persona appropriate to their class. In conventional terms, Edna's voyage of discovery is a process of becoming deviant: of becoming an adultress, a loose woman. If Edna were labeled such, there would be a taint on the family and a danger of its becoming déclassé. Léonce's effort is to prevent the status passage, both to save Edna and to save the family reputation. The respectability and reliability of the Pontellier family is essential if Léonce is to maintain his business connections and if the family is to maintain its class position. The problem here is analogous to the problem the Hamilton Mill operatives faced (see chapter 3). The difference is that they could maintain their high moral character by ostracizing the offender, but Léonce cannot very well ostracize his wife without tainting himself, his children, and his (and Edna's) kin. In moving to maintain respectability, he uses means ready to hand in his social world, for the problem is one that the class as a whole must deal with. If Léonce is concerned with maintaining a respectable family persona, his social world is concerned with maintaining a respectable class persona. In both cases, this requires hiding deviance by one means or another.

In maintaining a respectable persona, Léonce and other members of his class also regenerate the nature of the relationships through which Edna must somehow make her passage. Edna's world was marked by patriarchal dominance as well as class dominance. In the strongest terms, it was a world in which she, as a woman, wife, and mother, is supposed to nurture others and care for their selves, but without care for her own self. Or perhaps, in another sense, Edna's was the "the undernurtured woman's voice outside the 'man's world.'" (Smith, 1990a: 3). In the language of the "man's world" (which women also use), Edna would be labeled an outsider, a deviant, a fallen woman, a victim of irrational passions. From the inside, Edna Pontellier is an "innocent child," because there is no way to enact or name her values in the traditional, patriarchal, bourgeois world she lives in. And yet, for her to succeed in her self-overcoming, her new self must be collectively enacted. She must develop in relationship with others, as they develop.

In her novel, Chopin wrote fictional biography, not history, and it was the biography of a character whose moral passage constituted a criticism of her society. But in writing the novel, Chopin herself made a moral criticism of her own society. Chopin's novel was labeled—denounced and banned from bookstores and libraries. Willa Cather diagnosed Edna Pontellier as suffering from a disease that attacks women of brains (or at least, "rudimentary brains"), women who abuse their nerves with the result that the nerves get even.[4] Sharon O'Brien suggests that Cather feared that passion would prevent the self from rising to larger human concerns. In Edna's case (and in Margaret Sanger's), the moral passage required passion and leaving the old explanations behind. I'll return to the problem of "larger human concerns" at the close of the chapter, since it is a core issue for a collectivist moral theory and the idea of self in relationship.

The movement of Edna's passage in this context is a shadow play of hidden and public, of dream and reality. But although the dynamic of the passage takes place as a struggle between Edna's efforts toward self-overcoming and her husband's efforts to maintain respectability, Chopin is careful not to paint husband Léonce Pontellier in black and white. He is neither a blatant tyrant in the home nor a man without love for his wife. He fulfills his conventional responsibilities: they live very comfortably, in a fine house with servants, and he is generally considerate to Edna despite her shortcomings. He is a conventional man, and one who struggles to preserve their comfortable life. Throughout the novel, he maneuvers to hide Edna's missteps, to name them in a way that maintains the family respectability. He is fighting off what he sees as a status passage—Edna's slipping from being a respectable wife to her being a loose and dissolute woman. His is a conventional and very pragmatic vision of her passage. He struggles to maintain the conventional nature of their relationships.

It is by portraying Edna in marriage to this respectable man that Chopin is able to show an immorality in the fabric of her society, one not due to "the destroyer" of womanly virtue or the patriarchal tyranny of a husband over a wife—in fact, Chopin shows the resistance and negotiation that lie behind the respectable appearance of a patriarchal marriage. She gives a criticism of respectability itself as it was lived in upper-class New Orleans at the turn of the century. But in the end, her heroine cannot find the freedom she needs

---

4. I thank Jeanne and Barbara Addelson for bringing the Cather review to my attention. For a useful analysis of the Cather review, see O'Brien (1975). O'Brien argues that Cather fears passion will overwhelm the individual and prevent developing the artistic, intellectual, and emotional self.

for her newly forming self—the collective possibilities are not there, and particularly they are not there for her relationships to her children.

But it is time to turn to Edna Pontellier's awakening.

The Metamorphoses

Edna Pontellier is an upper-middle-class woman, married with two children, living in New Orleans. She has trouble living up to the ideal of what Kate Chopin calls a "mother woman." In the novel, the mother woman is exemplified by Adele Ratignolle:

> One of those women who idolized their children, worshiped their husbands, and esteemed it a holy privilege to efface themselves as individuals and grow wings as ministering angels. (Chopin, 1976: 8)

Adele Ratignolle also embodies an ideal of womanly beauty and grace. At one point, Edna stands watching her:

> The fair woman walked down the long line of galleries with the grace and majesty which queens are sometimes supposed to possess. Her little ones ran to meet her. Two of them clung to her white skirts, the third she took from its nurse and with a thousand endearments, bore it along in her own fond, encircling arms. Though as everybody well knew, the doctor had forbidden her to lift so much as a pin. (Chopin, 1976: 13)

Adele is in fact a healthy, capable woman. Her hands are always busy sewing for the children. Her household is well run, her meals delicious. She is a fine hostess. She is her husband's companion and finds his conversation fascinating. In short, she is an ideal, bourgeois, American woman of the time.

Even at the beginning, Edna Pontellier fails the ideal, and her husband has a certain vague dissatisfaction with her:

> It would have been a difficult matter for Mr. Pontellier to define to his own satisfaction or anyone else's wherein his wife failed in her duty toward their children. It was something he felt rather than perceived; and he never voiced the feeling without subsequent regret and ample atonement. (Chopin, 1976: 8)

Still and all, Edna starts out as a conventional woman, and we can see it in what happens in a scene early in the novel.

Edna and the children are spending the summer at Grand Isle, a Creole resort. Léonce Pontellier is with the family on weekends, spending the week in New Orleans at his brokerage business. On this particular Sunday night, he has been playing billiards with the clubmen who frequent Klein's Hotel just down the way from the resort. He returns at eleven o'clock, high spirited, wanting to share his experiences with Edna. She is overcome with sleep and answers with half utterances.

> He thought it very discouraging that his wife, who was the sole object of his existence, evinced so little interest in things which concerned him, and valued so little his conversation. (Chopin, 1976: 5)

Under the pretext of fatherly concern, he prods at the children until they begin to shift and talk in their sleep. Then he goes back and tells Edna that one of them has a high fever and needs looking after. She makes a brief inspection. He reproaches her with inattention to him and neglect of the children. Then he goes to bed and falls asleep.

Edna is now fully awake and goes out to sit on the porch. She begins to cry.

> She could not have told why she was crying. Such experiences as the foregoing were not uncommon in her married life. They seemed never before to have weighed much against the abundance of her husband's kindness and uniform devotion which had come to be tacit and self understood. An indescribable oppression, which seemed to generate in some unfamiliar part of her consciousness, filled her whole being with a vague anguish. It was like a shadow, like a mist passing across her soul's summer day. It was strange and unfamiliar; it was a mood. She did not sit there inwardly upbraiding her husband, lamenting at Fate, which had directed her footsteps to the path which they had taken. She was just having a good cry all to herself. (Chopin, 1976: 6–7)

Here I think we not only have a picture of Edna as a less-than-ideal woman, we have a glimpse of some of the controls that she will have to overcome to move on. She is critical of her husband's treatment and feels an affront to her moral humanity—she feels it through the "indescribable oppression." But she has no way to express this in terms of their conventional understanding. So she slides to a conventional interpretation: "it was strange and unfamiliar; it was a mood." A mood, after all, isn't anything to take seriously as a moral criticism of a relationship. To move to the next stage, Edna had to begin taking her inner thoughts and feelings seriously instead of dismissing them through conventional categories. She had to become candid, with herself at least.

Edna Pontellier came originally from old Presbyterian stock in Kentucky, daughter of a man who at one time raised race horses and a woman who was apparently driven to her grave as a victim of a patriarchal male. At Grand Isle, she is exposed to a more open, intimate society. Members of the Creole group understand how to behave as proper members of that society. However, Edna's background is quite different and the openness and intimacy have a different meaning for her. This is an important factor in her self-overcoming. Also important are her friendships with Robert Lebrun and Adele Ratignolle.

Robert is the son of the widowed owner of Grand Isle. He and Edna are nearly the same age, and Kate Chopin mentions that they look like brother and sister. Their relationship is one of more or less equality in which Robert only plays at protecting Edna, without the patriarchal underpinnings of Léonce Pontellier's genuine protection. He provides the romantic interest. Friend Adele is a wise and happy woman—a warning not to dismiss conventional wives out of hand. From Adele, Edna learns about candor, and in the end, she also learns what she cannot overcome.

These things offer the background for Edna's self-overcoming. Most important in making the first moves, perhaps, is the fact that she is momentarily relieved of her usual duties while she is at Grand Isle.

Dream and Reality

Edna's upbringing allowed her a way of preserving herself by dividing dream and reality—she learned to separate them.

> At a very early period, she had apprehended instinctively the dual life—that outward existence which conforms, the inward life which questions. (Chopin, 1976: 14)

and again,

> She had all her life been accustomed to harbor thoughts and emotions that never voiced themselves. They had never taken the form of struggles. They belonged to her and were her own and she entertained the conviction that they concerned no one but herself. (Chopin, 1976: 11)

The advantage here is that Edna's own reactions and feelings are preserved rather than denied and repressed. The danger is that they may simply be held inside and labeled as dream, without being acted on or even spoken of with others. They emerge into daylight in an interlude with Adele.

One sunny morning, the two women walk to the beach together, arm in arm, under a huge white sunshade. They sit alone by the sea and have a moment which is physically and spiritually intimate. Edna talks of an image of life from her girlhood, in which she moves alone through a meadow of tall grass, an endless sea of green. She talks of the dreams of her maidenhood and her infatuations with a cavalry officer and a famous tragedian. She remembers leaving these dreams behind with her marriage to Léonce Pontellier.

As the devoted wife of a man who worshipped her, she felt she would take her place with a certan dignity in the world of reality, closing the portals forever behind her upon the realm of romance and dreams. (Chopin, 1976: 19)

Edna, at that time, saw her possibilities for action in the world, and the possibilities of her whole and future lifetime, in the context of marriage. That (she felt) was the nature of the relationships in which she lived. That was reality. She has never before taken her romantic fancies to be real enough to mention to another person. In the course of sitting there with Adele Ratignolle, she sees her passionless attachment to Mr. Pontellier, and she sees the impulsiveness of her fondness for the children. Her candor lies not so much in revealing all this to Adele as in revealing it to herself:

Edna did not reveal so much as all this to Madame Ratignolle that summer day when they sat with faces turned to the sea. But a good part of it escaped her. She had put her head down on Madame Ratignolle's shoulder. She was flushed and felt intoxicated with the sound of her own voice and the unaccustomed taste of candor. It muddled her like wine, or like a first breath of freedom. (Chopin, 1976: 20)

At this point, Edna's "freedom" seems to be to admit, even as "mere" thoughts and feelings, how her world is, apart from the conventional interpretation of what she and her world should be. Before, she effaced herself. Now she begins to develop the kind of courage that candor requires.

It is after this intimate moment that Adele Ratignolle shows perception and wisdom. As an honorable young gentleman not yet ready to marry, Robert Lebrun is thoroughly trusted to be the companion of other men's wives. This summer, he has selected Edna as the object of his mock courtship. After their conversation on the beach, Adele grasps the import of what Edna is capable of. She makes an excuse to get Robert Lebrun alone, and then she warns him, "She is not one of us. She is not like us. She might make the serious blunder of taking you seriously" (Chopin, 1976: 21).

Edna admitted some of her inner feelings to herself and Adele at the seashore. On a Saturday evening several weeks later, she opens to herself even more. The Grand Isle guests are gathered for a social evening at "the house" (the Lebrun's house at the resort where they take meals and where the Lebruns live during the season). Mlle. Reicz, an unattractive spinster generally considered eccentric, is persuaded to play the piano. Edna listens.

It was not the first time she had heard an artist at the piano. Perhaps it was the first time she was ready, perhaps the first time her being was tempered to take an impress of the abiding truth. She waited for the material pictures she thought would gather and blaze before her imagination. She waited in vain.

She saw no pictures of solitude, of hope, of longing, or of despair. But the very passions themselves were aroused within her soul, swaying it, lashing it, as the waves daily beat upon her body. She was choking. The tears blinded her. (Chopin, 1976: 28)

Edna has left off conventionally experiencing passions in the "artistic" mode, which leaves them romantic illusions, safe and controlled, and she has begun feeling them—a deeper kind of candor than she showed with Madame Ratignolle. It is in a way her saying an internal "no" to the conventional world by refusing to hide her own stirrings under conventional images.[5]

Her next step comes immediately afterwards, when the Grand Isle guests go out for a moonlight swim. It involves an act of courage in saying no to the premise that women are fragile and must be protected. In a sense, she changes her nature by her action, and in changing it, she falsifies a conventional belief about women of her class by refusing to enact it.

Edna had attempted all summer to learn to swim. She had received instructions from both the men and women; in some instances from the children. Robert had pursued a system of lessons almost daily; and he was nearly at the point of discouragement in realizing the futility of his efforts. A certain ungovernable dread hung about her in the water, unless there was a hand near by that might reach out and reassure her.

But that night she was like the little, tottering, stumbling, clutching child, who of a sudden realizes its powers, and walks for the first time alone, boldly and with overconfidence. She could have shouted for joy, as with a sweeping stroke or two she lifted her body to the surface of the water.

A feeling of exultation overtook her, as if some power of significant import had been given her to control the working of her body and her soul. She grew daring and reckless, overestimating her strength. She wanted to swim far out, where no woman had swum before. (Chopin, 1976: 29)

She swims out, facing the expanse and solitude of the moonlit sea. When she turns to swim back, she suffers a sudden loss of nerve because of her distance from the shore.

A quick vision of death smote her soul and for a second time appalled and enfeebled her senses. But by an effort, she rallied her staggering faculties and managed to regain the land. (Chopin, 1976: 30)

---

5. Compare Tolstoy's *The Kreuzer Sonata,* in which music also whips up the passions. Author Chopin is using a conventional interpretation of her time to represent Edna's escape from conventional representation: music of certain sorts whips up the passions. I don't see any problem with this, since the point is to say that Edna has changed morally and now feels the passions for the first time. That point has to be represented in some way that reaches the readers of the time.

Edna now leaves the group and walks home alone, only to be overtaken by Robert Lebrun—somewhat to her annoyance. She is exhausted, and does not really understand what she has been through. Although she takes Robert's arm, she does not lean on it. "She let her hand lie listlessly, as though her thoughts were elsewhere—somewhere in advance of her body, and she was striving to overtake them" (Chopin, 1976: 31). In Kate Chopin's world, and throughout the novel, this leaning on the man's arm is symbol as well as enactment of the reality of the woman's fragility and the man's place in protecting her.

Edna lies in the hammock on the porch of the Pontellier cabin. Although she offers no encouragement, Robert stays with her. They don't speak, but "no multitude of words could have been more significant than those moments of silence, or more pregnant with the first-felt throbbings of desire" (Chopin, 1976: 33). Robert leaves when they hear the other bathers returning.

In a scene echoing the earlier one in which she had a "good cry," Edna once again gets into a struggle with her husband. But Edna has moved on in her passage. Mr. Pontellier returns from the swim and tells her to come into the house with him. When she declines, he goes in alone. He calls to her again, and she again refuses.

> She heard him moving around the room; every sound indicating impatience and irritation. Another time she would have gone in at his request. She would, through habit, have yielded to his desire; not with any sense of submission or obedience to his compelling wishes, but unthinkingly, as we walk, move, sit, stand, go through the daily treadmill of the life which has been portioned out to us. (Chopin, 1976: 33)

Mr. Pontellier asks again, "this time fondly, with a note of entreaty." When Edna again refuses, he moves to the "rational lord and master" position allowed to husbands:

> "This is more than folly," he blurted out. "I can't permit you to stay out here all night. You must come in the house instantly." (Chopin, 1976: 33)

That's all Edna needs.

> With a writhing motion she settled herself more securely in the hammock. She perceived that her will had blazed up, stubborn and resistant. She could not at that moment have done other than denied and resisted. She wondered if her husband had ever spoken to her like that before, and if she had submitted to his command. Of course she had; she remembered that she had. But she could not

realize why or how she should have yielded, feeling as she did then.

"Léonce, go to bed," she said. "I mean to stay out here. I don't wish to go in, and I don't intend to. Don't speak to me like that again; I shall not answer you." (Chopin, 1976: 33–34)

But there is a double meaning to Edna's situation. What seemed to be a newer, freer world is, in fact, something quite well-defined in the conventional world: a vacation. A vacation is a collectively made freedom that allows possibilities in relationships even as it controls them. Everything in her surroundings is on the side of convention. There she sits, at a family resort, on the porch of a cottage within which her children sleep. Léonce Pontellier gets himself a glass of wine and goes out to the porch.

> He drew up the rocker, hoisted his slippered feet on the rail and proceeded to smoke a cigar. He smoked two cigars; then he went inside and drank another glass of wine. Mrs. Pontellier again declined to accept a glass when it was offered to her. Mr. Pontellier once more seated himself with elevated feet, and after a reasonable amount of time, smoked some more cigars. (Chopin, 1976: 34)

The conventional meaning embodied in the furnishings, the meaning in Mr. Pontellier's elevated feet that signifies territorial possession, the meaning in the very cigar smoke that insists that her lungs acknowledge that she and the house are her husband's territory—these things overcome her. They drag her back to the conventional reality. All Léonce Pontellier needs to do is sit and wait.

> Edna began to feel like one who awakens gradually out of a dream, a delicious, grotesque, impossible dream, to feel again the realities pressing into her soul. The physical need for sleep began to overtake her; the exuberance which had sustained and exalted her spirit left her helpless and yielding to the conditions which crowded her in. (Chopin, 1976: 34)

By the close of the chapter, her position and Mr. Pontellier's are reversed—she asks him if he is coming in to bed, he says he'll be in when he finishes his cigar.

Room to Move

Edna's vacation at Grand Isle gave her time and space to develop within new relationships. The vacation reduced her involvement in a conventional way without affecting her usual commitment to conventional activities and a conventional place as her husband's helpmeet.[6] It did not have a serious effect on the nature of her relationships back home, with husband, children, servants, and people in their social worlds. To have room to move, she has to cut back on her commitments and begin changing the nature of the relationships. And she has to do this in a way that doesn't lead to her being labeled as some sort of deviant and being removed from the scene, either by being isolated someplace for a "cure" or by being ostracized to a deviant community.

Edna's first step is simply to stop her wifely duties. Every Tuesday in New Orleans, she has had her "reception day," receiving, among others, the female relatives of Mr. Pontellier's wealthy clients. She stops doing it.

Throughout her marriage, she has struggled (not always successfully) to discipline the household staff and conduct the household "en bonne menagere." She stops trying.

She leaves the children to the care of the nursemaid. She and her husband "meet in the morning at the breakfast table"; so far has she deserted wifely duties.

Mr. Pontellier tries to handle this as he has handled things before—by a patriarchal lecture or two, and by stalking out after giving a command. But this time it doesn't work.

> Her new and unexpected line of conduct completely bewildered him. It shocked him. Then her absolute disregard for her duties as a wife angered him. When Mr. Pontellier became rude, Edna grew insolent. She had resolved never to take another step backward. (Chopin, 1976: 61)

It's at this point that Edna runs a serious danger of being labelled and put out of commission.

Mr. Pontellier wants to make an accusation that will bring Edna into line. He needs help, because he is no longer able deal with her alone. But he must be careful where and how he gets help. Others could easily interpret things in a way he would find damaging socially, and damaging to his business prospects. He needs to find a suitable way to accuse Edna with a label that will stick, but that won't reflect badly on him. So he wonders if Edna is becoming mentally unbalanced. A conventional man, he chooses a conventional hypothesis. A rational man, he looks for an expert opinion to back him up—without it, his label would have no glue.

He visits his old friend and family physician, Doctor Madelet. The doctor asks if Edna has been "associating of late with a circle of pseudo-intellectual women."

---

6. Becker (1970) gives a useful definition of involvement in chapter 20 and of commitment in chapter 18. I am using the terms in something like his sense.

"That's the trouble," broke in Mr. Pontellier, "She hasn't been associating with any one. She has abandoned her Tuesdays at home, has thrown over all her acquaintances, and goes tramping about by herself, moping in the street-cars, getting in after dark. I tell you she's peculiar. I don't like it. I feel a little worried over it." (Chopin, 1976: 70)

The doctor advises Mr. Pontellier that most women are "moody and whimsical," and that he should just leave Edna alone for a while. Privately, he suspects there may be another man in the picture.[7] He doesn't mention this to Léonce Pontellier because "he knows his Creole too well to make a blunder such as that" (Chopin, 1976: 71).

At any rate, Edna has her room to move.

Stepping Out

Besides cutting her wifely commitments, Edna gradually stops presenting herself in the way women are conventionally understood to be "by nature"— something she must do to step out. The protection that is considered necessary for women and children is symbolically represented in the yards and yards of fabric in which they are swathed—even on vacation at a seaside resort. As the novel progresses, Edna becomes more and more casual about her dress, and author Kate Chopin is explicit in what it represents, saying that Edna "was becoming herself and daily casting aside that fictitious self which we assume like a garment with which to appear before the world" (Chopin, 1976: 60).

Edna breaks through the conventional women's presentation of herself as needing protection, a man's hand always nearby to support her. What Mr. Pontellier calls tramping about by herself and moping in streetcars is Edna's refusal to understand herself as needing that protection. Toward the end of the novel, Edna says to Robert Lebrun:

> "Isn't this a delightful place? . . . It's so out of the way, and a good walk from the [trolley] car. However I don't mind walking. I always feel so sorry for women who don't like to walk; they miss so much—so many rare little glimpses of life, and we women learn so little of life on the whole." (Chopin, 1976: 114)

This remark is one key to the nature of the relationships in Edna's patriarchal social world. Chopin's point seems to be that if women have trouble develop-

---

7. The doctor here sees an ordinary moral transgression rather than a rebellion against the social organization of morality. Pontellier's "mentally unbalanced" hypothesis makes a medical problem of the moral rebellion. See Ehrenreich and English (1979) or Barker-Benfield (1976). Both the doctor and Pontellier define the rebellion out of existence.

ing their moral selves, it may be because they are prevented from knowing and experiencing life. Women are protected, and that not only restricts their relationships with those they know, it keeps them from relationships with others with whom they might learn. Protection interferes with freedom as collective possibilities.[8]

Out on her own, Edna goes to visit Mlle. Reicz, the piano-playing eccentric from Grand Isle, now in her dreary spinster's quarters in New Orleans. But her dingy windows open to the ships on the Mississippi, and her life opens to a view that life in the Pontellier mansion cannot offer. For all her outward shabbiness, she has preserved her independence, and an understanding of passion and beauty, which she expresses in her artistry at the piano.[9]

By choosing her eccentric way, Mlle. Reicz has managed to preserve certain things, and Edna learns a great deal from her, beginning with the Grand Isle scene in which Edna experiences "the passions themselves," which I mentioned above. Basically, Mlle. Reicz accepts Edna's seeming eccentricities without labeling them. This enables her to offer an idea, which Edna can use to understand herself.

Edna tells Mlle. Reicz that she has taken up painting again and is becoming an artist. Mlle. Reicz says that Edna has pretentions. Edna answers,

> "Why pretensions? Do you think I could not become an artist?"
>
> "I do not know you well enough to say. I do not know your talent or your temperament. To be an artist includes much; one must possess many gifts—absolute gifts—which have not been acquired by one's own effort. And moreover, to succeed the artist must possess the courageous soul."
>
> "What do you mean by the courageous soul?"
>
> "Courageous, ma foi! The brave soul. The soul that dares and defies." (Chopin, 1976: 68)[10]

Later, Mlle. Reicz says more about the image, in a conversation Edna reports to her friend Alcée Arobin:

> "She says queer things sometimes in a bantering way that you don't notice at the time and you find yourself thinking about afterward."

8. This isn't true simply for women of Edna's day, of course, but for everyone. Protection comes in many guises, including the separation of deviants from normals (see theMaine Ministers of chapter 3) and the ghettoization of neighborhoods caused by differences in property values.

9. Mlle. Reicz's deviance is a good illustration of the importance of social position. She is apparently a very talented pianist. It she had been a male, she would likely have had a family and a concert career. Dismissing her as "eccentric" is of course a way of labeling her so that she isn't taken as a serious critic or as a counterexample of what women "really are."

10. Compare Margaret Sanger's remark about Lorenzo Portet—that he is "a spirit that flames in protest." Sanger seems to have a romantic ideal of the revolutionary, as Reicz (or Chopin) has a romantic ideal of the artist.

"For instance?"

"Well, for instance, when I left her today, she put her arms around me and felt my shoulder blades, to see if my wings were strong, she said. 'The bird that would soar above the level plain of tradition and prejudice must have strong wings. It is a sad spectacle to see the weaklings bruised, exhausted, fluttering back to earth.'" (Chopin, 1976: 89)

The image of a bird with a broken wing is used at the end of the novel to indicate Edna's failure. But at the moment, Alcée, a conventional deviant, offers a conventional label for Mlle. Reicz; "'I've heard she's partially demented.' said Arobin." Ignoring labels, Edna responds, "She seems to me wonderfully sane."

To continue stepping out, Edna needs new people, more freedom. She is exposed to new social circles when her father comes for a visit and they go to the races—following up her girlhood interest in horses. There she meets Mrs. Highcamp, Mrs. Merriman, and Alcée Arobin. Then Léonce Pontellier leaves for an extended business trip to New York. In the novel, this unusual husbandly behavior is explained by calling in Dr. Mandelet, who advises Léonce to take her "only if she wishes to go."

"If not, leave her here. Don't contradict her. The mood will pass, I assure you. It may take a month, two, three months—possibly longer, but it will pass. Have patience." (Chopin, 1976: 71)

When Léonce leaves, Grandmother Pontellier carries the children "off to Iberville with their quadroon" for a visit in the country. Edna now has all the room to move that she needs.

Left to herself, Edna begins to spend time with the group she met at the race track—particularly Alcée Arobin:

His manner was quiet, and at times a little insolent. He possessed a good figure, a pleasing face, not overburdened with depth of thought or feeling; and his dress was that of the conventional man of fashion. (Chopin, 1976: 79)

He also possesses a reputation. Adele Ratignolle says to Edna:

"You know how evil-minded the world is—some one was talking about Alcée Arobin visiting you. Of course, it wouldn't matter if Mr. Arobin had not such a dreadful reputation. Monsieur Ratignolle was telling me that his attentions alone are enough to ruin a woman's name." (Chopin, 1976: 103)

There is an ambiguity in Edna's relationship with Alcée that comes from the fact that she must understand her relationship with him neither from the point of view of the conventionally good (as Adele Ratignolle does), nor from that of the outsider who takes the conventionally bad as good (as perhaps Alcée himself does). At one point the ambiguity is explicit;

> He stood close to her, and the effrontery in his eyes repelled the old, vanishing self in her, yet drew all her awakening sensuousness. (Chopin, 1976: 82)

The need to understand without the usual labels leads Edna to be puzzled about herself as well:

> "One of these days," she says, "I'm going to pull myself together for a while and think—try to determine what character of a woman I am, for candidly, I don't know. By all the codes which I am acquainted with, I am a devilishly wicked specimen of the sex. But some way I can't convince myself that I am. I must think about it." (Chopin, 1976: 89)[11]

It is on the very evening that she says this to Alcee that she gains her first real knowledge of sensuality.

> Edna cried a little that night after Arobin left her. It was only one phase of multitudinous emotions which had assailed her. There was with her an overwhelming feeling of irresponsibility. There was the shock of the unexpected and the unaccustomed. There was her husband's reproach looking at her from the external existence. There was Robert's reproach making itself felt by a quicker, fiercer, more overpowering love which had awakened within her toward him. Above all there was understanding. She felt as if a mist had been lifted from her eyes, enabling her to look upon and comprehend the significance of life, that monster made up of beauty and brutality. (Chopin, 1976: 90)

Layers and layers of protection had kept that knowledge invisible. The knowledge was necessary to Edna's self-overcoming, but she could not have found it within the conventional relations of her social world. The question is whether she can find someone who can grow with her in a new relationship.

Stepping Outside

Edna has been making a little money selling her paintings. With this, supplemented by winnings at the racetrack, she rents a little cottage near the Pontellier mansion, the "Pigeon House." Shortly after her sexual awakening

---

11. This remark is made to Alcée Arobin, and he tells her not to think about it because he will tell her what manner of woman she is—and Edna responds that he will say she's adorable, captivating, and that he should spare himself the effort. Then follows the passage in which Alcée says Mlle. Reicz is demented and Edna says she is sane, quoted above.

with Alcée, she moves there, away from the things Mr. Pontellier had provided for her external existence. Edna now needs someone to make her new world with her. Although she and Alcée are doing something together, it is defined differently by each of them. He is having an illicit affair and she is gathering knowledge and self-respect.[12] Alcée simply isn't suitable for the new world Edna is trying to make—she and Alcée do not *care* for each other. Robert Lebrun seems the right choice.

Edna's sexual awakening with Alcée takes place on the evening of the day she learns that Robert has returned to New Orleans. His presence has been with her throughout the novel, however, and I believe he contributes one of the two barely formed ideas which she uses to understand her own awakening (the other being Mlle. Reicz's analogy with the defiant artist).

Robert is twenty-six, only two years younger than Edna, but his position as an unmarried member of his widowed mother's household has Adele Ratignolle calling him a "good boy." He isn't quite settled on a career line, and he makes large contributions to his mother's household, so he is understood as not yet ready to support a wife and household of his own.

The Creole social community at Grand Isle was like "one large family." Robert had a freedom with the married women like that of a young cousin, allowing Edna to have something of equality in a companionship with a man. Unfortunately, Edna overlooks the fact that this equality and freedom was possible because Léonce Pontellier was her protector, leaving Robert free to play at being protector. The image Edna builds around Robert is of a companionship, a freedom in love, something unclear—an ideal, a goal. Perhaps respect between lovers. Perhaps mutual care and moral growth in a relationship. If this isn't to be just a romantic whim, then there must be the freedom to make it happen—a freedom that includes both Edna's and Robert's capacities in the relationship and the collective possibilities offered in the relationships of their social worlds.

Edna runs into Robert at a little restaurant, and he accompanies her back to the Pigeon House. She kisses him, and he confesses his love. In the ensuing conversation, it becomes evident that they're coming from very different places indeed.

> "Something put into my head that you cared for me and I lost my senses. I forgot everything but a wild dream of you some way becoming my wife."
> "Your wife!"
> "Religion, loyalty, everything would give way if only you cared."
> "Then you must have forgotten that I was Léonce Pontellier's wife."

---

12. They bring their personal histories with them. Edna and Alcée aren't "coming from the same place," and so their affair means something different for each.

"Oh! I was demented, dreaming of wild, impossible things, recalling men who had set their wives free, we have heard of such things." (Chopin, 1976: 116)

When Edna asks why Robert didn't come to visit her after he returned, he replies, "I realized what a cur I was to dream of such a thing, even if you had been willing." And she responds,

"You have been a very, very foolish boy, wasting your time dreaming of impossible things when you speak of Mr. Pontellier setting me free! I am no longer one of Mr. Pontellier's possessions to dispose of or not. I give myself where I choose. If he were to say, 'Here, Robert, take her and be happy; she is yours,' I would laugh at you both."

His face grew a little white. "What do you mean?" he asked (Chopin, 1976: 116).

At this key moment, they are interrupted by the message that Mme. Ratignolle "has been taken sick" (that is, she is about to give birth). Edna runs off to be with Adele during the labor, while Robert, swept away, pleads with her to stay with him. After she is gone, however, he recovers his senses and writes a note: "I love you. Good-by—because I love you."

Robert is trying to protect Edna's virtue and her good name, and there's a certain amount of sense in what he's doing. Whatever the new values Edna is trying to create, she has to be able to live by them. I don't mean she has to be able to live up to them. In the crudest terms, she has to be able to survive— not be burned at the stake, not be imprisoned, be able to get food, drink, and shelter. Edna never really notices the way she is still protected by her husband and the conventional world in which she holds a higher-class position.[13] At one point, Adele had said, "In some way you seem to me like a child, Edna. You seem to act without a certain amount of reflection which is necessary in this life" (Chopin, 1976: 103). That of course is Edna's strength, as well as her weakness.

Robert has his own good name to protect as well as Edna's. If he takes up with Edna as she suggests, his whole past will be reread and he will become an incipient Alcée Arobin in everyone's eyes, and the social networks he needs even to get started earning a living will vanish. Edna says that Robert doesn't understand, and that is true. But there are things she doesn't understand as well.

Edna does finally come to grasp some inexorable realities, once again with the help of Adele Ratignolle.

---

13. This is true in the opportunities open to her—renting the Pigeon House, selling her paintings—as well as in the protection from the thousands of dangers non-white and poor women faced. Léonce explicitly protects her by making up a story about renovating the mansion, when he learns she's moved out. He is of course also protecting himself from scandal.

Adele is in labor and grouching at everyone in sight. Edna sits with her.

> Edna began to feel uneasy. She was seized with a vague dread. Her own like experiences seemed far away, unreal, and only half remembered. She recalled faintly an ecstasy of pain, the heavy odor of chloroform, a stupor which had deadened sensation, and an awakening to find a little new life to which she had given being, added to the great unnumbered multitude of souls that come and go. (Chopin, 1976: 119)

Edna's awakening here is to a perception of what seems to be, in her situation, certain inexorabilities.

> She began to wish she had not come; her presence was not necessary. She might have invented a pretext for staying away; she might even invent a pretext now for going. But Edna did not go. With an inward agony, with a flaming, outspoken revolt against the ways of nature, she witnessed the scene of torture.
>
> She was still stunned and speechless with emotion when later she leaned over her friend to kiss her and softly say goodby. Adele, pressing her check, whispered in an exhausted voice: "Think of the children! Remember them!" (Chopin, 1976: 119)

Edna leaves the house, and Dr. Mandelet walks her home. Kate Chopin repeats the phrase she used at the beginning of Edna's awakening, as she walked toward the cottage at Grand Isle, with Robert Lebrun, after the night she learned to swim. Edna walks "In an absent-minded way . . . as if her thoughts had gone ahead of her and she was striving to overtake them." She did not lean on Robert's arm then, and she does not lean on Dr. Mandelet's arm now. The doctor invites her to confide in him, but she does not feel moved to speak of things that trouble her. He leaves, and she sits on the porch step for a while.

Then she enters the Pigeon House to find Robert's note.

We next meet Edna at Grand Isle, not yet open for the season. As she walks down to the beach, she isn't thinking, but we get a review of her thoughts after she found Robert's note.

> She had said over and over to herself: "Today it is Arobin; tomorrow it will be some one else. It makes no difference to me, it doesn't matter about Léonce Pontellier—but Raoul and Etienne!" She understood now clearly what she had meant long ago when she said to Adele Ratignolle that she would give up the unessential, but she would never sacrifice herself for the children. (Chopin, 1976: 123)

At that time, earlier on Grand Isle, she had said she would give up her life for her children, but she would never give up herself.

The review of her thoughts continues:

> Despondency had come upon her there in the wakeful night and had never lifted. There was no human being whom she wanted near her except Robert; and she even realized that the day would come when he, too, and the thought of him would melt out of her existence, leaving her alone. The children appeared before her like antagonists who had overcome her; who had over-powered and sought to drag her into the soul's slavery for the rest of her days. (Chopin, 1976: 123)

She puts on her old bathing suit, walks to the water, then takes the suit off.

> For the first time in her life she stood naked in the open air, at the mercy of the sun, the breeze that beat upon her, and the waves that invited her.
> How strange and awful it seemed to stand naked under the sky! How delicious! She felt like some new-born creature, opening its eyes in a familiar world that it had never known. (Chopin, 1976: 124)

As she swims out into the sea, the thought passes her mind that Léonce Pontellier and the children were part of her life, "but they need not have thought they could possess her, body and soul." She thinks of Mlle. Reicz, and she thinks that she herself is a bird with a broken wing, not having the "courageous soul that dares and defies." She thinks of Robert who "didn't understand," who would "never understand." Then her thoughts drift without her volition, back to her childhood and the cavalry officer.

Discovery and Regeneration

Edna, in her way, honestly gazed at the face of eros and knew the paradox that her own world had to resolve. It is a paradox hidden in the myth of Psyche and Eros because theirs, like most love stories, reaches its *finis* before Psyche domesticates Eros to home, family, and neighborhood.

In Edna's respectable world, the "double standard" was a way of dealing with the paradox. The double standard is usually expressed in terms of sexual freedom—respectable women are to be virginal (or at least, limited to serial monogamy) and men are more or less free to satisfy their "sexual needs" (with their wives and, discreetly, with women who aren't respectable). But there is another side to this double standard, and it shows in Chopin's talk of "mother women." Women are free to be devoted to their children, their home, their community; while men are to be more distant— in fact forced to be more distant by the very work structure in which they must fulfill their roles as breadwinners. The double standard fractures eros. As the face of eros is gradually revealed to Edna in the process of her moral passage, she sees that there is no way to live the moral truth of what she has come to know. The fracture cannot be healed given the nature of relationships in her social worlds.

I mentioned the double standard, and the ideal of the mother woman. Talk of standards and ideals is a shorthand which must be understood in terms of the collective action through which people generate and regenerate the nature of their relationships. Otherwise, the talk is worse than useless—it is very deeply misleading. I've tried to give examples of collective action throughout the book. Here, let me review some of the themes that come up in Edna's passage.

When Edna quit her commitment to her wifely duties and took up with Alcée, Mrs. Highcamp, and Mrs. Merriman, she became a visitor to a social world on the margins of respectability and deviance. The world of Mlle. Reicz was also on the margins of respectability and deviance, though in a different way. Edna needed access to other worlds because there was knowledge hidden in them that she had to uncover as part of her moral passage. But the danger lay in taking the knowledge in the packages in which it was presented; i.e., in Mlle. Reicz's or Alcée Arobin's own definitions of themselves and their worlds and relationships. Unlike someone who "gets in with a bad crowd," Edna can't move from defining the world in conventional terms to defining it in deviant terms. Her process cannot be seen as a conversion from one set of labels to another, from one conventional kind of relationship to another. She has to operate for a while without labels, and without having a new set of her own. In this way, she steps out to a knowledge that is usually hidden by the official labels, whether conventional or deviant. This in fact is what Kate Chopin has her doing, and it is the reason that Edna's hope for a new life with Robert is dashed. Robert understands only the conventional labels and the conventional relationships. Robert, with a common sense as strong as Léonce's, accepts the fractured face of eros.

Léonce himself is struggling to keep his family secure in the ranks of the respectable bourgeoisie. The danger, given Edna's behavior, is that she and the family will go through a status passage and become déclassé. Though the status passage would begin in a process of moral judgement, it would end in damaging the family financial position so that their downfall would be cinched for economic reasons, not simply moral ones. We see one way in which the respectable (and powerful) classes discipline their members.

Léonce fights to control the status passage. He does it by coming up with labels for Edna that will minimize the damage—he wonders if she is becoming mentally unbalanced. He consults Dr. Mandelet for other, acceptable ways to label Edna's deviance.

I've said before that labels are not simply words that hide what is really going on. They define what is going on in the sense that people use them to enact truth. If Edna is judged mentally unbalanced by Léonce and his authority, Dr. Mandelet, then her behavior would be controlled in a variety of legitimate, established ways. Her relationships would change in certain well-known ways and the meaning of her passage would change—eventually it would change even for herself. At the same time, the label would hide what was going on. Léonce is good at hiding things—good at "keeping up appearances." He has taken great care to construct a family persona, and he is not about to have it damaged by his "unbalanced" wife. This is creativity in applying "the same" categories. And as is usual in such cases, it is not an intellectual exercise but a matter of survival—to survive as oneself, in the same social order and world.

Léonce is able to ward off a status passage for the family because there are conventional means at hand. The respectable world offers rich resources for its members to maintain respectability—in the process, regenerating the dominance of the respectable classes. These resources include ways of hiding and covering up, as well as an ample stock of labels. Some of the labels, like "mentally unbalanced," allow the family and other intimates of the deviant to maintain their own respectability without taint. They change their relationship to the deviant. Others, like "cheap woman," or "dissipate," or "destroyer" ostracize the deviant, often forcing them to other social worlds and relationships. This also changes relationships with the deviant, but it leaves behind a taint on the deviant's intimates and a taint on the respectable classes as well. To avoid taint, there may be institutionalized ways of hiding missteps and effecting a moral rescue—I discussed some of them in chapter 5.

The adult characters in *The Awakening* were not able to change their relationships in ways that Edna needed. But according to Kate Chopin, the adult relationships were not what defeated Edna. What defeated her were the children.

As I said, in Edna's world, the face of eros was fractured. Eros is not just romantic love or sex, it is also the mysteries of birth and the bond with children, and bonds between parents, kin, and community. This may be one point of Chopin's novel. In a sense, Edna sought to mend the fracture, and her deepest moral knowledge came when she discovered that she could not.

Edna had two primordial, archetypal experiences in the novel: the revelation of sex with Alcée and the revelation of birth in Adele's confinement. She comes to moral knowledge through the passionate impact of those moments. She experiences the passion of that knowledge, and she experiences it through relations with particular others—Alcée, Adele and the birth, the bond to her own children. She comes to the moral knowledge through relations with particular others, but the knowledge is not simply *of* those particular relations. It is, as I said, an archetypal, deeply moral knowledge.

In her early work, Margaret Sanger tried to mend the fracture in the face of eros. She tried to alter the truncated, distorted idea of mothering. Her hope was to bind together the joy in sex and the joy in having and raising children, all united in a good life and future for the community. She understood that relations between men and women would have to change, and that would require changing the nature of the relations; i.e., changing the social order. Change of some such sort was the only route to the woman of practical wisdom. Together with her sisters, the woman of practical wisdom had to invent herself, as she changed the nature of the relationships around her.

Personally, Sanger lived in a world in which the face of eros was fractured. She explored sex with revolutionary companions and she suffered sacrifice in the relationships with her children—most terrible in the death of her only daughter, but terrible too with her sons. The fracture was not so much the separation of sex and reproduction as the lack of collective possibilities for having a full relationship with her children and other intimates at the same time that she expanded her relationships in ways necessary for making a better answer to how we should live. This was (and is) a problem for men as well as women in the United States, for the face of eros has been fractured for all. At root, it is a problem of the market economy and the organization of work in the United States. Those things are rarely mentioned as the root of social problems of sex and reproduction, for the face of eros is fractured in that way as well. The domestication of eros requires some arrangement for winning the bread, after all. Becoming like the gods doesn't mean living off free nectar and ambrosia.

In her early work, Margaret Sanger saw the importance of change in economic arrangements. She approached the problem in terms of men's and women's spheres, industrial justice, and birth control. That was a division of moral labor that made sense in her time, at the beginning of the twentieth century. It makes no sense in the United States at the end of the century.

Earlier, I mentioned Sharon O'Brien's suggestion that Willa Cather feared that passion would prevent the self from rising to larger human concerns. Others have worried that moral focus on *particular* relationships would prevent the self from rising to larger human concerns. If we followed through on those fears, then the source of moral knowledge and self-overcoming would be cut off. Passion is essential for moral knowledge, and paradigmatically, passion is known in relationship with particular others. "Passion" here can't mean simply sexual or romantic passion—something which nowadays has come to resemble that old vice, lust. It is the fracture in the face of eros that leads many of us to magically transform passion in relationship into lust, with the diminution of all concerned. Passion may be natural to us as animals, but for all animals, lust is collectively enacted, with the meaning given in the social act. Erotic passion shows in other bonds and other acts, including the bonds with children or even (as in olden times) the bonds with God or our comrades.

Passion isn't simply something inside an individual. It is a fire in relationship. It is collectively given meaning as together, people interpret and create their worlds.

These words I write are just cool words on a printed page, of course. Scientists and other professionals (including myself) have been trained to drain knowledge of passion. For the moment, given the degree of our moral ignorance, that's all to the good. But it is important to remember that the knowledge we professionals offer is designed to hide the most important source of knowledge. And the relationships through which we professionals offer knowledge are designed to prevent reciprocity. That is the source of our cognitive authority. More important, it is how we are made trustworthy instruments of governance. But whether being trustworthy counts as being morally responsible is another question.

Bibliography

Acker, Joan, Kate Barry, and Johanna Esseveld. 1991. "Objectivity and Truth: Problems in Doing Feminist Research." In Mary Margaret Fonow and Judith Cook, eds. *Beyond Methodology: Feminist Scholarship as Lived Research.* Bloomington, IN:Indiana University Press.

Addams, Jane. 1907. *Democracy and Social Ethics.* New York: MacMillan.

Addelson, Kathryn Pyne. 1993. "Knower/Doers and their Moral Problems. In L. Alcoff and E. Potter. *Feminist Epistemologies.* New York: Routledge.

———. 1991. *Impure Thoughts: Essays in Philosophy, Feminism, and Ethics.* Philadelphia: Temple University Press.

———. 1987. "Moral Passages." In Eva Feder Kittay and Diana T. Meyers. *Women and Moral Theory.* Totowa, NJ: Rowman and Littlefield.

———. 1983a. "The Man of Professional Wisdom." In Sandra Harding and Merrill Hintikka. *Discovering Reality.* Dordrecht, Holland: D. Reidel.

———. 1983b. "Awakening." *Women's Studies Int. Forum* 6, no. 6: 583–95. Special first issue of Hypatia.

———. 1973. "Nietzsche and Moral Change." In R. Solomon, ed. *Nietzsche.* New York: Anchor Books.

Addelson, Kathryn, and Elizabeth Potter. 1991. "Making Knowledge." In J. Hartman and E. M. Davidow. *Engendering Knowledge: Feminists in Academe.* Knoxville: University of Tennessee Press.

Alcoff, Linda, and Elizabeth Potter. 1992. *Feminist Epistemologies.* New York: Routledge.

Alexander, Thomas M. 1987. *John Dewey's Theory of Art, Experience & Nature.* Albany, NY: SUNY Press.

Appiah, Anthony. 1992–93. "African American Philosophy." *Phil Forum* 24, nos. 1–3 (Fall-Spring).

———. 1992. *In My Father's House.* New York: Oxford University Press.

Arblaster, Anthony. 1984. *The Rise and Decline of Western Liberalism.* New York: Basil Blackwell.

Ardener, Edwin. 1987. "Remote Areas: Some Theoretical Considerations." In Anthony Jackson. *Anthropology At Home.* New York: Tavistock.

———. 1985. "Social Anthropology and the Decline of Modernism." In J. Overing, ed. *Reason and Morality.* ASA Monographs, no. 24. London: Tavistock.

———. 1975. "Belief and the Problem of Women." In Shirley Ardener, ed. *Perceiving Women.* New York: John Wiley and Sons.

Arnold, Mary Beth. 1989. "The Life of a Citizen—the Hands of a Woman: Sexual Assault in New York City, 1790–1820." In K. Peiss and C. Simmons, eds. *Passion and Power: Sexuality in History.* Philadelphia: Temple University Press.

Aubert, Vilhelm. 1965. *The Hidden Society.* NJ: Bedmister Press.

Baier, Annette. 1986. "Trust and Anti-Trust." *Ethics* 96 , no. 2: 231–60.

———. 1985. "What Do Women Want in a Moral Theory?" *Nous* 19 (March).

Bar-On, Bat Ami. 1993. "Marginality and Epistemic Privilege." In L. Alcoff and E. Potter, eds. *Feminist Epistemologies.* New York: Routledge.

Barker-Benfield, G. J. 1976. *The Horrors of the Half Known Life: Male Attitudes Toward Women and Sexuality in Nineteenth-Century America.* New York: Harper and Row.

Barnes, Barry and David Edge. 1982. *Science in Context: Readings in the Sociology of Science.* Cambridge, MA: MIT Press.

Becker, Howard S. 1986. *Doing Things Together.* Evanston, IL: Northwestern University Press.

———. 1982. *Art Worlds.* Berkeley: University of California Press.

———. [1963] 1973. *Outsiders.* New York: The Free Press.

———. 1970. *Sociological Work: Method and Substance.* Chicago: Aldine.

Belenky, Mary Field, et al. 1986. *Women's Ways of Knowing: The Development of Self, Voice, and Mind.* New York: Basic Books.

Bellah, Robert. 1982. "Social Science as Practical Reason." *Hastings Center Report* 12, no. 5: 32–39.

Bellah, Robert, et al. 1991. *The Good Society.* New York: Alfred A. Knopf.

———. 1985. *Habits of the Heart: Individuals and Commitment in American Life.* Berkeley: University of California Press.

Ben-Yehuda, Nachman. 1985. *Deviance and Moral Boundaries: Witchcraft, the Occult, Science Fiction, Deviant Sciences, and Scientists.* Chicago: University of Chicago Press.

Bernstein, Richard. 1983. *Beyond Objectivism and Relativism: Science, Hermeneutics and Praxis.* Philadelphia: University of Pennsylvania Press.

Bloor, David. 1976. *Knowledge and Social Imagery.* New York: Routledge and Kegan Paul.

Blum, Lawrence. 1980. *Friendship, Altruism, and Morality.* London: Routledge and Kegan Paul.

Blumer, Herbert. 1971. "Social Problems as Collective Behavior." *Social Problems* 18 (Winter): 298–306.

———. 1969. *Symbolic Interactionism: Perspective and Method.* Englewood Cliffs, NJ: Prentice Hall.

Boyer, Richard O., and Herbert M. Morais. 1955. *Labor's Untold Story.* New York: United Electrical, Radio & Machine Workers of America.

Breines, Wini. 1989. *Community Organization and the New Left, 1962–68.* New Brunswick, NJ: Rutgers University Press.

Briedis, Catherine. 1975. "Marginal Deviants: Teenage Girls Experience Community Response to Premarital Sex and Pregnancy." *Social Problems* 22, no 3 (April): 480–93.

Buff, Steven. 1973. *Labeling, Teenage Careers and Adult Socialization Among White, Working Class Youth.* Ph.D. diss., Northwestern University.

Burnham, John C. 1973. "The Progressive Era Revolution in American Attitudes Toward Sex." *Journal of American History* 59, no. 4: 885–908.

Calderone, Mary Steichen, ed. 1958. *Abortion in the United States: A Conference Sponsored by the Planned Parenthood Federation of America, Inc. at Arden House and the New York Academy of Medicine.* New York: Hoeber-Harper.

Callahan, Daniel. 1989. "Moral Theory: Thinking, Doing, and Living." *Journal of Social Philosophy* 20, nos. 1 and 2 (Spring/Fall).

Chamberlain, Neil. 1982. *Social Strategy and Corporate Structure.* New York: The Free Press.

Chatterjee, Partha, and Charles Taylor. 1990. "Modes of Civil Society." *Public Culture* 3, no. 1 (Fall): 95–118.

Chesler, Ellen. 1992. *Woman of Valor: Margaret Sanger and the Birth Control Movement in America.* New York: Simon and Schuster.

Chesney-Lind, Meda. 1973. "Judicial Enforcement of the Female Sex Role: The Family Court and the Female Delinquent." *Issues in Criminology* 8, no. 2: 51–69.

Chopin, Kate. 1976. *The Awakening.* New York: Duffield and Co.

Clarke, Adele E. 1991. "Social Worlds/Arenas Theory as Organizational Theory." In David Maines, ed. *Social Organization and Social Process: Essays in Honor of Anselm L. Strauss.* Hawthorne, NY: Aldine de Gruyter.

———. 1990a. "Controversy and the Development of Reproductive Sciences." *Social Problems* 37, no. 1: 18–37.

———. 1990b. "A Social Worlds Research Adventure: The Case of Reproductive Science." In Susan E. Cozzens and Thomas F. Feryn, eds. *Theories of Science in Society.* Bloomington: Indiana University Press.

Clarke, Adele, and Joan Fujimura. 1992. *The Right Tools for the Job: At Work in Twentieth-Century Life Sciences.* Princeton, NJ: Princeton University Press.

Clifford, James, and George E. Marcus. 1986. *Writing Culture: The Poetics and Politics of Ethnography.* Berkeley and Los Angeles: University of California Press.

Cohen, Jean L., and Andrew Arato. 1992. *Civil Society and Political Theory.* Cambridge, MA: MIT Press.

Cohn, Steven, and James Gallagher. 1984. "Gay Movements and Legal Change." *Social Problems* 32, no. 1 (October): 72–86.

Collier, Joan Fishburne, and Sylvia Junko Yanagisako. 1987. *Gender and Kinship: Essays Toward a Unified Analysis.* Stanford, CA: Stanford University Press.

Conrad, Peter, and Joseph Schneider. 1980. *Deviance and Medicalization: From Badness to Sickness.* St. Louis. MO: C. V. Mosby.

Corner, George. 1961. "Forword." In W. C. Young, ed. *Sex and Internal Secretions.* Baltimore, MD: Williams and Wilkins.

Cott, Nancy. 1975. "Young Women in the Second Great Awakening." *Feminist Studies* 3, no. 1/2 (Fall): 15–29.

Damico, Alfonso J. 1978. *Individuality and Community: The Social and Political Thought of John Dewey.* Gainesville: University Presses of Florida.

Davenport, Edward. 1987. "The New Politics of Knowledge: Rorty's Pragmatism and the Rhetoric of the Human Sciences." *Philosophy of Social Science* 17: 377–94.

Deegan, Mary Jo. 1988. *Jane Addams and the Men of the Chicago School, 1892–1918.* New Brunswick, NJ: Transaction Books.

DeLeon, David. 1978. *The American as Anarchist.* Baltimore, MD: Johns Hopkins University Press.

Dewey, John. 1929. *Experience and Nature.* London: Allen and Unwin.

———. 1896. "The Unit of Behavior (The Reflex Arc Concept in Psychology)." *Psychological Review* 3. Reprinted in H.S. Thayer, ed. *Pragmatism, The Classic Writings.* Indianapolis, IN: Hackett, 1982.

Diamond, Irene. 1983. *Families, Politics, and Public Policy: A Feminist Dialogue on Women and the State.* New York: Longman.

Dodge Luhan, Mabel. 1936. *Movers and Shakers* Intimate Memories, vol. 3. New York: Harcourt, Brace and Company.

Douglas, Emily Taft. 1970. *Margaret Sanger: Pioneer of the Future.* New York: Holt, Rinehart and Winston.

Dublin, Thomas. 1975. "Female Operatives in the Lowell Mills, 1830–1860." *Feminist Studies* 3, no. 1/2 (Fall): 30–39.

Dubofsky, Melvyn. 1969. *We Shall Be All: A History of the Industrial Workers of the World.* Chicago: Quadrangle.

Dye, Nancy Schrom. 1979. "Cleo's American Daughters: Male History, Female Reality." In J. Sherman and J. Beck, eds. *The Prism of Sex.* Madison: University of Wisconsin Press.

Ehrenreich, Barbara, and Dierdre English. 1979. *For Her Own Good: 150 Years of Experts' Advice to Women.* Garden City, NY: Anchor Press.

Ellis, Havelock. 1939. *My Life: An Autobiography of Havelock Ellis.* Boston: Houghton Mifflin.

———. 1910. *Sex in Relation to Society.* Studies in the Psychology of Sex, vol. 6. Philadelphia: F.A. Davis.

Elshtain, Jean. 1981. *Public Man, Private Woman.* Princeton, NJ: Princeton University Press.

Fee, Elizabeth. 1983. "Women, Nature, and Scientific Objectivity." In M. Lowe and R. Hubbard. *Women's Nature: Rationalizations of Inequality.* New York: Pergamon.

Flexner, Abraham. 1910. *Medical Education in the United States and Canada.* New York: Carnegie Foundation for the Advancement of Teaching. Bulletin 4.

Flynn, Elizabeth Gurley. 1973. *The Rebel Girl: An Autobiography, My First Life (1906–1926).* New York: International Publishers.

Flynn, Patricia. 1991a. "Just Decisions: Moral Ordering and the Social Construction of Bioethics." Ph.D diss., School of Nursing, University of California at San Francisco.

———. 1991b. "Moral Ordering: The Work of Bioethics Committees." Paper presented at Stone Symposium, Society for the Study of Symbolic Interactionism, San Francisco, CA (February).

Fonow, Mary Margaret, and Judith Cook, eds. 1991. *Beyond Methodology: Feminist Scholarship as Lived Research.* Bloomington: Indiana University Press.

Fox Keller, Evelyn. 1983. *A Feeling for the Organism: The Life and Work of Barbara McClintock.* New York: W. H. Freeman.

Freidson, Elliot. 1986. *Professional Powers: A Study of the Institutionalization of Formal Knowledge.* Chicago: University of Chicago Press.

———. 1982. "Occupational Autonomy and Labor Market Shelters." In P. L. Stewart and M. G. Cantor, eds. *Varieties of Work.* Beverly Hills, CA: Sage.

————. 1970. *Professional Dominance: The Social Structure of Medical Care.* Chicago: Aldine.

French, Peter. 1991. *The Spectrum of Responsibility.* New York: St. Martin's Press.

Fried, Amy. 1988. "Abortion Politics as Symbolic Politics: An Investigation into Belief Systems." *Social Science Quarterly* 69 (March): 137–54.

Furner, Mary. 1975. *Advocacy and Objectivity: A Crisis in the Professionalization of American Social Science.* Lexington: University Press of Kentucky.

Furstenberg, Frank F., J. Brooks-Gunn, and S. Philip Morgan. 1987. *Adolescent Mothers in Later Life.* Cambridge and New York: Cambridge University Press.

Garfinkel, Harold. 1967. *Studies in Ethnomethodology.* Englewood Cliffs, NJ: Prentice Hall.

Garry, Ann, and Marilyn Pearsall. 1989. *Women, Knowledge, and Reality.* Boston: Unwin Hyman.

Geertz, Clifford. 1984. "From the Native's Point of View." In R. Shweder and R. LeVine, eds. *Culture Theory.* Cambridge: Cambridge University Press.

Gelb, Joyce, and Marian Lief Palley. 1987. *Women and Public Policies.* Princeton, NJ: Princeton University Press.

Gerson, Elihu M. 1983. "Scientific Work and Social Worlds." *Knowledge: Creation, Diffusion, Utilization* 4, no. 3 (March).

Gilligan, Carol. 1982. *In a Different Voice.* Cambridge, MA: Harvard University Press.

————. 1977. "In a Different Voice: Women's Conceptions of Self and Morality." *Harvard Educational Review* 47, no. 4: 481–517.

Glaser, Barney, and Anselm Strauss. 1971. *Status Passage.* Chicago: Aldine-Atherton.

————. 1967. *The Discovery of Grounded Theory; Strategies for Qualitative Research.* Chicago: Aldine.

Goffman, Erving. 1961. *Asylums: Essays on the Social Situation of Mental Patients and Other Inmates.* Garden City, NJ: Doubleday.

Goldman, Emma. 1969. *Anarchism and Other Essays.* New York: Dover.

Gordon, Linda. 1977. *Woman's Body, Woman's Right: A Social History of Birth Control in America.* New York: Penguin.

Gray, Madeline. 1979. *Margaret Sanger: A Biography of the Champion of Birth Control.* New York: Richard Marek.

Greenwood, John D., ed. 1991. *The Future of Folk Psychology: Intentionality and Cognitive Science.* New York: Cambridge University Press.

Griffin, Susan. 1978. *Woman and Nature: The Roaring Inside Her.* New York: Harper and Row.

Grosskurth, Phyllis. 1980. *Havelock Ellis: A Biography.* New York: Knopf, distributed by Random House.

Gusfield, Joseph. 1984. "On the Side." In J. Schneider and J. Kitsuse, eds. *Studies in the Sociology of Social Problems.* NJ: Ablex.

———. 1981. *The Culture of Public Problems:Drinking, Driving, and the Symbolic Order.* Chicago: University of Chicago Press.

———. 1976 [1963]. *Symbolic Crusade: Status Politics and the American Temperance Movement.* Chicago: University of Illinois Press.

———. 1967. "Moral Passage: The Symbolic Process in Public Designations of Deviance." *Social Problems* 15, no.2 (Fall): 175–88.

Haraway, Donna. 1991. *Simians, Cyborgs, and Women: The Reinvention of Nature.* New York: Routledge.

———. 1989. *Primate Visions: Gender, Race and Nature in the World of Modern Science.* New York: Routledge.

Harding, Sandra. 1991. *Whose Science? Whose Knowledge?: Thinking from Women's Lives.* Ithaca, NY: Cornell University Press.

———. 1986. *The Science Question in Feminism.* Ithaca, NY: Cornell University Press.

Harding, Sandra, and Merrill Hintikka. 1983. *Discovering Reality.* Dordrecht, Holland: D. Reidel.

Harper, Anne. 1983. "Teenage Sexuality and Public Policy: An Agenda for Gender Education." In Irene Diamond, ed. *Families, Politics, and Public Policy: A Feminist Dialog on Women and the State.* New York: Longman.

Harrison, Beverly. 1983. *Our Right to Choose: Toward a New Ethic of Abortion.* Boston: Beacon.

Hart, H. L. A. 1981. *The Concept of Law.* Oxford: Clarendon.

Hartman, Joan, and Ellen Messer Davidow. 1991. *Engendering Knowledge: Feminists in Academe.* Knoxville: University of Tennessee Press.

Hauerwas, Stanley. 1981. *A Community of Character: Toward a Constructive Christian Social Ethic.* Notre Dame, IN: University of Notre Dame Press.

Hauerwas, Stanley, and Alasdair MacIntyre. 1983. *Revisions.* Notre Dame, IN: University of Notre Dame Press.

Hauerwas, Stanley, with Richard Bondi and David B. Burrell. 1977. *Truthfulness and Tragedy: Further Investigations in Christian Ethics.* Notre Dame, IN: University of Notre Dame Press.

Held, Virginia. 1987. "Feminism and Moral Theory." In Eva Feder Kittay and Diana T. Meyers. *Women and Moral Theory.* Totowa, NJ: Rowman and Littlefield.

Hersey, Harold. 1938. *Margaret Sanger: The Biography of the Birth Control Pioneer.* Printed by Emerson House, New York, but not distributed. Xerox in Sophia Smith Collection, Smith College.

Hountondji. 1983. *African Philosophy: Myth and Reality.* Bloomington: Indiana University Press.

Hughes, Everett C. 1984. *The Sociological Eye.* New Brunswick, NJ:Transaction Books.

Hursthouse, Rosalind. 1987. *Beginning Lives.* New York: Basil Blackwell.

Jackson, Anthony. 1987a. *Anthropology at Home.* New York: Tavistock.

———. 1987b. "Reflections on Ethnography at Home and the ASA." In A. Jackson. *Anthropology at Home.* New York: Tavistock.

Jaggar, Alison. 1989a. "Feminist Ethics: Some Issues for the Nineties." *Journal of Social Philosophy* 20, no. 1&2 (Spring/Fall).

———. 1989b. "Love and Knowledge: Emotion in Feminist Epistemology." In Ann Garry and Marilyn Pearsall, eds. *Women, Knowledge, and Reality.* Boston: Unwin Hyman.

———. 1983. *Feminist Politics and Human Nature.* Totowa, NJ: Rowman and Allanheld.

Jarvie, I. C. 1984. *Rationality and Relativism: In Search of a Philosophy and History of Anthropology.* Boston: Routledge and Kegan Paul.

Jensen, Joan M. 1981. "The Evolution of Margaret Sanger's Family Limitation Pamphlet, 1914–21." *Signs* 6, no. 3: 548–55.

Jonas, Hans. 1984. *The Imperative of Responsibility.* Chicago: University of Chicago Press.

Jordan, Judithet al. 1991. *Women's Growth in Connection.* New York: Guilford.

Kennedy, David M. 1970. *Birth Control: America, The Career of Margaret Sanger.* New Haven, CT: Yale University Press.

Kett, Joseph F. 1968. *The Formation of the American Medical Profession; The Role of Institutions, 1780–1860.* New Haven, CT: Yale University Press.

Kittay, Eva Feder, and Diana T. Meyers. 1987. *Women and Moral Theory.* Totowa, NJ:Rowman and Littlefield.

Kohlberg, Lawrence. 1981. *The Philosophy of Moral Development: Moral Stages and the Idea of Justice.* Essays on Moral Development, vol. 1. San Francisco: Harper and Row.

———. 1969. "Stage and Sequence: The Cognitive Developmental Approach to Socialization." In David A. Goslin, ed. *Handbook of Socialization Theory and Research.* Chicago: Rand McNally.

Kopp, Marie. 1933. *Birth Control in Practice.* New York: Robert M. McBride.

Kucklick, Bruce. 1984. "Seven Thinkers and How They Grew: Descartes, Spinoza, Leibniz, Locke, Berkeley, Hume, Kant." In *Philosophy in History.* R. Rorty, J. Schneewind, and Q. Skinner, eds. Cambridge: Cambridge University Press.

Kuhn, Thomas. 1970. *The Structure of Scientific Revolutions.* 2nd ed. Chicago: University of Chicago Press.

Kunitz, Stephen. 1974. "Professionalism and Social Control in the Progressive Era: The Case of the Flexner Report." *Social Problems* 22, no. 1: 16–17.

Ladd, John. 1983. "Philosophy and the Moral Professions." In Judith Swazey and Stephen Scher, eds. *Social Controls and the Medical Profession.* Boston: Oelgeschlager, Gunn Le Hain

———. 1982. "A Distinction Between Rights and Responsibilities." *Linacre Quarterly*: 121–42 (May).

———. 1975. "The Ethics of Participation." In J. Roland Pennock and John Chapman, eds. *Participation in Politics.* New York: Atherton-Leker.

Lader, Lawrence. 1955. *The Margaret Sanger Story and the Fight for Birth Control.* Garden City, NY: Doubleday.

Latour, Bruno. 1987. *Science in Action: How to Follow Scientists and Engineers through Society.* Cambridge, MA: Harvard University Press.

Latour, Bruno, and Steve Woolgar. 1986. *Laboratory Life: The Construction of Scientific Facts.* Princeton, NJ: Princeton University Press.

LeGuin, Ursula K. 1974. *The Dispossessed: An Ambiguous Utopia.* New York: Harper and Row.

Lemert, Charles. 1979. "Science, Religion and Secularization." *Sociological Quarterly* 20: 445–61.

Lemert, Edwin M. 1974. "Beyond Mead: The Societal Reaction to Deviance." *Social Problems* 21, no. 4: 457–68.

———. 1951. *Social Pathology: A Systematic Approach to the Theory of Sociopathic Behavior.* New York: McGraw Hill.

Lerner, Gerda. 1979. *The Majority Finds Its Past: Placing Women in History.* London: Oxford University Press.

Leval, Gaston. 1975. *Collectives in the Spanish Revolution.* London: Freedom Press.

Levins, R., and R. C. Lewontin. 1985. *The Dialectical Biologist.* Cambridge, MA: Harvard University Press.

Lewontin, R. C. 1992. *Biology as Ideology.* New York: Harper and Row.

Lieberman, James E., and Ellen Peck. 1982. *Sex and Birth Control: A Guide for the Young.* New York: Schocken.

Lofgren, Orvar. 1987. "Deconstructing Swedishness: Culture and Class in Modern Sweden." In A. Jackson. *Anthropology at Home.* New York: Tavistock.

Lukes, Steven. 1989. "Making Sense of Moral Conflict." In Nancy L. Rosenblum, ed., *Liberalism and the Moral Life.* Cambridge, MA: Harvard University Press.

Lynd, Robert S., and Helen Merrell Lynd. 1929. *Middletown.* Harcourt, Brace & World.

MacIntyre, Alasdair. 1981. *After Virtue: A Study in Moral Theory.* Notre Dame, IN: University of Notre Dame Press.

Marglin, Frederique Apffel. 1994 "Rationality, the Body, and the World: From Production to Regeneration." In F. Apffel Marglin and S. A. Marglin, eds., *Decolonizing Knowledge: From Development to Dialogue.* Clarendon: Oxford University Press.

Margold, Charles. 1926. *Sex Freedom and Social Control.* Chicago: University of Chicago Press.

Martin, Jane Roland. 1985. *Reclaiming a Conversation: The Ideal of the Educated Woman.* New Haven, CT: Yale University Press.

Mast, Coleen Kelly, ed. 1986. "Sex Respect: The Option of True Sexual Freedom." Manual for teachers; guide for parents; workbook for students. Respect, Inc.

Maticka-Tyndale, Eleanor. 1992. "Social Construction of HIV Transmission and Prevention Among Heterosexual Young Adults." *Social Problems* 39, no. 3): 238–52.

Matza, David. 1969. *Becoming Deviant.* Englewood Cliffs, NJ:Prentice Hall.

McCarthy, Thomas. 1990. "Private Irony and Public Decency: Richard Rorty's New Pragmatism." *Critical Inquiry* 16.

McLoughlin, William G. 1978. *Revivals, Awakenings, and Reform: An Essay on Religion and Social Change in America, 1607–1977.* Chicago: University of Chicago Press.

Mead, George Herbert. 1938. *The Philosophy of the Act.* Chicago: University of Chicago Press.

Mercer, Jane R. 1973. *Labeling the Mentally Retarded: Clinical and Social System Perspectives on Mental Retardation.* Berkeley: University of California Press.

Merchant, Carolyn. 1980. *The Death of Nature: Women, Ecology, and the Scientific Revolution.* San Francisco: Harper and Row.

Merton, Robert K. 1949. *Social Theory and Social Structure.* Glencoe, IL: The Free Press.

Messer-Davidow, Ellen. Forthcoming. "Acting Otherwise." In J. Gardiner, ed., *Provoking Agents.* Champaign-Urbana: University of Illinois Press.

Meyers, Diana. 1989. *Self, Society, and Personal Choice.* New York: Columbia University Press.

———. 1987. "Personal Autonomy and the Paradox of Feminine Socialization." *Journal of Philosophy* 84, no. 11 (November).

Mill, John Stuart. 1951. *Utilitarianism.* Everyman Edition.

Mills, C. Wright. 1963. *Power Politics and People.* Edited by Irving Louis Horowitz. New York: Ballantine.

Modell, John. 1983. "Dating Becomes the Way of American Youth." In L. P. Moch and G. D. Stark. *Essays on the Family and Historical Change.* College Station: Texas A&M Press.

Mohr, James C. 1978. *Abortion in America: The Origins and Evolution of National Policy, 1800–1900.* New York: Oxford University Press.

Moore, Kristin, and Martha Burt. 1982. *Private Crisis, Public Cost.* Washington, D.C.: Urban Institute Press.

Moynihan Report. 1965. "The Negro Family: The Case for National Action." Washington, D.C.: U.S. Government Printing Office.

Nathanson, Constance. 1991. *Dangerous Passage: The Social Control of Sexuality in Women's Adolescence.* Philadelphia: Temple University Press.

Nelson, Lynn Hankinson. 1993. "Epistemological Communities." In L. Alcoff and E. Potter, eds., *Feminist Epistemologies.* New York: Routledge.

———. 1990. *Who Knows: From Quine to a Feminist Empiricism.* Philadelphia: Temple University Press.

Neumann, Eric. 1956. *Amor and Psyche: A Commentary of the Tale by Apulius.* New York: Pantheon.

Newton, Lisa. 1983. "Professionalization: The Intractable Plurality of Values." In W. L. Robison, ed. *Profits and Professions: Essays in Business and Professional Ethics.* Clifton, NJ: Humana Press.

Nietz, Mary Jo. 1981. "Family, State, and God: Ideologies of the Right-to-Life Movement." *Sociological Analysis* 42, no. 3: 265–76.

Noddings, Nel. 1984. *Caring: A Feminine Approach to Ethics and Moral Education.* Berkeley: University of California Press.

Nussbaum, Martha. 1986. *The Fragility of Goodness.* New York: Cambridge University Press.

O'Brien, Sharon. 1975. "The Limits of Passion." *Women and Literature* 3 (Fall).

Oleson, Alexandra, and J. Voss. 1979. *The Organization of Knowledge in Modern America.* Baltimore, MD: Johns Hopkins University Press.

Osborne, Martha Lee, ed. 1979. *Women in Western Thought.* New York: Random House.

Overing, J, ed. 1985. *Reason and Morality.* ASA Monographs, no. 24. London: Tavistock.

Parsons, Kathryn Pyne. 1973. "Nietzsche and Moral Change." In R. Solomon, ed. *Nietzsche.* New York: Anchor Books.

Petchesky, Rosalind. 1983. *Abortion and Woman's Choice: The State, Sexuality, and Reproductive Freedom.* New York: Longman.

Peters, F. E. 1967. *Greek Philosophical Terms: A Historical Lexicon.* New York: New York University Press.

Pivar, David. 1973. *Purity Crusade.* Westport, CT: Greenwood Press.

Quine, W. V. 1969. *Ontological Relativity and Other Essays.* New York: Columbia University Press.

———. 1963. *From a Logical Point of View.* New York: Harper and Row.

———. 1960. *Word and Object.* Cambridge, MA: Technology Press of the Massachusetts Institute of Technology.

Rains, Prudence Mors. 1982. "Deviant Careers." In M. M. Rosenberg, R. Stebbins, and A. Turowetz, eds. *The Sociology of Deviance.* New York: St. Martin's Press.

———. 1971. *Becoming An Unwed Mother: A Sociological Account.* Chicago: Aldine-Atherton.

Rainwater, Lee. 1970. *Behind Ghetto Walls.* Chicago: Aldine.

———. 1960. *And the Poor Get Children.* Chicago: Quadrangle.

Rawls, John. 1971. *A Theory of Justice.* Cambridge, MA: Harvard University Press.

Reed, James. 1978. *From Private Vice to Public Virtue: The Birth Control Movement in American Society Since 1830.* New York: Basic Books.

Robinson, Paul. 1976. *The Modernization of Sex: Havelock Ellis, Alfred Kinsey, William Masters and Virginia Johnson.* New York: Harper and Row.

Rorty, Richard. 1991. *Philosophical Papers.* 2 vols. Cambridge and New York: Cambridge University Press.

———. 1989. "Solidarity or Objectivity?" In Michael Krausz, ed. *Relativism and Confrontation.* Notre Dame, IN: University of Notre Dame Press.

———. 1986. "On Ethnocentrism: A Reply to Clifford Geertz." *Michigan Quarterly Review* 25: 525–534.

———. 1979. *Philosophy and the Mirror of Nature.* Princeton, NJ: Princeton University Press.

Rosenberg, Charles E. 1979. "The Therapeutic Revolution: Medicine, Meaning, and Social Change in Nineteenth Century America." In Morris J. Vogel and Charles E. Rosenberg, eds. *The Therapeutic Revolution.* Philadelphia: University of Pennsylvania Press.

———. 1976. *No Other Gods: On Science and American Social Thought.* Baltimore, MD: Johns Hopkins University Press.

———. 1975. *The Family in History.* Philadelphia: University of Pennsylvania Press.

Rothstein, William G. 1972. *American Physicians in the Nineteenth Century: From Sects to Science.* Baltimore: Johns Hopkins University Press.

Ruddick, Sara. 1989. *Maternal Thinking: Toward a Politics of Peace.* Boston: Beacon.

———. 1984. "Maternal Thinking." In Joyce Treblicot, ed. *Mothering: Essays in Feminist Theory.* Totowa, NJ: Rowman & Allenheld.

Sandel, Michael, ed. 1984. *Liberalism and Its Critics.* New York: New York University Press.

———. 1982. *Liberalism and the Limits of Justice.* New York: Cambridge University Press.

Sanger, Alexander Campbell. 1969. *Margaret Sanger: The Early Years, 1910–1917.* Senior Thesis, Princeton University.

Sanger, Margaret. 1938 *An Autobiography.* New York: W. W. Norton.

———. 1931. *My Fight for Birth Control.* New York: Farrar and Rinehart.

———. 1922. *The Pivot of Civilization.* New York: Brentano.

———. 1920a. *What Every Girl Should Know.* (Reprinted, New York, 1980).

———. 1920. *Women and the New Race.* New York: Blue Ribbon Books.

Scheman, Naomi. 1983. "Individualism and the Objects of Psychology." In Sandra Harding and Merrill Hintikka. *Discovering Reality.* Dordrecht, Holland: D. Reidel.

Schneider, Joseph W. 1991. "Troubles with Textual Sociology." *Symbolic Interaction* 14, no. 3: 295–319.

Schneider, Joseph and Peter Conrad. 1980. "The Medical Control of Deviance." In Julius Roth, ed. *Research in the Sociology of Health Care,* vol. 1. Greenwich CT: JAI Press.

Schutz, Alfred. 1962, 1964, 1966. *Collected Papers, Volumes 1–3.* The Hague: Martinus Nijhoff.

Shalin, Dmitri N. 1988. "G. H. Mead, Socialism, and the Progressive Agenda." *American Journal of Sociology* 93, no. 4 (January): 913–51.

———. 1986. "Pragmatism and Social Interactionism." *American Sociological Review* 51 (February): 9–29.

Shryock, Richard H. 1967. *Medical Licensing in America.* Baltimore, MD: Johns Hopkins University Press.

Smith, Dorothy E. 1990a . *The Conceptual Practices of Power: A Feminist Sociology of Knowledge.* Boston: Northeastern University Press.

———. 1990b . *Texts, Facts, and Femininity: Exploring the Relations of Ruling.* New York: Routledge.

———. 1987. *The Everyday World as Problematic: A Feminist Sociology.* Boston: Northeastern University Press.

Smith-Rosenberg, Carroll. 1975. "The New Woman and the New History." *Feminist Studies* 3, no. 1/2 (Fall): 185–98.

———. 1971a. "Beauty and the Beast and Militant Women: A Case Study in Sex Roles and Social Stress in Jacksonian America." *American Quarterly* 23, no. 4: 563–84.

———. 1971b. *Religion and the Rise of the American City: The New York City Mission Movement, 1812–1870.* Ithaca, NY: Cornell University Press.

Solinger, Rickie. 1992. *Wake Up Little Susie: Single Pregnancy and Race Before Roe vs. Wade.* New York: Routledge.

Solomon, Robert. 1993. *The Passions: Emotions and the Meaning of Life.* Indianapolis, IN: Hacking.

Spector, Malcolm, and John Kitsuse. 1977. *Constructing Social Problems.* Menlo Park, CA: Cummings.

Spelman, Elizabeth V. 1989a. *Inessential Woman.* Boston: Beacon.

———. 1989b. "Anger and Insubordination." In Ann Garry and Marilyn Pearsall, eds. *Women, Knowledge, and Reality.* Boston: Unwin Hyman.

Stacey, Judith. 1988. "Can There Be a Feminist Ethnography?" *Women's Studies International Forum* 11, no. 1: 21–27.

Stack, Carol B. 1974. *All Our Kin: Strategies for Survival in a Black Community.* New York: Harper and Row.

Starr, Paul. 1982. *The Social Transformation of American Medicine: The Rise of a Sovereign Profession and the Making of a Vast Industry.* New York: Basic Books.

Stewart, Granis Jane. 1993. *The 'Postmodern Turn' in Anthropology: A Critique.* Senior Thesis, Anthropology Department, Smith College.

Stich, Stephen. 1990. *The Fragmentation of Reason: Preface to a Pragmatic Theory of Cognitive Evaluation.* Cambridge, MA: MIT Press.

Storer, Horatio. 1860. *On Criminal Abortion in America.* Philadelphia: Lippincott.

Strathern, Marilyn, ed. 1987. "The Limits of Auto-Anthropology." In A. Jackson. *Anthropology at Home.* New York: Tavistock.

Strauss, Anselm L. 1993. *Continual Permutations of Action.* New York: Aldine de Gruyter.

———. 1987. *Qualitative Analysis for Social Scientists.* Cambridge: Cambridge University Press.

———. 1978. "A Social Worlds Perspective." In Norman Denzin, ed. *Studies in Symbolic Interaction* vol. 1. Greenwich, CT: JAI Press.

———. 1975. *Professions, Work, and Careers.* New Brunswick, NJ: Transaction Press.

Strauss, Anselm, and Berenice Fischer. 1978. "Interactionism." In Tom Bottomore and Robert Nesbit, eds. *A History of Sociological Analysis.* New York: Basic Books.

Sumner, L. W. 1981. *Abortion and Moral Theory.* Princeton, NJ: Princeton University Press.

Taylor, Charles. 1989. *Sources of the Self.* Cambridge, MA: Harvard University Press.

Taylor, Charles, and Partha Chatterjee. 1990. "Modes of Civil Society." *Public Culture* 3, no. 1 (Fall): 95–118.

Thomson, Judith Jarvis. 1971. "A Defense of Abortion." *Philosophy and Public Affairs* 1, no. 1. (September): 47–66.

Tong, Rosemarie. 1993. *Feminine and Feminist Ethics*. Belmont, CA: Wadsworth.

Traweek, Sharon. 1988. *Beamtimes and Lifetimes: The World of High Energy Physicists*. Cambridge, MA: Harvard University Press.

Treblicot, Joyce, ed. 1984. *Mothering: Essays in Feminist Theory*. Totowa, NJ: Roman and Allanheld.

Turner, Roy. 1974. *Ethnomethodology*. Baltimore: Penguin.

Verran, Helen Watson, and David Wade Chambers. 1989. *Singing the Land, Signing the Land*. Geelong, Victoria, Australia: Deakin University Press,

Vincent, Clark. 1961. *Unmarried Mothers*. New York: Free Press.

Vinovskis, Maris A. 1981. "An 'Epidemic' of Adolescent Pregnancy? Some Historical Questions." *Journal of Family History* 6, no. 2 (Summer).

Waller, Willard. 1932. *The Sociology of Teaching*. New York: John Wiley and Sons.

Wattleton, Faye. 1990. "Teenage Pregnancy: A Case for National Action." In Evelyn C. White, ed. *The Black Women's Health Book*. Seattle, WA: Seal Press.

Wells, H. G. 1920. *The Outline of History*. New York: Garden City Publishers.

Whitbeck, Caroline. forthcoming. *Understanding Moral Problems in Engineering*. Cambridge: Cambridge University Press.

———. 1989. "A Different Reality: Feminist Ontology." In Ann Garry and Marilyn Pearsall, eds. *Women, Knowledge, and Reality: Explorations in Feminist Philosophy*. Boston: Unwin Hyman.

———. 1984. "The Maternal Instinct." In Joyce Treblicot, ed. *Mothering: Essays in Feminist Theory*. Totowa, NJ: Roman and Allanheld.

———. 1983. "The Moral Implications of Regarding Women as People: New Perspectives on Pregnancy and Personhood." In William Bondism, et al. *Abortion and the Status of the Fetus*. Boston: D. Reidel.

White, Evelyn C., ed. 1990. *The Black Women's Health Book*. Seattle, WA: Seal Press.

Whyte, William Foote. 1943. "A Slum Sex Code." *American Journal of Sociology* 49, no. 1 (July).

Will, George. 1992. "The Children of the Rainbow." *Boston Globe,* 6 Dec. 1992, Focus section.

Williams, Bernard. 1985. *Ethics and the Limits of Philosophy*. Cambridge, MA: Harvard University Press.

Williams, Dorothy, ed. 1991. "Human Sexuality: Values and Choices." A collaborative project of the Search Institute of Minneapolis and Healthstart of St. Paul, MN.

Willis, Paul. 1981. *Learning to Labor: How Working Class Kids Get Working Class Jobs.* New York: Columbia University Press.

Winch, Peter. 1964. "Understanding a Primitive Society." *American Philosophical Quarterly* 1: 307–24.

———. 1958. *The Idea of a Social Science.* London: Routledge and Kegan Paul.

Windt, Peter, et al. 1989. *Ethical Issues in the Professions.* Englewood Cliffs, NJ: Prentice Hall.

Wolfe, Alan. 1989. *Whose Keeper? Social Science and Moral Obligation.* Berkeley: University of California Press.

Wolfe-Devine, Celia. 1989. "Abortion and the Feminine Voice." *Public Affairs Quarterly* 3, no. 3 (July): 81–97.

Young, R. M. 1985. *Darwin's Metaphor.* Cambridge: Cambridge University Press.

Zelnik, Melvin, John Kanter, and Kathleen Ford. 1981. *Sex and Pregnancy in Adolescence.* Beverly Hills, CA: Sage Library of Social Research.

Index